D1567905

Books by African-American Authors and Illustrators

for Children and Young Adults

This book is dedicated to three groups of creative people of color—

those who went before
those who now are
those who will come

Books by
African-American
Authors and
Illustrators

for Children and Young Adults

Helen E. Williams

American Library Association
Chicago and London 1991

Helen E. Williams is a professor of literature for children and young adults. She was a Fulbright professor in the South Pacific Islands where she assisted in curriculum development. Her previous experiences also include being a teacher-librarian, public librarian, and university librarian. She has promoted reading through workshops conducted nationally in Africa, the Caribbean, and in the South Pacific region. Her two previous books are *The High/Low Consensus* and *Independent Reading, K–3.*

Cover and text design by Publishers Services, Inc.
Composed in Omega on the Quadex 5000
Compugraphic 9800 system by Publishers Services, Inc.

Printed on 50-pound Galtfelter B-16, a pH-neutral stock,
and bound in Holliston Roxite B51590 Vellum Finish cover stock
by Edwards Brothers, Inc.

The paper used in this publication meets the minimum requirements of American National Standard for Information Sciences—Permanence of Paper for Printed Library Materials, ANSI Z39.48-1984. ∞

Library of Congress Cataloging-in-Publication Data

Williams, Helen E.
    Books by African-American authors and illustrators for children
and young adults / by Helen E. Williams.
        p. cm.
    Includes index.
    ISBN 0-8389-0570-6
    1. Children's literature, American—Afro-American authors—
Bibliography. 2. Young adult literature, American—Afro-American
authors—Bibliography. 3. Children's literature, American—Afro-
American authors—Illustrations—Catalogs. 4. Young adult
literature, American—Afro-American authors—Illustrations—
Catalogs. 5. Illustrated books, Children's—United States—
Bibliography. 6. Afro-Americans in literature—Bibliography.
7. Afro-Americans in art—Catalogs. I. Title.
Z1037.W672   1991
[PN1009.A1]
016.8108'09282—dc20   91-13931

Printed in the United States of America.

95 94 93 92 91   5 4 3 2 1

Contents

Preface

The objective of this work is to provide a representative identification of the books which are written and illustrated by black writers and artists. One of its purposes is to facilitate the identification of these books especially for the benefit of young readers, their nurturers and teachers, and for the general public, as well. The dispersed, and thus concealed, status of many of these books has contributed inadvertently to the paucity of information about the true extent of the contributions made by black writers and artists to the field of literature for children and young adults. In addition, the common omission of blacks from many standard reference and biographical information sources increases the value of this book and its focus. It should prove useful in providing meaningful responses to frequently asked questions regarding the identification of indigenous textual and graphic materials for young readers and students.

A black perspective is the preferred focus because promotion of black writers and illustrators is noticeably sacrificed in the publicity of works by popular or prestigious other ethnic artists whose perspectives are tacitly assigned a greater value. Additionally, "by and about" bibliographies often provide references to books about black experiences from other ethnic perspectives, some of which distort, trivialize, or otherwise misrepresent the cultural essence upon which the stories are based. The imperative to allow a people to speak for and about themselves is addressed throughout this compilation, which is also intended to promote increased attention to and study of black writers and artists.

Verifying content information necessitated the study and research of many books, databases, special collections, exhibits, ephemeral items such as pamphlets, bookmarks, newspaper and magazine articles, as well conferences with writers, illustrators, and scholars. An effort was made to include everything available. However, the lack of success in locating reviews in major reviewing sources contributed to many omissions. Additional factors included a lack of time and resources to collect, read, and review all of the unfamiliar books for which reviews were not available. Therefore, the resulting contents represent, although not comprehensively, works published during the twentieth century up to the beginning of 1990. An intended future update will endeavor to resolve the dilemma of current omissions.

The organizational structure is a grouping of books deemed to be appropriate for use by or with young people at three scholastic levels. Chapter 1 contains descriptions of books suitable for use by and with preschoolers up to those having fourth-grade cognitive abilities and skills. Chapter 2 represents books considered appropriate for middle and junior high school level needs, interests, and abilities. Books cited in Chapter 3 should prove useful to readers with interests and abilities at the senior high school level and above. Chapter 4 describes and identifies the artistic contributions of black illustrators of books intended or appropriate for the previously defined groups.

Grateful acknowledgment is extended to the American Library Association for its Whitney-Carnegie Fund grant which made possible the competent research assistance of Virginia Bradley Moore. Appreciation is hereby given to the reviewing media and bibliographers who allowed me to use their works as a basis for description. Warm expressions of gratitude go to David Driskell, a co-worker and friend who is one of America's leading specialists in African-American art. For helpful and patient tutoring on the techniques of indexing, I offer sincere thanks to William Pitt, an accomplished indexer, recently deceased. Golda May Haines, my wonderfully patient and competent typist, deserves considerably more thanks than she has already received, so I recognize her invaluable assistance with this published expression of deep appreciation. Finally, I am grateful to my friends around the world who cared about this effort and encouraged me when discouragements and problems abounded.

In paraphrase of words by Ann Allen Shockley, writing requires a certain amount of self-confidence and a deep interest and concern for scholarship and humanity. Some say that black writers and illustrators are no different than white ones. But to be a black writer or illustrator takes a great deal of determination and spirit, because blacks in the United States continue to encounter an inequitable society and the insensitivity of a predominantly white publishing world. Writing and graphic creations by blacks are responses to American society as well as vehicles for the expression and illumination of the black experience through personal revelations, ideas, thoughts, and reactions. May they be encouraged to continue.

List of Abbreviations

This list of abbreviations represents the sources from which all annotations in Chapters 1 through 3 were based. An abbreviation appears in parentheses at the end of each annotation.

ALR	ALAN Review
ATL	Atlantic
BCCB	Bulletin of the Center for Children's Books
BK	Bookmark
BL	Booklist
BRD	Book Review Digest
BW	Book World
C	Choice
CC	Children's Catalog
CHR	Christian Century
CIP	Cataloging in Publication
CLW	Catholic Library World
CSM	Christian Science Monitor
DCPL	District of Columbia Public Library
DLB	Dictionary of Literary Biography
ED	Editor
EJ	English Journal
EPL	Enoch Pratt Free Public Library
ESLC	Elementary School Library Collection
H	Harpers magazine
HB	Horn Book
IBCB	Interracial Books for Children Bulletin
JAMHIS	Journal of American History
JHS	Junior High School Library Catalog
KIR	Kirkus Review of Books
LA	Language Arts
LJ	Library Journal
MS	Ms Magazine
N	Nation
ND	Negro Digest
NR	New Republic

NUC	National Union Catalog
NW	Newsweek
NY	New Yorker
NYHT	New York Herald Tribune Book Review
NYTBR	New York Times Book Review
OCLC	Online Computer Library Center
P	Poetry magazine
PLC	Public Library Catalog
PW	Publishers Weekly
SHS	Senior High School Library Catalog
SLJ	School Library Journal
SR	Saturday Review
SS	School and Society
TCR	Teachers College Record
TLS	Times Literary Supplement
USQ	U.S. Quarterly Book Advocate
VOYA	Voice of Youth Advocates
WLB	Wilson Library Bulletin
YALE	Yale Review

Chapter 1

Books for Very Young Children

Advocates of multiculturality without bias in books for young children often emphasize the importance of children seeing and experiencing positive and joyful aspects of their own culture, as well as other cultures. Because it is believed that black writers portray more sensitively their own cultural experiences and history, the books represented in this chapter reflect black authorship and interpretation. While all the books are not concerned with ethnicity or are inclusive of black characters, they present subjects of interest and cognitive benefit to young readers. Included are wordless picture books, story picture books, concept books, folk and fairy tales, biographies, alphabet and counting books, and poetry.

Each entry has a unique number by which the information it represents is indexed. The entries are listed alphabetically by the primary author's last name and each book is described with bibliographic data which includes the names of authors, illustrators (where appropriate), publisher and date of publication. A description of the book's contents is provided with a code to represent the reviewing source from which it is fashioned. Books which have won literary awards are noted with a concluding statement of award name and year identification.

1   Arkhurst, Joyce Cooper, reteller. **The adventures of Spider: West African folk tales; retold.** Illustrated by Jerry Pinkney. Little, 1964.

Spider (usually called Anansi), the popular and cunning trickster of West African folktales, is featured in six stories. (BRD)

2   Baker, Augusta, comp. **The talking tree: fairy tales from fifteen lands.** Illustrated by Johannes Troyer. Lippincott, 1955.

This collection represents choices of young listeners at the New York Public Library's story hours. Each story is characteristic of the culture it represents. (BRD)

3   Baker, Augusta, comp. **Young years: best loved stories and poems for little children.** Home Library Pr., 1960.

This anthology of literary classics for very young children includes sections of nursery rhymes and stories, fables, fairy tales, and poetry. The preface explains to parents the importance of reading to children and provides techniques for successful reading experiences. (ED)

4   Baker, Bettye F. **What is black?** Watts, 1969.

Black can be many things, such as a friendly puppy, a delicious licorice stick, a strong locomotive, rich soil, and black children. (NUC)

5   Baldwin, James. **Little man, little man.** Illustrated by Yoran Cazac. Dial, 1977.

TJ's Harlem block is introduced through his fantasy which is peopled by his neighbors: the janitor, Mr. Man; his friends, WT and Blinky; Miss Lee; and Miss Beanpole. (KIR)

6   ben-Moring, Alvin Loctor. **Balthazar, the black and shining prince.** Illustrated by John Gretzer. Westminster, 1974.

Here is a jazzed-up version of the story of the biblical three kings. It portrays Balthazar as a black who lives in Harlem and rides a famous horse called Black Spirit. (LJ)

7   Bontemps, Arna Wendell and Conroy, Jack. **Fast Sooner hound.** Illustrated by Virginia Lee Burton. Houghton, 1942.

Sooner was a hound dog that belonged to a railroad fireman who was not allowed to have his dog ride with him in the cab.

When Sooner demonstrated his speed, the chagrined roadmaster relented.   (BRD)

8   Bontemps, Arna Wendell. **Mr. Kelso's lion.** Illustrated by Len Ebert. Lippincott, 1970.

Because of zoning ordinances, life for people in a small Alabama town is made miserable by a lion that is boarded there. Percy and his grandfather, visitors to the town, confront local governmental agencies without success.   (LJ)

9   Bontemps, Arna and Hughes, Langston. **Popo and Fifina.** Illustrated by Elmer Simms Campbell. Macmillan, 1932.

This story describes the everyday happenings in the lives of two black children in Haiti when their parents move from a farm to a village where Papa Jean plans to earn a living as a fisherman.   (BRD)

10   Bontemps, Arna Wendell. **Sad-faced boy.** Illustrated by Virginia Lee Burton. Houghton, 1937.

Three small boys leave their Alabama home for Harlem because they want to see the tall buildings. After a visit to their Uncle Jasper and experiences with their own musical group, they remember that persimmons are ripe in Alabama and they head for home.   (BRD)

11   Bontemps, Arna Wendell and Conroy, Jack. **Sam Patch, the high, wide and handsome jumper.** Illustrated by Paul Brown. Houghton, 1951.

This retelling of the Sam Patch legend shows him growing up and learning to take bigger and better jumps until he defeats Hurricane Harry, the snapping turtle who boasted that he was the best jumper of all times.   (BRD)

12   Bontemps, Arna Wendell. **You can't pet a possum.** Illustrated by Ilse Bischoff. Morrow, 1934.

The amusing escapades of an eight-year-old black boy and his dog during hot, sunny days in the Alabama countryside are told in dialect.   (BRD)

13   Breinburg, Petronella. **Doctor Shawn.** Illustrated by Errol Lloyd. Crowell, 1975.

Mom goes shopping and leaves the children alone with instructions not to mess up the house. They play doctor with Shawn as the doctor and his sister as the nurse.   (SLJ)

14   Breinburg, Petronella. **Sally-Ann's skateboard.** Illustrated by Ossie Murray. Bodley Head, 1979.

This story is about being forced to disobey an order and doing something dangerous on a skateboard.   (SLJ)

Winner: Children's Book of the Year Award, 1979.

15   Breinburg, Petronella. **Shawn goes to school.** Illustrated by Errol Lloyd. Crowell, 1974.

Shawn has always wanted to go to school, but when the big day comes he panics and cries. Comfort and support from a kind teacher, his mother, and an older sister ease his fears.   (BL)

16   Brooks, Gwendolyn. **Bronzeville boys and girls.** Illustrated by Ronnie Solbert. Harper, 1956.

This collection of thirty-six poems about everyday experiences of black children in one section of Chicago reveals the basic elements of a good life in warm, human terms.   (BRD)

17   Brown, Margery W. **Animals made by me.** Illustrated by author. Putnam, 1970.

A child finds a piece of chalk on the sidewalk and draws animals with imaginary distinctions, such as a zebra with plaid skin and a polar bear on ice skates. Rhyming text describes the child's experiences and encourages readers to create their own zoo of funny animals.   (BCCB)

18   Brown, Margery W. **Yesterday I climbed a mountain.** Illustrated by author. Putnam, 1977.

During imaginative play, a small girl talks of sandbox activities—a jungle gym in the playground is a mountain, crayons are the city streets, etc. Someday she hopes to travel to real mountains, forests, etc., but presently she is limited to what is just outside her door.   (BCCB)

19   Bryan, Ashley, reteller. **The adventures of Aku.** Illustrated by Ashley Bryan. Atheneum, 1976.

Subtitled: Or, how it came about that we shall always see Okra the cat lying on a velvet cushion, while Okraman the dog sleeps among the ashes. When the gods send Mother Onyema a son, Aku, his foolish behavior results in his lowered status, translating into the dog's less luxurious sleeping place.   (BL)

20   Bryan, Ashley, reteller. **Beat the story-drum, pum-pum.** Illustrated by Ashley Bryan. Atheneum, 1980.

Five Nigerian stories are retold with a faint American bouquet without comprising their ethnicity.   (BL)

Winner: Notable Children's Books (American Library Association), 1980; Coretta Scott King Award, 1981; Parents' Choice Award for Illustration in Children's Books, 1980.

21   Bryan, Ashley, reteller. **The cat's purr.** Illustrated by Ashley Bryan. Atheneum, 1985.

The reason why cats purr is retold in this story of the former friendship of Cat and Rat. It is based upon Rat's insistence to play a tiny Cat family drum even though he had been told not to do so.   (BL)

Winner: Notable Children's Books (American Library Association), 1985.

22   Bryan, Ashley, reteller. **The dancing Granny.** Illustrated by Ashley Bryan. Atheneum, 1977.

Granny Anika, Anansi the spider—a trickster, and Granny's garden spider who raids repeatedly before he is tricked—are central in this story from the Antilles.   (BL)

23   Bryan, Ashley, comp. **I'm going to sing: Black American spirituals, volume 2.** Illustrated by Ashley Bryan. Atheneum, 1982.

This companion volume to *Walk Together Children* presents the melody lines and words of twenty-five spirituals in creative design.   (BL)

Winner: Notable Children's Books (American Library Association), 1982; Coretta Scott King Honorable Mention Book, 1983.

24   Bryan, Ashley, reteller. **The ox of the wonderful horns and other African folk tales.** Illustrated by Ashley Bryan. Atheneum, 1971.

Five stories tell how Spider Anansi makes a fool of himself

while seeking to make a fool of another; the troubles of a frog with two wives; how Tortoise outwits Hare; about Frog's claim that Elephant is his horse; and about a boy who makes a fortune with nothing but a pair of horns.   (BL)

25   Bryan, Ashley, ed. **Walk together children: Black American spirituals.** Illustrated by Ashley Bryan. Atheneum, 1974.

More than twenty Black American spirituals are provided with treble clef music and verse.   (LJ)

26   Burroughs, Margaret G., comp. **Did you feed my cow?** Illustrated by Margaret G. Burroughs. Follett, 1969.

In this revision of the 1956 edition are street games, chants, rhymes, and songs—all collected on Chicago's South Side and all involving group actions and reactions.   (LJ)

27   Caines, Jeannette Franklin. **Abby.** Illustrated by Steven Kellogg. Harper, 1973.

Abby is adopted and enjoys reading her baby book which documents the event. Kevin, an older sibling, is slow to realize Abby's need to feel important. Later, he wants to take her to show-and-tell to brag that his family gets to keep her forever.   (LJ)

28   Caines, Jeannette Franklin. **Chilly stomach.** Illustrated by Pat Cummings. Harper, 1986.

Child abuse is implied when Sandy reveals to her best friend that she is uncomfortable around her uncle who sometimes hugs her and kisses her on the lips. She is afraid that if she tells her parents about her feelings, they won't believe her or love her.   (BCCB)

29   Caines, Jeannette Franklin. **Daddy.** Illustrated by Ronald Himler. Harper, 1977.

A little girl describes the anxious wait for her Saturday visits with her father. They enjoy coloring, talking and teasing, and cooking chocolate pudding.   (BL)

30   Caines, Jeannette Franklin. **Just us women.** Illustrated by Pat Cummings. Harper, 1982.

A young girl and her favorite aunt share the excitement of planning a very special car trip for just the two of them.   (ED)

Winner: Coretta Scott King Honorable Mention Book, 1983.

31   Caines, Jeannette Franklin. **Window wishing.** Illustrated by Kevin Brooks. Harper, 1980.

Window wishing is window shopping and two black children enjoy this delightful activity when they visit their lively Grandma during vacation. (BCCB)

32   Carew, Jan. **Children of the sun.** Illustrated by Leo and Diane Dillon. Little, 1980.

The young and restless Sun falls in love with an earth woman who bears twin sons. The children develop opposite natures and experience different destinies. (BL)

33   Carew, Jan. **The third gift.** Illustrated by Leo and Diane Dillon. Little, 1974.

This story tells of the Jubas and how their prophet Amakosa brings them to Nameless Mountain where they receive, in time, the gifts of work, beauty, and imagination. (BL)

Winner: American Institute of Graphic Arts Certificate of Excellence, 1974.

34   Childress, Alice. **"Let's hear it for the queen."** Illustrated by Loring Eutemey. Coward, 1976.

A play based on the rhyme "The Queen of Hearts/She made some tarts. . . . " Knave is the central figure. A girl who conceives the idea of dramatization plays the defendant's lawyer, winning acquittal for the tart stealer and a round of applause for the Queen who "baked some swingin' cookies." (BCCB)

35   Clifton, Lucille. **All us come across the water.** Illustrated by John Steptoe. Holt, 1973.

A young black boy learns the meaning of nationhood when he searches for the response to his teacher's request that each student name his or her country of origin. (LJ)

36   Clifton, Lucille. **Amifika.** Illustrated by Thomas Di Grazia. Dutton, 1977.

In making room for Amifika's dad who is returning home

from military service, his mother seeks to get rid of things he won't remember. Because Amifika doesn't remember his dad, he feels that the reverse is also true, so he hides away outdoors and falls asleep, but wakes as his dad carries him inside. (BCCB)

37   Clifton, Lucille. **The black BC's.** Illustrated by Donald George Miller. Dutton, 1970.

The alphabet provides a unifying theme for prose and poetry by describing the achievements of black men and women in history and highlighting some meaningful expressions.   (LJ)

38   Clifton, Lucille. **The boy who didn't believe in Spring.** Illustrated by Brinton Turkle. Dutton, 1973.

King Shabazz doubted his teacher's talk of Spring, so he and a friend crossed the street alone for the first time and found proof of Spring in a vacant lot.   (BCCB)

39   Clifton, Lucille. **Don't you remember?** Illustrated by Evaline Ness. Dutton, 1973.

Four-year-old Tate remembers special promises from her parents, and she also wants to drink coffee with her older brothers. But they all seem to forget until, on her birthday, special requests are remembered.   (BL)

Winner: Coretta Scott King Honorable Mention Book, 1974.

40   Clifton, Lucille. **Everett Anderson's Christmas coming.** Illustrated by Evaline Ness. Holt, 1971.

The five days before Christmas are described by verses and graphics which depict happiness in Apartment 14A.   (BRD)

41   Clifton, Lucille. **Everett Anderson's friend.** Illustrated by Ann Grifalconi. Holt, 1976.

A small black boy is delighted to see a new family move in across the street but is disappointed at first when he realizes that all the children are girls.   (CC)

Winner: Coretta Scott King Honorable Mention Book, 1977.

42   Clifton, Lucille. **Everett Anderson's good-bye.** Illustrated by Ann Grifalconi. Holt, 1983.

After listing the five stages of grief (denial, anger, bargaining, depression, and acceptance), this story tells (in verse) of a young boy's reactions to his father's death. (BRD)

Winner: Coretta Scott King Award, 1984.

43   Clifton, Lucille. **Everett Anderson's nine month long.** Illustrated by Ann Grifalconi. Holt, 1978.

A small black boy is helped to accept his new stepfather and the expected baby. Dethronement receives gentle attention during walks and assuring talks about love enough for all. (BCCB)

44   Clifton, Lucille. **Everett Anderson's 1-2-3.** Illustrated by Ann Grifalconi. Holt, 1977.

This is not a counting book. In verse, Everett ponders the new neighbor, Mr. Perry, and his willingness to fill the place of Everett's dad. (BCCB)

45   Clifton, Lucille. **Everett Anderson's year.** Illustrated by Ann Grifalconi. Holt, 1974.

Everett's seventh year of life is described in twelve poems which reveal the intimacy of his immediate world. (BCCB)

46   Clifton, Lucille. **Good, says Jerome.** Illustrated by Stephanie Douglas. Dutton, 1973.

Poetry in a question-and-answer format shows how a small boy's fears are assuaged by an older sister. His questions have universality and her answers are encouraging. (BCCB)

47   Clifton, Lucille. **The lucky stone.** Illustrated by Dale Payson. Delacorte, 1979.

Anecdotes from a great-grandmother's life reflect stories within a story. The lucky stone is the linking device—how it was given to great-grandmother when she was a girl; how it saved the life of the woman who gave it to her; and how it brought her and her future husband together. (BCCB)

48   Clifton, Lucille. **My brother fine with me.** Illustrated by Moneta Barnett. Holt, 1975.

An eight-year-old girl gladly helps her nuisance five-year-old brother pack when he decides to leave home. However, when he is gone, the house is too quiet, she is restless and has nobody to play with. She looks outside and is delighted to find him sitting on the front steps.   (BCCB)

49   Clifton, Lucille. **My friend Jacob.** Elsevier-Dutton, 1980.

Warm friendship is celebrated between eight-year-old Sam and sixteen-year-old Jacob, a retarded youth who lives next door. (BL)

50   Clifton, Lucille. **Some of the days of Everett Anderson.** Illustrated by Evaline Ness. Holt, 1970.

Nine short poems interpret the thoughts and activities of a lively six-year-old black boy from Monday morning to the following Sunday night.   (BL)

51   Clifton, Lucille. **Three wishes.** Illustrated by Stephanie Douglas. Viking, 1976.

Nobie finds a penny with her birth year on it. This lucky penny provides her with three wishes. When her friend leaves after a quarrel, she is reminded that the best thing to wish for is good friends.   (BCCB)

52   Cornish, Sam. **Grandmother's pictures.** Illustrated by Jeanne Johns. Bookstore Pr., 1974.

A small boy narrates a story of a black community in New England by explaining what he learns and feels when he visits his grandmother who shows him snapshots of relatives and explains their destinies.   (PW)

53   Cornish, Sam. **Your hand in mine.** Illustrated by Carl Owens. HBJ, 1970.

A small black boy is lonely and writes verses about things around him. He fends for himself because both parents work, but when he forgets his lunch, he realizes that his teacher is his friend.   (LJ)

54   Crews, Donald. **Bicycle race.** Illustrated by Donald Crews. Greenwillow, 1985.

Twelve bicyclists in numbered helmets are the focus of this counting book which enumerates the changing order of numbers as riders continually switch positions.   (BL)

55   Crews, Donald. **Carousel.** Illustrated by Donald Crews. Greenwillow, 1982.

Color photography of paintings in Art Deco style and words without a story line describe the waiting horses, the carousel ride, and the end of the whirling joy.   (CC)

Winner: Notable Children's Books (American Library Association), 1982.

56   Crews, Donald. **Flying.** Illustrated by Donald Crews. Greenwillow, 1986.

A propeller airplane takes off, flies over cities, highways, countrysides, mountains, clouds, and lands with its solo passenger— a little boy. This full-color study in movement has very little text.   (BL)

Winner: New York Times Choice of Best Illustrated Children's Books of the Year, 1986.

57   Crews, Donald. **Freight train.** Illustrated by Donald Crews. Greenwillow, 1978.

This train book presents colors and the different cars of a train that move in and out of a tunnel, past cities, and across trestles on a track along the bottom of the page.   (BCCB)

Winner: Art Books for Children Citation, 1979; Randolph Caldecott Honor Book, 1979.

58   Crews, Donald. **Harbor.** Illustrated by Donald Crews. Greenwillow, 1982.

Many kinds of boats and ships are shown as modes of transportation. A busy harbor, docks, piers, wharves, and warehouses are portrayed in simple drawings and bright colors.   (BCCB)

59   Crews, Donald. **Light.** Illustrated by Donald Crews. Greenwillow, 1981.

Distinctions are made among the different kinds of lights— artificial and natural, garish neon, and the tracery of lights glimmering on a large bridge.   (BCCB)

60   Crews, Donald. **Parade.** Illustrated by Donald Crews. Greenwillow, 1983.

The gathering crowd, vendors, a marching band, baton twirlers, floats, antique cars and bicycles, a fire engine, and the sanitation truck which cleans the deserted parade route depict a parade and its excitement.   (BCCB)

61   Crews, Donald. **School bus.** Illustrated by Donald Crews. Greenwillow, 1984.

Clear color blocks show empty buses being boarded by children, which take them to schools around the town. The buses are then parked in school lots until it is time for the children and buses to go home.   (BCCB)

Winner: School Library Journal "Best Books of the Year" Award, 1984.

62   Crews, Donald. **Ten black dots.** Illustrated by Donald Crews. Greenwillow, 1986.

Objects from one to ten are introduced with colors and textures for visual variety.   (SLJ)

63   Crews, Donald. **Truck.** Illustrated by Donald Crews. Greenwillow, 1980.

This picture book follows a truck from its loading station to its destination as it encounters road signs, other trucks on the highway, a truck stop, and the intricate road system.   (BCCB)

Winner: Notable Children's Books (American Library Association), 1980; Randolph Caldecott Honor Book, 1981; School Library Journal "Best Books of the Year" Award, 1980.

64   Crews, Donald. **We read: A to Z.** Illustrated by Donald Crews. Greenwillow, 1967.

Alphabet letters are combined with illustrations to provide definite concepts that children can see and use.   (CC)

Winner: New Jersey Institute of Technology New Jersey Author Award, 1967.

65   Cullen, Countee. **The lost zoo (a rhyme for the young, but not too young)** by Christopher Cat and [the author]. Harper, 1940.

Christopher, Cullen's cat, relates stories from his father in rhyme about the queer animals that did not get into Noah's ark.   (BRD)

66   Cummings, Pat. **C.L.O.U.D.S.** Illustrated by Pat Cummings. Lothrop, 1986.

In a spoof of the business management sector, Chuku works for C.L.O.U.D.S. (Creative Lights, Opticals, and Unusual Designs in the Sky) and is assigned the unenviable job of designing the skies over New York City which has tall buildings, dirty air, and people who don't look up.   (SLJ)

67   Cummings, Pat. **Jimmy Lee did it.** Lothrop, 1985.

Whenever Artie gets into trouble, his imaginary friend, Jimmy Lee, must take the blame.   (EPL)

68   De Veaux, Alexis. **An enchanted hair tale.** Illustrated by Alexis De Veaux. Harper, 1987.

Enchanted hair refers to the dreadlocks which Sudan wears. When others see his hair as unsightful rather than enchanted, he runs away and finds a circus with performers who all wear their hair in dreadlocks.   (KIR)

Winner: Notable Children's Books (American Library Association), 1987.

69   De Veaux, Alexis. **Na-nl; a story and pictures** [by the author]. Illustrated by Alexis De Veaux. Harper, 1973.

Na-ni waits outside with her friend for the mailman to deliver the welfare check which her mother has promised will buy a bicycle. The check is stolen from the mailbox while they are inside the house. Na-ni, now devastated, goes to her room and writes her story as a sad poem.   (BL)

70   Dodson, Owen. **Boy at the window.** Farrar, 1951.

This first novel by Dodson portrays one year in a nine-year-old black boy's life in a Brooklyn neighborhood.   (BRD)

71   Dunbar, Paul Laurence. **Little brown baby.** Illustrated by Erick Berry. Dodd, 1940.

Poems for young readers from the author's works are written in dialect. A biographical sketch is also included.   (BRD)

72   Egypt, Ophelia Settle. **James Weldon Johnson.** Illustrated by Moneta Barnett. Crowell, 1974.

This book is a mildly fictionalized introduction to Johnson's life, interests, and accomplishments.   (BL)

73   Evans, Mari. **I look at me!** Third World Press, 1974.

This reader manual to teach two-year-olds is also useful in instruction to counteract racism against blacks.   (LJ)

74   Evans, Mari. **J. D.** Illustrated by Jerry Pinkney. Doubleday, 1973.

Eight-year-old J.D. lives with his mother in a housing project. Four short stories portray him as lonely, sometimes frightened, and wise beyond his years.   (LJ)

75   Evans, Mari. **Jim flying high.** Illustrated by Ashley Bryan. Doubleday, 1979.

This story is told in black idiom by one of the boys who sees Jim, a flying fish, get stuck in a tree. Jim gasps and dries out but refuses to acknowledge that he needs help. An act of pity helps him to recuperate and return to the water.   (BCCB)

76   Feelings, Muriel. **Jambo means hello; Swahili alphabet book.** Illustrated by Tom Feelings. Dial, 1974.

This introduction to the Swahili alphabet couples words with a sentence or two that imparts information on their meaning in terms of African culture.   (BL)

Winner: Art Books for Children Citation, 1976; Boston Globe-Horn Book Award, 1974; Randolph Caldecott Honor Book, 1975.

77   Feelings, Muriel. **Moja means one; Swahili counting book.** Illustrated by Tom Feelings. Dial, 1971.

Softly shaded paintings depict mountains, villages, trees, animals, markets, and musical instruments of East Africa in accord with the Swahili numbers moja to kumi.   (LJ)

Winner: Art Books for Children Citation, 1974, 1975, 1983; Randolph Caldecott Honor Book, 1972.

78   Feelings, Muriel. **Zamani goes to market.** Illustrated by Tom Feelings. Seabury, 1970.

This story set in West Africa shows Zamani of age and going to market for the first time. He chooses to buy a necklace for his mother and is delighted to discover that his father bought him his first grown-up garment.   (BCCB)

79   Flournoy, Valerie. **The patchwork quilt.** Illustrated by Jerry Pinkney. Dial, 1985.

Tanya, a young black girl, helps her grandmother and mother make a quilt using scraps cut from the family's old clothing. The beautiful quilt tells the story of her family's life.   (SLJ)

Winner: Notable Children's Books (American Library Association), 1985; Christopher Award, 1987; Coretta Scott King Award, 1986.

80   Fufuka, Karama. **My daddy is a cool dude, and other poems.** Illustrated by Mahiri Fufuka. Dial, 1975.

An easy-feeling familiarity with big city black experience provides expressions of friendship.   (BL)

81   Gibbs, Ruth Duckett. **Black is the color.** Illustrated by Tom Feelings. Center for Media Development, 1973.

Each poem in this book speaks primarily to black children by expressing a single aspect of black pride. Notes suggesting uses of the poems are provided to teachers and parents.   (BL)

82   Giovanni, Nikki. **Ego-tripping and other poems for young people.** Illustrated by George Cephas Ford. Lawrence Hill Bks., 1974.

Angry, tender, and impassioned poems about children and the poet's childhood celebrate blackness.   (BCCB)

83   Giovanni, Nikki. **Spin a soft black song.** Illustrated by Charles Bible. Hill & Wang, 1985.

These poems are about black children on the themes of mommies, daddies, babies, haircuts, basketball, and dreams.   (ED)

84   Giovanni, Nikki. **Vacation time; poems for children.** Morrow, 1980.

Brief, humorous, lyrical, and narrative poems covering subjects related to vacation time.   (BCCB)

85   Goss, Clay. **Bill Pickett: black bulldogger.** Illustrated by Chico Hall. Hill & Wang, 1970.

Pickett is a cowhand of 1910 who stands to lose his chance for a bulldogging prize because of an accident to his horse.   (LJ)

86   Graham, Lorenz. **David he no fear.** Illustrated by Ann Grifalconi. Crowell, 1971.

Based on the story of David and Goliath as told by an African storyteller in the colloquial cadence of the oral tradition. (BCCB)

87   Graham, Lorenz. **Every man heart lay down.** Illustrated by Colleen Browning. Crowell, 1970.

This African retelling and interpretation of events of the first Christmas comes from the author's collection of retold Bible stories—*How God Fix Jonah.* (BCCB)

Winner: Coretta Scott King Honorable Mention Book, 1971.

88   Graham, Lorenz. **God wash the world and start again.** Illustrated by Clare Romano Ross. Crowell, 1971.

Using the rhythmic parlance and imagery of English-speaking Liberian storytellers, the story of Noah and the flood is retold. (BL)

89   Graham, Lorenz. **Hongry catches the foolish boy.** Illustrated by James Brown. Crowell, 1973.

African speech patterns adapt biblical language in a single-story picture book of the young prodigal son's return home and his older brother's reaction. (BCCB)

90   Graham, Lorenz. **How God fix Jonah.** Illustrated by Letterio Calapai. Reynal, 1946.

Twenty-one Bible stories are told in the idiom of a West African native. (BRD)

91   Graham, Lorenz. **A road down in the sea.** Illustrated by Gregorio Prestopino. Crowell, 1970.

This biblical story of the exodus from Egypt, retold in Liberian dialect, comes from the author's *How God Fix Noah.* (BCCB)

92   Graham, Lorenz. **Song of the boat.** Illustrated by Leo and Diane Dillon. Crowell, 1975.

Momolu, the son of an African tribesman, helps his father find just the right tree for making a boat to replace the canoe broken by an alligator. (BCCB)

Winner: Boston Globe-Horn Book Award, 1976; Children's Book Showcase Award, 1976.

93 Greenfield, Eloise. **Africa dream.** Illustrated by Carole M. Byard. Day, 1977.

Poetic text and swirling pictures describe a child's dream (daydream?) of going back across the sea, back in time, to the Africa of long ago. (BCCB)

Winner: Coretta Scott King Award, 1978.

94 Greenfield, Eloise. **Darlene.** Illustrated by George Cephas Ford. Methuen, 1980.

A physically handicapped black girl learns to feel less different and to relax with her relatives who love her. (BCCB)

95 Greenfield, Eloise. **Daydreamers.** Illustrated by Tom Feelings. Dial, 1981.

This book is a poetic mood piece about a child who daydreams and who is changed by the introspective quietness of that process. (BCCB)

Winner: Notable Children's Books (American Library Association), 1981; Coretta Scott King Honorable Mention Book, 1982.

96 Greenfield, Eloise. **First pink light.** Illustrated by Moneta Barnett. Crowell, 1976.

In order to avoid missing his daddy's homecoming, Tyree's mother allows him to get his pillow and blanket and watch by the window for the first pink light. Of course, he falls asleep. (BL)

97 Greenfield, Eloise. **Good news.** Illustrated by Pat Cummings. Coward, 1977.

When a little boy comes home from school excited about his ability to read, he isn't able to capture his busy mother's attention, so he tells his baby sister who is too young to understand. (BCCB)

98   Greenfield, Eloise. **Grandmama's joy.** Illustrated by Carole M. Byard. Collins, 1980.

When grandmother must move from her home, granddaughter Rhondy reminds her that love will endure wherever they live. (EPL)

Winner: Coretta Scott King Honorable Mention Book, 1981.

99   Greenfield, Eloise. **Grandpa's face.** Illustrated by Floyd Cooper. Philomel Bks., 1988.

Tamika is a little black girl who loves her grandpa—especially his face. When she peeks while he is rehearsing for a play, she sees a face which upsets her greatly. They take a talk-walk to the park and Grandpa reassures her of his love. (ED)

Winner: School Library Journal "Best Books of the Year" Award, 1988; Notable Children's Books (American Library Association), 1988.

100   Greenfield, Eloise. **Honey, I love, and other love poems.** Illustrated by Diane and Leo Dillon. Crowell, 1978.

Beautiful black girls illustrate sixteen poems about a child's love and enjoyment of people, places, and doing things. (BCCB)

101   Greenfield, Eloise. **Mary McLeod Bethune.** Illustrated by Jerry Pinkney. Crowell, 1977.

The author outlines Bethune's childhood, years of schooling, and pioneering work in the area of fostering education among blacks. (BL)

Winner: Coretta Scott King Honorable Mention Book, 1978.

102   Greenfield, Eloise. **Me and Neesie.** Illustrated by Moneta Barnett. Crowell, 1975.

Janell's insistence that she has an imaginary friend exasperates her mother, but Aunt Bea acts aggressively to encourage Janell to find new friends at school. (BCCB)

103   Greenfield, Eloise. **Nathaniel talking.** Illustrated by Jan Spivey Gilchrist. Black Butterfly Children's Bks., 1988.

Nine-year-old Nathaniel B. Free is a poet who raps and

rhymes about his world, his education, his family life, and what it is like to be nine. He is playful, curious, enthusiastic, and intelligent as he synthesizes information and questions contradictions. (ED)

104   Greenfield, Eloise. **Paul Robeson.** Illustrated by George Cephas Ford. Crowell, 1975.

This biography of a great singer emphasizes his role as a political activist and covers the major points of his childhood. (BCCB)

Winner: Jane Addams Book Award, 1976; Coretta Scott King Honorable Mention Book, 1976.

105   Greenfield, Eloise. **Rosa Parks.** Illustrated by Eric Marlow. Crowell, 1973.

This book sketches Parks's life up to the point when her refusal to give up her bus seat sparked the modern civil rights movement. (BL)

Winner: Carter G. Woodson Book Award, 1974.

106   Greenfield, Eloise. **She come bringing me that little baby girl.** Illustrated by John Steptoe. Lippincott, 1974.

When Kevin sees his infant sister for the first time, he is downright disturbed at the adults' responses to her. His Uncle Ray helps him to appreciate his big brother role. (BL)

Winner: Boston Globe-Horn Book Award, 1975; Irma Simonton Black Award, 1975.

107   Greenfield, Eloise. **Talk about a family.** Illustrated by James Calvin. Lippincott, 1978.

This book views a young girl's experience when parental strife disrupts her family. A neighbor helps her to understand that broken things can assume new shapes and be made to work again. (BL)

108   Greenfield, Eloise. **Under the Sunday tree; poems.** Paintings by Amos Ferguson. Harper, 1988.

Familiar figures and everyday events in the life of a Bahamian community are presented in twenty poems and paintings. Included in the celebrations are subjects such as nature, family, occupations, special places, and dreams. (BRD)

Winner: Notable Children's Books (American Library Association), 1988.

109   Gregg, Ernest. **And the Sun God said: that's hip.** Illustrated by G. Falcon Beazer. Harper, 1972.

This poem and artwork celebrate the creation of the Third World of red, yellow, brown, and black creations with hip language. (LJ)

110   Griffin, Judith Berry. **The magic mirrors.** Illustrated by Ernest Crichlow. Coward, 1971.

A modern fairy tale about a beautiful young African princess of long ago tells how she was loved by all but one of her fifty-three stepmothers. (BCCB)

111   Griffin, Judith Berry. **Nat Turner.** Illustrated by Leo Carty. Coward, 1970.

This book is a biography of the slave whose unsuccessful rebellion was one of the events that paved the way for the abolition of slavery. (BCCB)

112   Griffin, Judith Berry. **Phoebe and the general.** Illustrated by Margot Tomes. Coward, 1977.

The thirteen-year-old daughter of a free black businessman in New York City is sent to serve as a housekeeper for General George Washington. While serving the general, she prevents a murder attempt on his life. (BCCB)

113   Grimes, Nikki. **Something on my mind.** Illustrated by Tom Feelings. Dial, 1978.

Poems are illustrated with children waiting, hopeful and expectant, and brooding. (LA)

Winner: Coretta Scott King Award, 1979.

114   Guy, Rosa. **Mother Crocodile: an Uncle Amadou tale from Senegal.** Illustrated by John Steptoe. Delacorte, 1981.

This cautionary tale describes how the vengeful and foolish

monkey abuses the wisdom of Mother Crocodile so that her children no longer listen to her stories of the dangers brought by men. (SLJ)

Winner: Notable Children's Books (American Library Association), 1981; Coretta Scott King Award, 1982.

115 Halliburton, Warren J. **The picture life of Jesse Jackson.** Watts, 1972.

This brief look at the life and works of Jackson, a Chicago-based, nationally known civil rights leader, emphasizes his image as a determined and gifted young black man. (BL)

116 Halliburton, Warren J. **The picture life of Michael Jackson.** Watts, 1984.

The Jacksons' career history is telescoped as attention is given to Michael's private and public life and to his record-breaking "Thriller" album and video. (BL)

117 Hamilton, Virginia. **Jahdu.** Illustrated by Jerry Pinkney. Greenwillow, 1980.

Carved and lucid beads on a storyteller's chain are linked to form a story about Jahdu who is taunted by other creatures, is told that he has lost his power, and is upset that he has lost his shadow. (BCCB)

118 Hamilton, Virginia. **Time-ago lost: more tales of Jahdu.** Macmillan, 1973.

Further adventures of Jahdu, the strong, black hero, are told as Mama Luka reaches into the air to catch a story and entertain Lee Edward. (BL)

119 Hamilton, Virginia. **The time-ago tales of Jahdu.** Illustrated by Nonny Hogrogian. Macmillan, 1969.

Each day Lee Edward stayed with Mama Luka after school, she told a story of Jahdu, the crafty boy who grew wiser and more powerful. (BCCB)

120 Hansen, Joyce. **The gift-giver.** Houghton, 1980.

A fifth-grade girl in the Bronx tells of her friendship with a foster boy who intrigues her with his quiet self-possession.

She learns from him the maturity to accept her parents' rules as evidence of their love and to be helpful during her father's temporary unemployment. (BRD)

121   Haskett, Edythe Rance, ed. **Grains of pepper: folktales from Liberia.** Illustrated by Musu Miatta. Abelard-Schuman, 1970.

An American school teacher captures Liberian folktales in the pidgin English in which she probably encountered them. (TLS)

122   Haskett, Edythe Rance, ed. **Some gold, a little ivory: country tales from Ghana and the Ivory Coast.** Illustrated by Edythe Haskett. Day, 1971.

Dilemma stories, didactic tales, and pourquoi stories are told in simple, expository style with frequent direct conversations, much humor, and often with a proverb at the end. (LJ)

123   Haskins, James. **Barbara Jordan.** Dial, 1977.

As the first black woman elected to the state senate in Texas, Jordan went to Washington and to the Democratic National Convention in 1976. (ESLC)

Winner: Coretta Scott King Honorable Mention Book, 1978.

124   Haskins, James. **Diana Ross, star Supreme.** Illustrated by Jim Spence. Viking, 1985.

This book portrays the ups and downs of the personal and professional lives of this ambitious and determined singer and movie star. (ESLC)

125   Hollingsworth, A. C. **I'd like the Goo-gen-heim.** Illustrated by Alvin C. Hollingsworth. Reilly & Lee, 1970.

While his dad naps in Central Park, Andy takes a solitary tour of the museum across the street, and when asked what he would like for his birthday, the title is his response. (BCCB)

126   Hughes, Langston. **First book of rhythms.** Illustrated by Robin King. Watts, 1954.

An invitation to make rhythm with a pencil on paper progresses to explanations of rhythms of music, painting, sculpture, nature, athletics, and machines. (BRD)

127   Hughes, Langston. **First book of the West Indies.** Illustrated by Robert Bruce. Watts, 1956.

After giving a general view of the West Indies, each island is presented with a discussion of famous persons born there, customs, trade, plants, etc. (BRD)

128   Hunter, Kristin. **Boss cat.** Illustrated by Harold Franklin. Scribner, 1971.

When a cat becomes a member of a poor black and proud family, the superstitious mother presents a problem because she believes cats to be bad luck. (PW)

129   Jordan, June. **Fannie Lou Hamer.** Illustrated by Albert Williams. Crowell, 1972.

A black woman with only a sixth-grade education assumed leadership for registering blacks to vote. Of the many highlights of Hamer's life, she was jailed and beaten, founded the Freedom Farm Cooperative, and became a public figure. (BCCB)

130   Jordan, June. **Kimako's story.** Illustrated by Kay Burford. Houghton, 1981.

Seven-year-old Kimako describes the sights and sounds of the city beyond her home as she walks the neighbor's dog. (SLJ)

131   Jordan, June. **New life, new room.** Illustrated by Ray Cruz. Crowell, 1975.

When the birth of their fourth child nears, Mr. and Mrs. Robinson give their large bedroom to their children, ages ten, nine, and six, and leave everything to them. Their childlike solutions form a warm, violence-free happening in which the process is central. (BL)

132   Jordan, June and Bush, Terri, comp. **The voice of the children.** Holt, 1970.

This collection of poetry and short pieces written by black and Puerto Rican children contains stridence, anger, abrasiveness, joy, and sadness. (PW)

Winner: Nancy Block Memorial Award, 1971; Coretta Scott King Honorable Mention Book, 1971.

133   King, Helen H. **The soul of Christmas.** Johnson, 1972.

A black family in the city prepares to celebrate Christmas. (NUC)

134   King, Helen H. **Willy.** Illustrated by Carole M. Byard. Doubleday, 1971.

A nameless ten-year-old feels responsible for capturing a rat (Willy) who has ravaged the family's food supply.   (BCCB)

135   Lee, George L. **Interesting people: Black American history makers.** Illustrated by George Lee. McFarland & Co., 1989.

Cartoon-style drawings are accompanied by biographical highlights of notable people from contemporary leaders in government, civil rights, entertainment, and sports.   (ED)

136   Lester, Julius. **Black folktales.** Illustrated by Tom Feelings. R. W. Baron, 1969.

These are tales of African origin, slavery time, and the recent past with human and animal subjects.   (BCCB)

137   Lester, Julius. **How many spots does a leopard have? and other tales.** Illustrated by David Shannon. Scholastic, 1990.

This collection of African and Jewish folktales is told with colloquial language and is easy to read aloud. Full-page color paintings accompany each story.   (NYTBR)

138   Lester, Julius. **The knee-high man, and other tales.** Illustrated by Ralph Pinto. Dial, 1972.

Six animal stories from black folklore about cleverness and self-dissatisfaction are presented in this book.   (BCCB)

Winner: Lewis Carroll Shelf Award, 1973.

139   Lester, Julius. **More tales of Uncle Remus; further adventures of Brer Rabbit, his friends, enemies, and others.** Illustrated by Jerry Pinkney. Dial, 1988.

This companion volume to *The Tales of Uncle Remus: The Adventures of Brer Rabbit* includes retellings of thirty-seven stories from Joel Chandler Harris's compilation of African-American animal fables.   (BRD)

Winner: Notable Children's Books (American Library Association), 1988; School Library Journal "Best Books of the Year" Award, 1988.

140   Little, Lessie Jones. **Children of long ago: poems.** Illustrated by Jan Spivey Gilchrist. Philomel Bks., 1988.

Poems reflecting simpler days portray grandmothers who read aloud and children who walk barefoot on damp earth and pick blackberries for their paper dolls to eat.   (CIP)

141   Little, Lessie Jones and Greenfield, Eloise. **I can do it by myself.** Illustrated by Carole M. Byard. Crowell, 1978.

It is Mama's birthday and Donny knows just the right plant he can get for his precious dollar, but first he must overcome his apprehension about his solo shopping spree.   (CC)

142   Lynch, Lorenzo. **The hot dog man.** Illustrated by Lorenzo Lynch. Bobbs-Merrill, 1970.

A day in the life of a big city hot dog man is portrayed.   (LJ)

143   McKissack, Frederick. **Look what you've done now, Moses.** Illustrated by Patricia McKissack. Chariot Bks., 1984.

This story presents incidents from the life of Moses, including Pharaoh's daughter finding him in the Nile River and later receiving God's laws on Mount Sinai.   (NUC)

144   McKissack, Patricia C. **The Apache.** Childrens Pr., 1984.

This book describes the history, customs, religion, government, homes, and day-to-day life of the Apache people of the Southwest.   (CC)

145   McKissack, Patricia C. **Aztec Indians.** Photos. Childrens Pr., 1985.

The daily life, religion, government, and present-day descendants of the Aztec Indians are covered in this book.   (SLJ)

146   McKissack, Patricia C. and McKissack, Frederick. **Cinderella.** Illustrated by Tom Dunnington. Childrens Pr., 1985.

This adaptation of the original tale is illustrated with cartoon-style drawings and features a word list at the end of the story.   (SLJ)

147   McKissack, Patricia C. **Country mouse and city mouse.** Illustrated by Anne Sikorski. Childrens Pr., 1985.

This adapted version of the original tale brings the story to the present and is told by the country mouse who is frightened away from the city by a noisy garbage truck.   (SLJ)

148   McKissack, Patricia C. **Flossie and the fox.** Illustrated by Rachel Isadora. Dial, 1986.

A feisty little black girl outwits a sly fox who tries to steal the eggs she is sent to deliver to a neighbor.   (ED)

Winner: School Library Journal "Best Books of the Year" Award, 1986.

149   McKissack, Patricia C. **The Incas.** Photos. Childrens Pr., 1985.

The daily life, religion, government, and present-day descendants of the Incas are presented here.   (SLJ)

150   McKissack, Patricia C. **The little red hen.** Illustrated by Dennis Hockerman. Childrens Pr., 1985.

This adaptation and condensation of the original tale is illustrated in cartoon style and has a word list at the end of the story.   (SLJ)

151   McKissack, Patricia C. **The Mayas.** Photos. Childrens Pr., 1985.

The daily life, religion, government, and present-day descendants of the Mayas are covered in this book.   (SLJ)

152   McKissack, Patricia C. **Mirandy and Brother Wind.** Illustrated by Jerry Pinkney. Knopf, 1988.

For the fast-approaching junior cakewalk contest, Mirandy would like Brother Wind to be her partner. She follows through on a suggestion from Mis' Poinsettia and captures him. At the dance, she is paired with a clumsy boy named Ezel and calls on Brother Wind for help. They give a prizewinning performance.   (BRD)

Winner: Notable Children's Books (American Library Association), 1988; Coretta Scott King Award, 1989.

153   McKissack, Patricia C. **Who is who?** Illustrated by Elizabeth M. Allen. Childrens Pr., 1983.

Twin boys, Johnny and Bobby, display their preferences for

red or blue, over or under, front or back, and hot or cold. (SLJ)

154   Mathis, Sharon Bell. **Brooklyn story.** Illustrated by Charles Bible. Hill & Wang, 1970.

The daughter is hopeful and the son skeptical when their mother returns home after years of absence. (NUC)

155   Mathis, Sharon Bell. **The hundred penny box.** Illustrated by Leo and Diane Dillon. Viking, 1975.

Michael's 100-year-old great-great aunt shares memories of her life with him as she recalls people and places associated with her hundred pennies—one for each year of her life. (BL)

Winner: Boston Globe-Horn Book Award, 1975; John Newbery Honor Book, 1976.

156   Mathis, Sharon Bell. **Ray Charles.** Illustrated by George Cephas Ford. Crowell, 1973.

This is a short biography of the black jazz musician from his impoverished childhood to success despite obstacles, including blindness. (LJ)

Winner: Coretta Scott King Award, 1974.

157   Mathis, Sharon Bell. **Sidewalk story.** Illustrated by Leo Carty. Viking, 1971.

This easy-to-read book is a story of a little black girl who persists in trying to help a friend in trouble. (BL)

Winner: Council on Interracial Books for Children Award, 1969.

158   Michels, Barbara and White, Bettye. **Apples on a stick: the folklore of black children.** Illustrated by Jerry Pinkney. Coward, 1983.

This book is a collection of playground poetry and games captured from black children in Houston, Texas, and includes favorites of children throughout the United States. (ED)

159   Myers, Walter Dean. **The dancers.** Illustrated by Ann Rockwell. Parents Magazine Pr., 1972.

When Michael accompanies his dad to his job at the theatre,

the world of ballet is opened to him and the children in his neighborhood. (BCCB)

160   Myers, Walter Dean. **The dragon takes a wife.** Illustrated by Ann Grifalconi. Bobbs-Merrill, 1972.

An ambitious young dragon can't best a knight and win a wife, so he seeks help from a good fairy who turns herself into a dragon for demonstration purposes and decides to remain one because they have so much fun. (BCCB)

161   Myers, Walter Dean. **Fly, Jimmy, fly!** Illustrated by Moneta Barnett. Putnam, 1974.

Jimmy's inner city world is explored through a quiet, suggestive, fluent prose poem as he dreams of flying like a bird. (KIR)

162   Myers, Walter Dean. **The golden serpent.** Illustrated by Alice and Martin Provensen. Viking, 1980.

This is an abstract tale in which a wise Indian man and his young attendant are summoned by the king to solve what is defined only as "a mystery." (BL)

163   Myers, Walter Dean. **Mr. Monkey and the Gotcha bird.** Illustrated by Leslie Morrill. Delacorte, 1984.

Monkey, caught by the huge white bird who says "Gotcha" when he catches his prey, cleverly talks his way out of being eaten. (BCCB)

164   Myers, Walter Dean. **Where does the day go?** Illustrated by Leo Carty. Parents Magazine Pr., 1969.

A concept book about adult-child relationships in which the father explains, during a family outing in the park, that day and night are like people—different. (BL)

165   Palmer, C. Everard. **Baba and Mr. Big.** Illustrated by Lorenzo Lynch. Bobbs-Merrill, 1972.

Jim moves to a rural Jamaican community and finds it difficult to make friends until he solicits and receives assistance from lonely old Baba. (LJ)

166   Palmer, C. Everard. **A cow called Boy.** Illustrated by Charles E. Gaines. Bobbs-Merrill, 1972.

A small boy trains a young bull to perform at his command, and pandemonium results when the bull follows him to school.   (LJ)

167   Patterson, Lillie. **Birthdays.** Illustrated by Erica Merkling. Garrard, 1965.

This is a simplified survey for primary readers of past and present birthday customs in other countries, as well as changes in our customs.   (BCCB)

168   Patterson, Lillie. **Christmas feasts and festivals.** Illustrated by Cliff Schule. Garrard, 1968.

Topics such as Christmas music, national legendary gift givers (Santa Claus, Father Christmas, etc.), the holiday feast, and the use of greens enjoy separate chapters.   (BCCB)

169   Patterson, Lillie. **Christmas in America.** Illustrated by Vincent Colabella. Garrard, 1969.

Here is a chronological presentation of Christmas traditions and customs.   (BCCB)

170   Patterson, Lillie. **Christmas in Britain and Scandinavia.** Illustrated by Kelly Oechsli. Garrard, 1970.

Ethnic derivations and contributions are stressed and a cross-fertilization of national customs is shown.   (BCCB)

171   Patterson, Lillie. **Christmas trick or treat.** Illustrated by Kelly Oechsli. Garrard, 1979.

This book contains two tales—an ornery pixie king brings good fortune to three penniless boys; an elf plays tricks on a farmer who doesn't believe in fairies.   (SLJ)

172   Patterson, Lillie. **Coretta Scott King.** Garrard, 1977.

This biography emphasizes King's musical and scholastic abilities and her use of special skills to assist her husband's efforts during his lifetime and after his death.   (BL)

Winner: Coretta Scott King Honorable Mention Book, 1978.

173   Patterson, Lillie. **David, the story of a king.** Abingdon, 1985.

This is a retelling of the Old Testament story of David, the shepherd, who became King of Israel.   (NUC)

174   Patterson. Lillie. **Easter.** Illustrated by Kelly Oechsli. Garrard, 1966.

This book describes Easter customs, legends, and games, in both the pagan and Christian tradition. The styles of celebration and foods are also contrasted.   (BCCB)

175   Patterson, Lillie. **Frederick Douglass: freedom fighter.** Garrard, 1965.

This book introduces the life of the famous antislavery fighter, Frederick Douglass—his achievements, his escape to freedom, and his abolitionist activities.   (BL)

176   Patterson, Lillie. **The grouchy Santa.** Illustrated by Lou Cunette. Garrard, 1979.

A grumpy man takes a midnight ride to a lamenting widow who must wear rags and tatters, but who changes the grump into a do-gooder.   (SLJ)

177   Patterson, Lillie. **Halloween.** Illustrated by Gil Miret. Garrard, 1963.

Traces the origin of Halloween and its celebration from the ancient Celts and Romans to the present collection day for UNICEF.   (ESLC)

178   Patterson, Lillie. **Haunted house on Halloween.** Illustrated by Doug Cushman. Garrard, 1979.

This is a retelling of two spooky folktales—a man stays overnight in a house where bones thump around and assemble into a skeleton; a man outwits a witch cat.   (SLJ)

179   Patterson, Lillie. **Jack-o-lantern trick.** Illustrated by William Hutchinson. Garrard, 1979.

Two colonial girls cause hostile Indians to retreat by convincing them that grinning faces are evil spirits.   (SLJ)

180   Petry, Ann. **Drugstore cat.** Illustrated by Susanne Suba. Crowell, 1949.

The new drugstore cat, with a short tail and a shorter temper, scratches a customer and prompts the druggist's daughter to consider returning him to the country. (BRD)

181   Petry, Ann. **Legends of the saints.** Illustrated by Anne Rockwell. Crowell, 1971.

This book provides accounts of the lives of Christopher, Genesius, George, Blaise, Catherine of Alexandria, Nicholas, Francis of Assisi, Joan of Arc, Thomas More, and Martin de Porres. (BRD)

182   Robinson, Matt. **Giveaway Gibson.** Illustrated by Lou Myers. Random, 1971.

A generous emperor loads twenty-six camels, one for each letter of the alphabet, with giveaway goodies beginning with the appropriate letters. (NUC)

183   Robinson, Matt. **Gordon of Sesame Street storybook.** Illustrated by Edward Koren and others. Random, 1972.

Four brief stories convey the results of pollution and waste, playing with fire, bad manners, and stubbornness. (LJ)

184   Robinson, Matt. **A lot of hot water.** Illustrated by Stan Mack. Random, 1971.

Lonesome Lewis's dislike of people brings him much unnecessary trouble. (NUC)

185   Robinson, Matt. **The pecan tree.** Illustrated by Robert Velde. Random, 1971.

A farmer's pecan tree grows so high that it becomes a menace to the village. (NUC)

186   Robinson, Matt. **The six-button dragon.** Illustrated by Brumsic Brandon, Jr. Random, 1971.

Short-stick Stokes rescues Little Louella from Fire-Breathing Brown, the Six-Button Dragon. (NUC)

187   Rollins, Charlemae Hill, comp. **Christmas gif'.** Illustrated by Tom O'Sullivan. Follett, 1963.

Subtitle: An anthology of Christmas poems, songs, essays, stories, and recipes written by and about blacks. The title is from a game played by slaves on Christmas Day—two people meeting would compete to be the first to call out the words; the loser would pay the forfeit of a simple present.   (BRD)

188   Sanchez, Sonia. **The adventures of Fathead, Smallhead and Squarehead.** Illustrated by Taiwo DuVall. Third World Press, 1974.

A fable of three friends who set out for Mecca has as its moral "slow is not always dumb and fast is not always smart." (PW)

189   Shearer, John. **Billy Jo Jive and the case of the missing pigeons.** Illustrated by Ted Shearer. Delacorte, 1978.

Billy Jo Jive and his crime-fighting partner, Susie Sunset, track down several false leads before their photographic experience helps them catch the pigeon thief.   (ESLC)

190   Shearer, John. **Billy Jo Jive and the walkie-talkie caper.** Illustrated by Ted Shearer. Dell, 1982.

Supersleuth Billy Jo Jive and his sidekick Susie Sunset are called for help when someone steals the walkie-talkie which Steam Boat Lewis needs to build a secret communications system for the Bugaloo Smackers club.   (NYTBR)

191   Shearer, John. **The case of the missing ten speed bike.** Delacorte, 1977.

Billy Jo and his partner Susie Sunset solve this mystery set against an intercity background.   (ESLC)

192   Shearer, John. **Case of the sneaker snatcher.** Illustrated by Ted Shearer. Delacorte, 1977.

Billy Jo and Susie track down lots of clues and recover the missing lucky basketball shoes which were ripped off just before the big Bugaloo Smackers game.   (ESLC)

193   Shearer, John. **I wish I had an Afro.** Cowles, 1970.

Both the parents and their eleven-year-old son narrate a portion of the story by relating personal ideals and dreams. Little John begins to take pride in his blackness and wants to wear an Afro, something which his father forbids.   (BRD)

194   Shearer, John. **Little man in the family.** Illustrated by John Shearer. Delacorte, 1972.

This photographic essay shows similarities and differences in the lives of a Puerto Rican boy and an upper-middle-class white boy. (ESLC)

195   Shepard, Mary and Shepard, Ray. **Vegetable soup activities.** Scholastic, 1975.

This book consists of crafts, games, recipes, language activities, and answers to children's questions. It is intended as a follow-up to the television program "Vegetable Soup." (SLJ)

196   Sherlock, Philip Manderson. **Anansi, the spider man; Jamaican folk tales.** Illustrated by Marcia Brown. Crowell, 1954.

In this retelling of some Caribbean folktales, Anansi, the spider man, is central. Being both man and spider, Anansi becomes a spider when he is in great danger. (BRD)

197   Sherlock, Philip Manderson. **The iguana's tail; crick crack stories from the Caribbean.** Illustrated by Gioia Fiammenghi. Crowell, 1969.

Six short, self-explanatory animal tales are connected by the device of travelers swapping stories to shorten a journey. Each story is introduced and concluded by a traditionally Caribbean, ritualistic, attention-calling dialogue between the storyteller and the audience. (BRD)

198   Sherlock, Philip Manderson. **West Indian folk-tales.** Illustrated by John Kiddell-Monroe. Walck, 1966.

Some of the more serious tales here stem from the mythology of the Caribs. The lively ones feature Anansi, the tricky spider brought to the islands by African slaves. (BRD)

199   Steptoe, John. **Baby says.** Illustrated by John Steptoe. Lothrop, 1988.

Loving exchanges in few words happen between two brothers—one of whom is trying to construct a building block castle while his baby brother in the play pen does all he can to upset the process. (SLJ)

200   Steptoe, John. **Birthday.** Illustrated by John Steptoe. Holt, 1972.

Javaka's eighth birthday is the occasion for a very special celebration because he was the first child born in the new town of Yoruba. (LJ)

201   Steptoe, John. **Daddy is a monster . . . sometimes.** Illustrated by John Steptoe. Lippincott, 1980.

Two black children talk about their relationship with Daddy and how he behaves when they misbehave and anger him. (BCCB)

202   Steptoe, John. **Jeffrey Bear cleans up his act.** Illustrated by John Steptoe. Lothrop, 1983.

Bears act out a scenario of boredom in the classroom when a man from the sanitation department talks to the second grade. (BCCB)

203   Steptoe, John. **Mufaro's beautiful daughters: an African tale.** Illustrated by John Steptoe. Lothrop, 1987.

This story of two sisters, alike in beauty but opposite in disposition, is based on an animal-groom tale collected at the end of the nineteenth century from the Zimbabwe region of southern Africa. (BCCB)

Winner: Notable Children's Books (American Library Association), 1987; Boston Globe-Horn Book Award, 1987; Coretta Scott King Award, 1988; Randolph Caldecott Honor Book, 1987; School Library Journal "Best Books of the Year" Award, 1987.

204   Steptoe, John. **My special best words.** Illustrated by John Steptoe. Viking, 1974.

Steptoe's children are featured in their daily routines that end with a bedtime story and "I love you." (BL)

205   Steptoe, John. **Stevie.** Illustrated by John Steptoe. Harper, 1969.

Stevie enjoys, without reserve, a day-care arrangement at Robert's house and leads Robert to admit that he is lonely as an only child. (BCCB)

Winner: Art Books for Children Citation, 1973; Lewis Carroll Shelf Award, 1978.

206   Steptoe, John. **The story of jumping mouse.** Illustrated by John Steptoe. Lothrop, 1984.

This is an adaptation of a Native American legend in which a young mouse dreams of and sets out to find a wonderful, faraway land. (BL)

Winner: Randolph Caldecott Medal, 1984.

207   Steptoe, John. **Train ride.** Illustrated by John Steptoe. Harper, 1971.

Four black boys, wanting something to do, sneak onto a subway train in Brooklyn and ride to Times Square where they spend their money in a penny arcade and earn the spanking of their lives upon returning home. (BL)

208   Stokes, Olivia P., comp. **The beauty of being black; folktales, poems and art from Africa.** Edited by Louise Crane and illustrated by Karen Turek. Friendship Pr., 1971.

This collection of folktales, poems, and short stories from Africa is enhanced by photographs and discussions of Africa's art. (OCLC)

209   Stokes, Olivia P. **Why the spider lives in corners; African facts and fun.** Edited by Louise Crane and illustrated by Allan Eitzen. Friendship Pr., 1971.

This book is an introduction to Ghana, Liberia, Congo, Uganda, and Zambia by giving a description of the flag, an article about a typical child, a factual portrait of the country, a folktale, and a native game or song. (OCLC)

210   Tarry, Ellen. **Hezakiah Horton.** Illustrated by Oliver Wendell Harrington. Viking, 1942.

A small black boy with a large admiration for automobiles gets a ride in a beautiful shiny red car and makes friends with the owner. (BRD)

211   Tarry, Ellen and Ets, Marie Hall. **My dog Rinty.** Photos by Alexander and Alexandra Alland. Viking, 1946.

A small black boy and his much misunderstood dog give an idea of life in Harlem. (BRD)

212   Tarry, Ellen. **Runaway elephant.** Illustrated by Oliver Wendell Harrington. Viking, 1950.

Hezekiah and his friend with the big red car are tracking down a runaway circus elephant, for which the small boy has the one piece of information needed for successful capture. (BRD)

213 Tate, Eleanora. **Just an overnight guest.** Dial, 1987.

A nine-year-old black girl explains her emotional growth when her four-year-old biracial cousin Ethel is brought home to escape neglect and abuse from her mother. (BCCB)

214 Taylor, Mildred. **The friendship.** Dial, 1987.

Four young black children patronize a country store they had been warned about. In Mississippi of 1933, the youngest experiences his first racial harassment, but later they all witness the humiliation and injury of an old black man who refuses to address the store's owner as "Mister." (WLB)

Winner: Notable Children's Books (American Library Association), 1987; Boston Globe-Horn Book Award, 1988; Coretta Scott King Award, 1988.

215 Taylor, Mildred. **The gold Cadillac.** Illustrated by Michael Hays. Dial, 1987.

A young black girl explains the fears which she and her sister experience as they take a trip with their parents to visit their grandparents in the South. Their father's new gold-colored Cadillac attracts racist reactions from the whites they encounter. This is a youthful perspective on racism and its dehumanizing intentions. (SLJ)

Winner: Christopher Award, 1988.

216 Taylor, Mildred D. **Song of the trees.** Illustrated by Jerry Pinkney. Dial, 1975.

Cassie, one of four children, tells the story of a Depression-era incident in Taylor's family history in the Deep South. (BCCB)

Winner: Children's Book Showcase Award, 1976; Council on Interracial Books for Children Award, 1973; Coretta Scott King Honorable Mention Book, 1976.

217 Teague, Bob. **Adam in Blunderland.** Illustrated by Floyd Sowell. Doubleday, 1971.

Fantasy features ten-year-old Adam in Fun City which is in-

habited only by boys and girls, but which replicates many
societal ills of the real world. (LJ)

218 Teague, Bob. **Agent K-13, the super spy.** Illustrated by Geoffrey
Moss. Doubleday, 1974.

Agent K-13, of the Secret Service, outwits Simon La Greedy,
kidnapper of the most dangerous super weapon ever
invented—the Crumble-Bomb. (BL)

219 Teague, Bob. **Super-spy K-13 in outer space.** Illustrated by Sammis
McLean. Doubleday, 1980.

Stripped of his secret spy kit, Agent K-13 must use ingenuity
and the enemy's weapons to prevent an immobilization of all
machines on Earth. (LJ)

220 Thomas, Dawn C. **A bicycle from Bridgetown.** Illustrated by
Donald George Miller. McGraw-Hill, 1975.

Edgar dreams of having a bicycle like those of the famous
cyclists. Then he could help earn money for the family and
use his free time to explore the island of Barbados beyond his
impoverished village. (SLJ)

221 Thomas, Dawn C. **Downtown is.** Illustrated by Colleen Browning.
McGraw-Hill, 1972.

When a boy from uptown New York makes his first trip downtown, he finds a dollar bill in the street and takes a ride on the
A train. The story explains the sights he sees as he discovers
that downtown isn't everything he dreamed it would be.
(BCCB)

222 Thomas, Dawn C. **Mira! Mira!** Illustrated by Harold L. James. Lippincott, 1970.

After arriving in New York City from Puerto Rico, Ramon and
two friends experience new and wonderful things, including a
snowstorm! (BL)

223 Thomas, Dawn C. **Pablito's new feet.** Illustrated by Paul Frame.
Lippincott, 1973.

Polio renders a young Puerto Rican boy unable to walk. When
his family moves to New York City, he has two operations and

finally walks when a famous baseball player visits the hospital to dispense autographed baseballs. (BCCB)

224   Thomas, Dawn C. **A tree for Tompkins Park.** Illustrated by Leo Carty. McGraw-Hill, 1971.

A Cub Scout conceived the idea of a large and glorious Christmas tree for the local park in the Bedford-Stuyvesant section of Brooklyn, like the tree in Rockefeller Center. This effort brought the entire community together. (BCCB)

225   Thomas, Ianthe. **Hi, Mrs. Mallory!** Illustrated by Ann Toulmin-Rothe. Harper, 1979.

This is a story of friendship and death told by a young black girl about her elderly white neighbor and their lives in a farm community. The void left by Mrs. Mallory's death is mitigated when her pet moves to the little girl's house. (BRD)

226   Thomas, Ianthe. **Willie blows a mean horn.** Illustrated by Ann Toulmin-Rothe. Harper, 1981.

Willie's young son narrates the story of an evening spent listening to his father play the trumpet at a jazz jamboree, visiting him backstage, and finally going to bed with dreams of playing a horn with his dad someday. (BRD)

227   Turner, Glennette T. **Surprise for Mrs. Burns.** Albert Whitman, 1971.

When the elementary students learn that their black teacher is leaving, they are inspired to plan a surprise party to honor her. The story focuses on their preparations for the party. (LJ)

228   Turner, Glennette T. **Take a walk in their shoes.** Illustrated by Elton Clay Fax. Dutton, 1990.

Here are fourteen biographical sketches of Black Americans who made significant social contributions. Each chapter is accompanied by the script for a short skit capturing a key event. (NYTBR)

229   Walker, Alice. **Langston Hughes, American poet.** Illustrated by Donald George Miller. Crowell, 1974.

This biography relates the high points of Hughes's life by emphasizing his youth and his relationship with his family. (LJ)

230   Walter, Mildred Pitts. **Brother to the wind.** Illustrated by Leo and Diane Dillon. Lothrop, 1985.

This folktale in an African setting shows how Emeke is jeered by his peers because he wants to fly and plans to ask Good Snake to grant his wish.   (BCCB)

231   Walter, Mildred Pitts. **My mama needs me.** Illustrated by Pat Cummings. Lothrop, 1983.

When Jason confines himself to the house to be near his mother and new baby sister, he is allowed to hold the baby and to help bathe her before he is given the hug he craves. (BCCB)

Winner: Coretta Scott King Award, 1984.

232   Walter, Mildred Pitts. **Ty's one-man band.** Four Winds Pr., 1980.

Andro seems miraculous to Ty because he can jiggle his eating utensils and make rhythms with them. He further proves his musical skills when Ty brings a washboard, a comb, wooden spoons, a tin pail, and his family and friends.   (BL)

233   White, Edgar. **Omar at Christmas.** Illustrated by Dindga McCannon. Lothrop, 1973.

From the South Bronx, Omar accompanies his mother, a black maid to rich whites, to her job in a fashionable Manhattan residence on Christmas Eve. On the way Omar is most delighted by the falling snow.   (LJ)

234   White, Edgar. **Sati, the Rastifarian.** Illustrated by Dindga McCannon. Lothrop, 1973.

Lilting text describes the adjustment which Sati must make when his aunt brings him to New York from his home in the mountains of the West Indies.   (LJ)

235   Williamson, Mel and Ford, George. **Walk on!** Illustrated by Mel Williamson and George Cephas Ford. Third World Press, 1972.

A story of few words depicts the energetic romp through the day by three black children who, while walking, see a hopscotch game, a spurting hydrant, a storefront church service, gangs, and the movies.   (LJ)

236   Wilson, Beth P. **Martin Luther King, Jr.** Illustrated by Floyd Sowell. Putnam, 1971.

This easy-to-read biography presents the activities of the young black leader from 1955 to 1968 and chronicles the advances in civil rights for that period.   (OCLC)

237   Yarbrough, Camille. **Cornrows.** Illustrated by Carole M. Byard. Coward, 1979.

A black mother and Great-Grammaw tell a young sister and brother stories of ancestral life in Africa, sing a litany to Black American activists, and explain the origin and significance of the cornrow hairstyle.   (BCCB)

Winner: Coretta Scott King Award, 1980.

238   Young, Bernice Elizabeth. **The picture story of Frank Robinson.** Messner, 1975.

This book delves into the personality and playing technique that earned Robinson Most Valuable Player awards in both the National and American leagues, and his distinction of being the first black major league manager.   (BL)

239   Young, Bernice Elizabeth. **The picture story of Hank Aaron.** Messner, 1974.

Black-and-white photographs help to describe Aaron's childhood sandlot team experiences and years with the Indiana Clowns and other minor league teams before he joined the Milwaukee Braves.   (BCCB)

240   Young, Margaret Buckner. **Picture life of Martin Luther King, Jr.** Watts, 1968.

This easy-to-read biography, which is enhanced with numerous photographs, highlights King's life.   (BL)

241   Young, Margaret Buckner. **The picture life of Ralph J. Bunche.** Watts, 1968.

The contribution of Bunche to peace maintenance, information about the United Nations, and additional biographical information are presented through text and photographs. (BCCB)

242   Young, Margaret Buckner. **Picture life of Thurgood Marshall.** Watts, 1971.

Plentiful black-and-white photographs enhance this easy-to-read biography which highlights the life of the first black justice of the U.S. Supreme Court, with particular emphasis on his work for the NAACP. (LJ)

Chapter 2

Books for Intermediate Readers

Books represented in this chapter are appropriate for use by readers at the middle and junior high school achievement levels, which encompass grades five through eight. As in chapters 1 and 3, the books discussed are written by black authors; however, all do not treat black ethnicity and portray black characters. They largely reflect the extent of literary contributions intended for this audience and show the range of the writers' subject expertise.

Included among the types of books listed in this chapter are folk literature; mystery and detective stories; adventure stories; poetry; informational books in various subjects such as biographies, sports, music, dance, science, history, and careers; and general fiction and fantasy. These books may also be appropriate for some readers in the scholastic range above or below that for which this chapter is structured. This is because interest, informational needs, and learning abilities vary greatly and deserve to be respected and encouraged. What speaks to the reader of the black experience in these books will vary with each author's or illustrator's choice of subject and intent as well as each reader's ability and willingness to comprehend and accept.

243   Abdul, Raoul. **Famous black entertainers of today.** Illustrated. Dodd, 1974.

Included in this book is a broad sampling of contemporary black performing artists and entertainers, such as opera singer Martina Arroyo, conductor James De Priest, choreographer Alvin Ailey, and more recognizable personalities.   (BL)

244   Abdul, Raoul, ed. **The magic of black poetry.** Illustrated by Dane Burr. Dodd, 1972.

Especially chosen to present positive black images for young people, this collection includes materials, some anonymous, from many sources—the United States, Ancient Egypt, South Africa, Moorish Spain, Cuba, Jamaica, Latin America, the Arab world, and many African countries.   (BCCB)

245   Adams, Russell L. **Great Negroes, past and present,** 3rd ed. Edited by David P. Ross, Jr. and illustrated by Eugene Winslow. Afro-Am, 1969.

A simplified presentation with numerous illustrations makes this book useful to persons with limited reading ability.   (BL)

246   Archer, Elsie. **Let's face it; the guide to good grooming for girls of color,** rev. ed. Lippincott, 1968.

Originally published in 1959, this revision is a practical guide which considers recent trends and includes frank discussions of health and personal hygiene, pleasing personality, and acceptable behavior.   (LJ)

247   Attaway, William. **Hear America singing.** Illustrated by Carolyn Cather. Lion Press, 1967.

The stages of American musical evolution from the nature-dominated chants of various Indian tribes to folk rock are described.   (BRD)

248   Baker, Augusta, comp. **The golden lynx and other tales.** Illustrated by Johannes Troyer. Lippincott, 1960.

Folktales from seven countries and selected from out-of-print books are included because they have stood the supreme test of children's interest and approval.   (BL)

Winner: Regina Medal, 1981.

249   Bambara, Toni Cade. **Gorilla, my love.** Random, 1972.

Fifteen short stories, set mostly in the black milieux, evoke the authentic notes of life in the 1970s for the proud, angry, gifted, and the ineluctably feminine.   (LJ)

250   ben-Moring, Alvin Lester. **Quadrus and Goliath.** Illustrated by George Malick. Westminster, 1976.

When his beloved "second daddy" is killed by a renegade bear, a young black boy sets out to avenge his death by going after the animal with his only weapon—a slingshot.   (NUC)

251   Bennett, Lerone. **Pioneers in protest.** Johnson Chgo., 1968.

These are detailed biographies of leaders of black protest movements from the eighteenth century forward.   (ED)

252   Bontemps, Arna Wendell. **Chariot in the sky: a story of the Jubilee Singers.** Illustrated by Cyrus Leroy Baldridge. Winston, 1951.

This is the story of a slave who later became a Fisk University student. The plot reveals how black spirituals grew out of slavery and how the Fisk Jubilee singers made this music known to the world.   (BRD)

253   Bontemps, Arna Wendell. **Famous Negro athletes.** Dodd, 1964.

Biographies present the struggle of each subject to succeed as both athlete and person. Included are Joe Louis, Sugar Ray Robinson, Jackie Robinson, Leroy (Satchel) Paige, Willie Mays, Jesse Owens, Wilt Chamberlain, James Nathaniel Brown, and Althea Gibson.   (BRD)

254   Bontemps, Arna Wendell. **Frederick Douglass: slave-fighter-freeman.** Illustrated by Eugene Harper Johnson. Knopf, 1959.

This book chiefly covers the boyhood and youth of the first great black abolitionist—the early years that were dramatized by the awakening of a human spirit trapped by an inhumane system, the escape from slavery, and the beginning of a career dedicated to the cause of freedom for all men.   (BRD)

255   Bontemps, Arna Wendell, comp. **Golden slippers.** Illustrated by Henrietta Bruce Sharon. Harper, 1941.

This anthology of black poetry for young readers

includes many old favorites and brief biographical information on the poets represented. (BRD)

256 Bontemps, Arna Wendell, comp. **Great slave narratives.** Beacon, 1969.

This is a collection of autobiographies written by slaves. (BRD)

257 Bontemps, Arna Wendell, comp. **Hold fast to dreams; poems old and new.** Follett, 1969.

This is an anthology of poetry selected from English and American poets. (BRD)

258 Bontemps, Arna Wendell. **Lonesome boy.** Illustrated by Feliks Topolski. Houghton, 1955.

Here is a picture story about a little black boy who only wanted to play his trumpet, and what happened. (BRD)

259 Bontemps, Arna Wendell. **100 years of Negro freedom.** Greenwood, 1980.

Black ideas and advances since the Civil War are provided. Frederick Douglass, Booker T. Washington, W. E. B. Du Bois, the NAACP, and the Urban League represent various goals and experiments. (CC)

260 Bontemps, Arna Wendell and Conroy, Jack. **Slappy Hooper; the wonderful sign painter.** Illustrated by Ursula Koering. Houghton, 1946.

This is a tall tale from American folklore about a painter whose signs were so real that they caused considerable trouble. (BRD)

261 Bontemps, Arna Wendell. **Story of George Washington Carver.** Illustrated by Eugene Harper Johnson. Grosset, 1954.

Young George was alert and curious enough to leave home in search of a place where a black boy could go to school. Later, he worked diligently to help his people. (BRD)

262 Bontemps, Arna Wendell. **Story of the Negro.** Illustrated by Raymond Lufkin. Knopf, 1948.

This history of blacks from the days of antiquity provides a chronology of events from 1700 B.C. with comparable dates in world history. (BRD)

Winner: Jane Addams Book Award, 1956; John Newbery Honor Book, 1949.

263   Booker, Simeon. **Susie King Taylor, Civil War nurse.** Illustrated by Harold L. James. McGraw-Hill, 1969.

This is the biography of Susie King Taylor, a black teenager who was given her freedom when the Yankees invaded South Carolina. She subsequently found a home with a famous slave regiment and served as a laundress and nurse during the Civil War. (BRD)

264   Brewer, J. Mason. **American Negro folklore.** Illustrated by Richard Lowe. Quadrangle Bks., 1968.

This anthology includes tales of religion, songs, superstitions, proverbs, rhymes, riddles, names, personal experiences and children's rhymes and pastimes. (BRD)

265   Brooks, Gwendolyn. **Maud Martha.** Harper, 1953.

Here are sketches about the life of a young black girl growing up in Chicago who loved special moments—her youth, marriage, and motherhood. (BRD)

266   Brooks, Gwendolyn. **Selected poems.** Harper, 1963.

These selections from other volumes also include a section of new poems. (BRD)

267   Brooks, Gwendolyn. **A street in Bronzeville.** Harper, 1945.

This is the Pulitzer Prize–winning author's first book of poetry. (BRD)

268   Brooks, Gwendolyn. **The world of Gwendolyn Brooks.** Harper, 1972.

Five previously published volumes are combined into one publication—four of which are poetry: *A Street in Bronzeville, Annie Allen, The Bean Eaters,* and *In the Mecca. Maud Martha* is fiction. (BRD)

269 Brown, Margery W. **The second stone.** Illustrated by Margery W. Brown. Putnam, 1974.

Fifteen-year-old Henry is cared for by his older brother, a policeman, after both parents die. When he is cautioned that his best friend is a gang member, he resents his older brother until an older woman is injured and his friend is killed. (LJ)

270 Burroughs, Margaret G. **Jasper the drummin' boy.** Illustrated by Margaret G. Burroughs. Follett, 1970.

In this revision of the 1947 edition, Jasper wants to be a drummer like his grandfather and he drums on any handy surface. This keeps him in trouble with his parents, neighbors, minister, and teacher. When he plays at a street fair, a famous drummer detects talent and encourages lessons. (LJ)

271 Campell, Barbara. **A girl called Bob and a horse called Yoki.** Dial, 1982.

Bob (Barbara Ann) is black, bright, and filled with compassion for the old milk wagon horse that is to be sold to a glue factory. (BCCB)

272 Chesnutt, Charles Waddell. **Conjure tales.** Retold by Ray Anthony Shepard, and illustrated by John Ross and Clare Romano. Dutton, 1973.

Seven short stories comprise this collection: "Poor Sandy," "The Conjurer's Revenge," "The Gray Wolf's Haint," "Master James' Nightmare," "The Goophered Grapevine," "Hot-foot Hannibal," and "Sister Becky's Child." (OCLC)

273 Childress, Alice. **A hero ain't nothin' but a sandwich.** Illustrated by David Scott Brown. Coward, 1973.

The story of thirteen-year-old Benjie, a drug addict, is told from viewpoints of people in Harlem who know him—the pusher, his friends, teacher, mother, grandmother, mother's common-law husband, and Benjie himself. (LJ)

Winner: Coretta Scott King Honorable Mention Book, 1974.

274 Childress, Alice. **Rainbow Jordan.** Coward, 1981.

Three personalities are spotlighted: Rainbow, a teenager; Kathie, her flighty, self-centered and occasionally abusive mother; and Josephine, a foster mother, middle-aged and clinging to a much younger husband who eventually leaves her. (BCCB)

Winner: Coretta Scott King Honorable Mention Book, 1982; School Library Journal "Best Books of the Year" Award, 1981.

275   Childress, Alice. **When the rattlesnake sounds: a play.** Coward, 1975.

This one-act play, set in a hotel laundry room in Cape May, New Jersey, in the 1860s, describes an incident which occurred when Harriet Tubman worked as a laundress to raise money for the abolitionist cause. (BRD)

276   Clifton, Lucille. **Good times; poems.** Random, 1969.

These are words of black pride on a personal level and as an abstraction. The title poem cautions children to remember occasions of family happiness. (BL)

277   Clifton, Lucille. **Sonora Beautiful.** Illustrated by Michael Garland. Dutton, 1981.

Sonora dislikes her name (her parents met at the edge of the Sonora Desert). She is embarrassed by her father's occupation (poet), so she receives gentle assurances from her mother. (BCCB)

278   Clifton, Lucille. **The times they used to be.** Illustrated by Susan Jeschke. Holt, 1974.

A black woman recounts to her children her twelfth year when she became a woman, saw her uncle chase a ghost to his own death, and revealed the magic of television. (BL)

279   Davis, Ossie. **Escape to freedom; a play about young Frederick Douglass.** Viking, 1978.

Five scenes and a prologue present life episodes of Frederick Douglass—his childhood in a slave cabin; his zeal in learning how to read; his treatment on a slave-breaking plantation; his experiences in Baltimore; and his escape to New York. (HB)

Winner: Coretta Scott King Award, 1979.

280   Davis, Ossie. **Langston: a play.** Delacorte, 1982.

The story of Langston Hughes is told within a play. Hughes

appears to youngsters who are dramatizing his biography and tells the young actors of his life while they act out the appropriate roles.   (ED)

281   Douglass, Frederick. **Life and times of Frederick Douglass.** Adapted by Barbara Ritchie. Crowell, 1966.

Born a slave, self-taught, and a fugitive at twenty-one, Douglass at twenty-four years old became an outstanding spokesman for his race and continued this emphasis throughout his life.   (BRD)

282   Douglass, Frederick. **The mind and heart of Frederick Douglass; excerpts from speeches of the great Negro orator.** Adapted by Barbara Ritchie. Crowell, 1968.

This book presents a picture of a Black American and the status of his people through selections from speeches made between 1841 and 1886.   (BRD)

283   Duckett, Alfred. **The changing of the guard: the new black political breed.** Coward, 1972.

Young readers are provided these brief sketches of the roles, philosophies, and long-range goals of blacks who are involved in the American political mainstream. Duckett compares old and new stratagems and profiles notables. A final chapter is devoted to the congressional Black Caucus.   (LJ)

284   Dunbar, Paul Laurence. **The complete poems of Paul Laurence Dunbar.** Dodd, ©1913, 1980.

This volume includes *Lyrics of Lowly Life* (1896); *Lyrics of the Hearthside* (1899); *Lyrics of Love and Laughter* (1903); *Lyrics of Sunshine and Shadow* (1905); and some poems never before published.   (JHS)

285   Dunbar, Paul Laurence. **I greet the dawn, poems.** Compiled and illustrated by Ashley Bryan. Atheneum, 1978.

These poems are written in standard English rather than in dialect.   (BRD)

286   Durham, John. **The long haul, and other stories.** Illustrated by Norman Nodel. McGraw-Hill, 1968.

Twelve short stories are compiled into two volumes edited by

John Durham, Warren Halliburton, and Laurence Swinburne. (OCLC)

287   Durham, John. **Me and Arch and the Pest.** Illustrated by Ingrid Fetz. Four Winds Pr., 1970.

Two boys acquire a stray German shepherd which they name Pest. When the dog disappears, they become involved in a crime involving a gang of dognappers. (BL)

288   Fax, Elton, C. **Contemporary black leaders.** Photos by Elton C. Fax. Dodd, 1970.

Fourteen profiles of contemporary black men and women prominent in the struggle for equal rights include Fannie Lou Hamer, Ruby Dee, Coretta King, Bayard Rustin, Edward Brooke, Charles Evers, and Thurgood Marshall. (JHS)

289   Feelings, Tom. **Black pilgrimage.** Illustrated by Tom Feelings. Lothrop, 1972.

Here is an autobiographical sketch with statements of his beliefs about black consciousness, black art, and the freedom of black people everywhere. (BL)

290   Fenderson, Lewis H. **Daniel Hale Williams: open-heart doctor.** Illustrated by Donald George Miller. McGraw-Hill, 1971.

With focus on this doctor's medical training and career, this book explains how Williams became nationally prominent in 1893 after he performed the first open-heart surgery on a man who had been stabbed. He also worked consistently to improve the medical care available to black people. (LJ)

291   Fenderson, Lewis H. **Thurgood Marshall: fighter for justice.** Illustrated by David Hodges. McGraw-Hill, 1969.

This biography highlights important events in the private life and public career of the lawyer who in 1967 became the first black justice appointed to the United States Supreme Court. (OCLC)

292   Gaines, Ernest J. **A long day in November.** Illustrated by Don Bolognese. Dial, 1971.

Earthy, funny, and sad tale of a marital spat and a wise "hoodoo'' woman who patches it up, as seen through the egocentric eye of six-year-old Sonny. (LJ)

293   Giovanni, Nikki. **Those who ride the night winds.** Morrow, 1983.

This collection of poems describes people who have lived guided by their consciences and who have tried to change difficult situations. (ED)

294   Gordy, Berry. **Movin' up; Pop Gordy tells his story.** Harper, 1979.

The son of a Georgia slave tells of his childhood in the South and of his business experience there and in Detroit where he raised a family. His son is founder and president of Motown Records. (BRD)

Winner: Coretta Scott King Honorable Mention Book, 1980.

295   Graham, Lorenz. **I, Momolu.** Illustrated by John Thomas Biggers. Crowell, 1966.

Momolu is required to journey with his father down river to a distant coastal city. At fourteen, he first observes the bewildering and exciting wonder of modern civilization and then makes an important decision about his future. (BL)

296   Graham, Lorenz. **John Brown: a cry for freedom.** Crowell, 1980.

This is a biographical description of the abolitionist's religious upbringing and growing commitment to aiding runaway slaves, his eloquent trial speech, eulogies about him, and a description of the effects of his ill-fated raid on Harper's Ferry. (CC)

297   Graham, Lorenz. **North Town.** Crowell, 1965.

A sequel to *South Town* in which the Williams family moves to a city near Detroit where sixteen-year-old David faces more than the usual problems of adjustment as he preserves his dream of becoming a doctor. (BL)

298   Graham, Lorenz. **Return to South Town.** Crowell, 1976.

Fourth in a series, this book describes David Williams's return to the place his family had left fifteen years earlier as the result of racial hostilities. He is now a medical doctor and observes many changes in the still imperfect society. (BCCB)

299   Graham, Lorenz. **South Town.** Follett, 1958.

Sixteen-year-old David Williams lives on a small farm in the South and has ambitions of becoming a doctor. Racial tensions develop over his father's refusal to accept less pay than his white co-workers. (BL)

300   Graham, Lorenz. **Whose town?** Crowell, 1969.

This is a sequel to *South Town* and *North Town.* David Williams, eighteen, is in conflict about the best stance for Black Americans as he experiences discrimination and is torn between the moderate path and that advocated by a Black Power figure. (BCCB)

301   Graham, Shirley. **Booker T. Washington: educator of hand, head and heart.** Messner, 1955.

Washington's life episodes are explained to help young readers understand the essential gifts of this great black educator. (BRD)

302   Graham, Shirley. **Jean Baptiste Pointe de Sable, founder of Chicago.** Messner, 1953.

This is the life story of a Santa Domingo black who came to America in 1764. With the help of his Indian wife and others, he built a trading post which later became Chicago. (BRD)

303   Graham, Shirley. **Julius K. Nyerere: teacher of Africa.** Messner, 1975.

President Nyerere is portrayed as a dedicated, modest leader-teacher who worked to liberate Tanganiyka and Zanzibar, and to join them as the new country of Tanzania. (SLJ)

Winner: Coretta Scott King Honorable Mention Book, 1976.

304   Graham, Shirley. **Paul Robeson, citizen of the world.** Messner, 1946.

This biography of a great black singer and actor details his struggle upward. (BRD)

305   Graham, Shirley. **Story of Phillis Wheatley.** Illustrated by Robert Burns. Messner, 1949.

This book covers the period from the day that Phillis was

rescued from the Boston slave market by the kindly Mrs. Wheatley until Phillis's death in 1784. (BRD)

306   Graham, Shirley. **There was once a slave: the heroic story of Frederick Douglass.** Messner, 1947.

This is a semifictional account of a slave who escaped from bondage before the Civil War, who educated himself and became one of the leaders of the abolitionist movement, and who was a friend of Abraham Lincoln, John Brown, and William Lord Garrison. (JHS)

307   Graham, Shirley. **Your most humble servant.** Messner, 1949.

Here is the life story of Benjamin Banneker who invented a clock, who was an assistant in the planning of Washington, D.C., and an author of a letter to Thomas Jefferson that was a sharp reminder of the human rights of blacks. (BRD)

308   Graham, Shirley and Lipscomb, George D. **Dr. George Washington Carver, scientist.** Illustrated by Elton C. Fax. Messner, 1944.

This is the biography of the great black scientist who gave up personal success and wealth to work for forty-six years among blacks at Tuskegee Institute. It portrays his early handicaps, the versatility of his genius, and his achievements in scientific agriculture and chemurgy. (BL)

309   Greenfield, Eloise. **Sister.** Illustrated by Moneta Barnett. Crowell, 1974.

Doretha, thirteen, black, and confused about herself and her adolescent groping for security, finds that her diary reveals something about her and the people she has loved. (BCCB)

310   Greenfield, Eloise and Little, Lessie Jones. **Childtimes: a three-generation memoir.** Illustrated by Jerry Pinkney. Crowell, 1979.

Reminiscences of Eloise, her mother, and her grandmother form a century-wide collage of growing-up experiences. (BL)

Winner: Coretta Scott King Honorable Mention Book, 1980.

311   Greenfield, Eloise and Revis, Alesia. **Alesia.** Illustrated by George Cephas Ford and photos by Sandra Turner Bond. Philomel Bks., 1981.

These dated journal entries explain Alesia's handicap as the result of being hit by a car when she was nine years old, and show her persistent and successful efforts to improve and to accept what she couldn't change. (BCCB)

312   Guy, Rosa. **And I heard a bird sing.** Delacorte, 1987.

This is a sequel to *The Disappearance* and *New Guys around the Block*. Now eighteen years old, Imamu Jones is a grocery delivery boy living with his insecure mother and foster sister in Brooklyn. When the niece of a wealthy customer is murdered and the trustee of the estate accuses Imamu, the detective does not arrest him. They work together and it is Imamu who confronts the criminal and solves the case. (BRD)

313   Guy, Rosa. **Children of longing.** Holt, 1971.

Young blacks between thirteen and twenty-three years old speak out about the black experience and consciousness in the United States. (BL)

314   Guy, Rosa. **Edith Jackson.** Viking, 1978.

A seventeen-year-old girl tries to keep her orphaned siblings together, but they desert her, and leave her desperate for love and exploitation. (BL)

315   Guy, Rosa. **The friends.** Holt, 1973.

Phillisia, who recently arrived in Harlem from the West Indies, receives hostile reception from her classmates, except one who yearns to be accepted. (LJ)

316   Guy, Rosa. **Mirror of her own.** Delacorte, 1981.

Plain and timid Mary understands that John prefers her beautiful and self-confident sister, but she is not totally discouraged by this fact. (BCCB)

317   Guy, Rosa. **New guys around the block.** Delacorte, 1983.

This is a sequel to *The Disappearance* in which Imamu is back in his Harlem tenement planning to paint it for his mother's return from the hospital, and feeling resentful because the police suspect him of burglary and violence. (BCCB)

318   Guy, Rosa. **Paris, Pee Wee, and Big Dog.** Illustrated by Caroline Binch. Delacorte, 1985.

Three black boys who live in Harlem enjoy a roller skating adventure around town and escape bullies and other dangers.   (SLJ)

319   Haley, Alex. **A different kind of Christmas.** Doubleday, 1988.

A white southerner, Fletcher Randall, and a black slave, Harpin' John, work toward a mutual goal of getting slaves to the Underground Railroad and ultimate freedom. Moral courage and spiritual regeneration are reflected in the characters' actions.   (ED)

320   Halliburton, Warren. **The fighting redtails: America's first black airmen.** Silver Burdett, 1978.

Here is a brief and concise history of the highly decorated first black army air unit.   (DCPL)

321   Hamilton, Virginia. **Arilla Sun Down.** Greenwillow, 1976.

A twelve-year-old girl of black and Native American parentage feels overshadowed by her attractive, assured, and dramatic brother. She later overcomes these feelings and becomes more confident.   (BCCB)

322   Hamilton, Virginia. **Dustland.** Greenwillow, 1980.

This sequel to *Justice and Her Brothers* shows eleven-year-old Justice discovering that she has supersensory powers, as do her friend and her twin brothers.   (BCCB)

323   Hamilton, Virginia. **The gathering.** Greenwillow, 1981.

This is a third book in a trilogy involving the mind travels of Justice, her twin brothers, and their friend. Their combined power is called "the unit."   (SLJ)

Winner: Notable Children's Books (American Library Association), 1981.

324   Hamilton, Virginia. **The house of Dies Drear.** Macmillan, 1968.

Young Thomas Small and his family move into a house that once was a station on the Underground Railroad and haunted with its own history.   (SLJ)

325   Hamilton, Virginia. **In the beginning; creation stories from around the world.** Told by Virginia Hamilton and illustrated by Barry Moser. HBJ, 1988.

Explanations of how the world was created are presented in this illustrated collection of twenty-five myths from various parts of the world.   (BCCB)

Winner: Notable Children's Books (American Library Association), 1988.

326   Hamilton, Virginia. **Junius over far.** Harper, 1985.

Grandfather Jackabo's home on a small, beautiful Caribbean island brings him less happiness because he misses his son and grandson who are far away in the United States when strange activities begin to unfold and confuse him.   (BCCB)

327   Hamilton, Virginia. **Justice and her brothers.** Greenwillow, 1978.

Eleven-year-old Justice spends the summer trying to keep up with her thirteen-year-old twin brothers who take her with them when they travel into the future.   (BL)

Winner: Coretta Scott King Honorable Mention Book, 1979.

328   Hamilton, Virginia. **A little love.** Philomel Bks., 1984.

Sheema longs for the father she never knew and learns to understand the love which surrounds her from caring grandparents and Forrest, whom she loves.   (BCCB)

Winner: Coretta Scott King Honorable Mention Book, 1985.

329   Hamilton, Virginia. **M. C. Higgins, the great.** Macmillan, 1974.

M. C. takes care of his younger siblings while his parents work. He enjoys sitting atop a forty-foot pole to survey the mountain that his family owns, and dreaming about getting his family away from the danger they face from a heap left from strip mining.   (BCCB)

Winner: John Newbery Medal Award, 1975.

330   Hamilton, Virginia. **The mystery of Drear House.** Greenwillow, 1987.

A black boy living in a house that served the Underground Railroad makes a discovery.   (ED)

331 Hamilton, Virginia. **The people could fly: American black folk tales.** Illustrated by Leo and Diane Dillon. Knopf, 1985.

Twenty-four representative folktales are organized into four sections—tales of animals; the supernatural; the real, extravagant, and fanciful; and freedom tales. (BL)

Winner: Notable Children's Books (American Library Association), 1985; International Board on Books for Young People (Honor): United States, 1988; Coretta Scott King Award, 1986; New York Times Choice of Best Illustrated Children's Books of the Year, 1985; Other Award, 1986; School Library Journal ''Best Books of the Year'' Award, 1985.

332 Hamilton, Virginia. **The planet of Junior Brown.** Macmillan, 1971.

An overweight musical prodigy and a homeless boy who lives by his wits find an affinity in their loneliness and seek refuge from society. (BL)

333 Hamilton, Virginia. **Sweet whispers, Brother Rush.** Putnam, 1982.

Through the ghost of her dead uncle, Tree works out the frustrations she feels about her mother's long absences and having to care for her retarded brother alone. (BL)

Winner: Notable Children's Books (American Library Association), 1982; Boston Globe-Horn Book Award, 1983; International Board on Books for Young People (Honor): United States, 1984: Coretta Scott King Award, 1983; School Library Journal ''Best Books of the Year'' Award, 1982.

334 Hamilton, Virginia. **W. E. B. Du Bois: a biography.** Crowell, 1972.

This biography for young readers treats the significance of Du Bois in today's black movements. (BL)

335 Hamilton, Virginia. **Willie Bea and the time the Martians landed.** Greenwillow, 1983.

In 1938 on Halloween, children and grandchildren of an Ohio farm family are gathered for dinner when a dramatic aunt brings news from the famous Orson Wells broadcast that Martians have landed in New Jersey. (BCCB)

Winner: Notable Children's Books (American Library Association), 1983.

336   Hamilton, Virginia. **Zeely.** Illustrated by Symeon Shimin. Macmillan, 1967.

Geeder Perry lives in a world of daydreams and insists that mysterious, stately Zeely is a Watusi queen.   (BL)

337   Hansen, Joyce. **Out from this place.** Walker & Co., 1988.

This story continues experiences begun in *Which Way Freedom?* Fourteen-year-old Easter escapes from the Phillips plantation with other recently emancipated blacks. They arrive at the Union-held Sea Islands off South Carolina where the Union Army pays them to work a plantation and promises that they will receive title to the land after the war. However, President Andrew Johnson reneges on this promise and returns confiscated land to white owners in 1865. In Easter's community, an armed rebellion results in a compromise and the blacks become landowners after tragic bloodshed.   (KIR)

Winner: Notable Children's Books (American Library Association), 1988.

338   Hansen, Joyce. **Which way freedom?** Walker & Co., 1986.

Obi escapes from slavery during the Civil War, joins a black Union regiment, and soon becomes involved in the bloody fighting at Fort Pillow, Tennessee. This story illustrates the contributions made by many black soldiers during this conflict.   (BCCB)

Winner: Notable Children's Books (American Library Association), 1986.

339   Hansen, Joyce. **Yellow Bird and me.** Clarion, 1986.

When a black sixth grader loses her best friend because his foster parents place him in a group home, her efforts to earn money to visit him are encroached upon by Yellow Bird, a dyslexic classmate who needs and receives her help.   (BRD)

340   Harrison, Deloris. **The Bannekers of Bannaky Springs.** Illustrated by David Hodges. Hawthorn, 1970.

This biography concentrates on the family background of the eighteenth century black man, self-taught naturalist, astronomer, and mathematician who helped to survey Washington, D.C.   (NUC)

341   Haskins, James. **Adam Clayton Powell: portrait of a marching black.** Dial, 1974.

This is the biography of a man who worked effectively for the liberation of blacks during his twenty-five years as a congressman from Harlem. (LJ)

342   Haskins, James. **Always movin' on: the life of Langston Hughes.** Watts, 1976.

This is a portrait of a sensitive black writer known as the poet laureate of his people, who, though criticized for perpetuating stereotypes, spent most of his career writing about poor, uneducated blacks who fought for their dignity and individuality. (JHS)

343   Haskins, James. **Black music in America: a history through its people.** Crowell, 1987.

This panoramic overview of black music from the earliest slave songs through ragtime, the blues, classic jazz, bop, soul, disco, modern jazz and beyond also provides portraits of some of the artists. (ED)

Winner: Carter G. Woodson Book Award, 1988.

344   Haskins, James. **Bob McAdoo, superstar.** Lothrop, 1978.

Here are reflections of formative influences of a supportive family life, his determination to receive a good education, and the unsettled climate in the struggle for civil rights and integration. (JHS)

345   Haskins, James. **Break dancing.** Lerner, 1985.

This highly illustrated explanation of break dancing includes a brief history, profiles of famous performers, and descriptions of some dance steps. (SLJ)

346   Haskins, James. **The child abuse help book.** By James Haskins with Pat Connolly. Addison-Wesley, 1982.

Physical abuse, sexual abuse, and physical neglect are identified and distinguished. Emotional abuse and neglect are also discussed. (JHS)

347   Haskins, James. **The consumer movement.** Watts, 1975.

This book pictures the numerous industries involved in the

consumer movement, including a long-range view of industries such as food, clothing, tobacco, and automobiles. Problems related to selling on credit are also discussed.   (JHS)

348   Haskins, James. **Corazon Aquino: leader of the Philippines.** Enslow Pubs., 1988.

This political biography traces events in the life of the woman who became the first elected woman president of the Philippines in 1986. She entered the political arena after the murder of her husband, Benigno Aquino.   (BRD)

349   Haskins, James. **Creoles of color of New Orleans.** Illustrated by Donald George Miller. Crowell, 1975.

This book traces the history of the Creoles of New Orleans and describes their occupations, religion, education, political activities, and their contributions of famed cooking and the development of jazz.   (ESLC)

350   Haskins, James. **Donna Summer: an unauthorized biography.** By James Haskins and J. M. Stifle. Little, 1983.

Problems encountered in making records and doing concert tours, and the special joys of success are recounted.   (JHS)

351   Haskins, James. **Fighting Shirley Chisolm.** Dial, 1975.

The first black woman ever to be elected to the United States Congress was forceful, highly principled, and warmly human.   (ESLC)

352   Haskins, James. **From Lew Alcindor to Kareem Abdul-Jabbar,** rev. ed. Lothrop, 1978.

Kareem's brilliant career in the National Basketball Association is traced through the end of the 1976–77 season.   (JHS)

353   Haskins, James. **Gambling—who really wins?** Watts, 1979.

This overview of gambling is concerned with abuse. Legal and illegal games are described and moral and philosophical considerations are probed.   (BL)

354   Haskins, James. **The Guardian Angels.** Enslow Pubs., 1983.

Here is a profile of the group founded by Curtis Sliwa to prevent crime on New York City subways.   (JHS)

355 Haskins, James. **I'm gonna make you love me: the story of Diana Ross.** Dial, 1980.

This biography traces Ross's life from her birth in Detroit, through her teen years with a singing group, and into the development of her performing talents which led to stardom. (ESLC)

356 Haskins, James. **James Van Der Zee, the picture takin' man.** Dodd, 1979.

This is an interview-based life story of the man whose photographs chronicled the people and life of Harlem in the early to mid-1900s. (ESLC)

Winner: Coretta Scott King Honorable Mention Book, 1980.

357 Haskins, James. **Katherine Dunham.** Coward, 1982.

This book chronologically presents choreographer Katherine Dunham's work in anthropology, the fortunes of her various dance companies and schools, and her work in films and on Broadway which impacted the black community and the dance world. (CC)

358 Haskins, James. **Lena Horne.** Coward, 1983.

Lena Horne's early life and career are described, including the social milieus of the Cotton Club, Harlem Renaissance, and Hollywood of the 1940s. (JHS)

Winner: Coretta Scott King Honorable Mention Book, 1984.

359 Haskins, James. **The life and death of Martin Luther King, Jr.** Lothrop, 1977.

By using a theory of conspiracy, this book explains the development of the Civil Rights Movement, the FBI's and the CIA's harassments, and King's assassination. (CC)

360 Haskins, James. **The long struggle: the story of American labor.** Westminster, 1976.

Here is a historical assessment, from nineteenth century organizational efforts, its successes, the differences in idealogy and purpose, and recent trends of a stagnating movement. The role of blacks in unionization is also covered. (JHS)

361   Haskins, James. **Mabel Mercer: a life.** Atheneum, 1987.

This anecdotal portrait of Mabel Mercer draws on the recollections of people who knew her in Europe and her friends and neighbors in Chatham, New York.   (BRD)

362   Haskins, James. **Mr. Bojangles: the biography of Bill Robinson.** By James Haskins and N. R. Mitgang. Morrow, 1988.

By presenting the life and career of the famous dancer, this book attempts to show him as one who challenged the white entertainment establishment and succeeded in opening doors for other entertainers of color.   (BRD)

363   Haskins, James. **New Americans: Cuban boat people.** Enslow Pubs., 1982.

This book details conditions which prompted the two waves of exodus from Cuba to the United States in 1965–1971 and 1980, problems encountered in America, and the differing values of the two groups of immigrants.   (ESLC)

364   Haskins, James. **New Americans: Vietnamese boat people.** Enslow Pubs., 1980.

This book presents the history of Vietnam and events which led to United States intervention in the war. It describes the mass exodus as a result of the war and the settlement of refugees in the United States.   (ESLC)

365   Haskins, James. **A piece of the power: four black mayors.** Dial, 1972.

The careers of four black mayors are examined with respect to family, educational background, and political significance. The four mayors discussed are Carl Stokes (Cleveland, Ohio), Richard Hatcher (Gary, Indiana), Charles Evers (Fayette, Mississippi) and Kenneth Gibson (Newark, New Jersey).   (BL)

366   Haskins, James. **Profiles in Black Power.** Doubleday, 1972.

This book provides a chronology of the Black Power movement with brief profiles of persons associated with militancy— Adam Clayton Powell, Malcolm X, Eldridge Cleaver, H. Rap Brown, and others.   (JHS)

367   Haskins, James. **Queen of the blues: a biography of Dinah Washington.** Morrow, 1987.

Here is a portrayal of the African-American singer whose career spanned the years from 1943 to 1963, and whose music ranged from salty blues to "Top Ten" hits.   (BRD)

368   Haskins, James. **The quiet revolution: the struggle for the rights of disabled Americans.** By James Haskins with J. M. Stifle. Crowell, 1979.

Here is an overview of efforts made by organizations and individuals that is structured around the United Cerebral Palsy's "Bill of Rights for the Handicapped."   (CC)

369   Haskins, James. **Ralph Bunche: a most reluctant hero.** Hawthorne, 1974.

Activities from childhood forward relate his progress from poverty and discrimination to outstanding student and athlete, a Harvard Ph.D. in political science, the first black American to hold an important State Department position, and winner of the Nobel Peace Prize in 1950 for negotiating peace between the Israelis and the Arabs.   (JHS)

370   Haskins, James. **Religions.** Lippincott, 1973.

The five major religions in the world—Hinduism, Buddhism, Judaism, Christianity, and Islam—are explained by giving broad overviews with the practices and beliefs of each.   (JHS)

371   Haskins, James. **Revolutionaries: agents of change.** Lippincott, 1971.

This book presents the lives of eleven people who represent a cross section of the types of men who have come to symbolize revolution.   (JHS)

372   Haskins, James. **Space challenger: the story of Guion Bluford; an authorized biography.** By James Haskins and Kathleen Benson. Carolrhoda Books, 1984.

From his boyhood interest in flight to earning his Ph.D. in aerospace engineering, training and mission projects, Bluford became the first black American in space on the space shuttle *Challenger* in August 1983.   (CC)

373   Haskins, James. **The story of Stevie Wonder.** Lothrop, 1976.

The problems of Stevie Wonder's blindness and his way of compensating, his career, his professional relationships, and his evolution as a musician are documented.   (JHS)

Winner: Coretta Scott King Award, 1977.

374   Haskins, James. **Street gangs: yesterday and today.** Hastings, 1974.

This book traces the history of street gangs from Colonial times and discusses reasons for their existence and who joins them.   (ESLC)

375   Haskins, James. **Sugar Ray Leonard.** Lothrop, 1982.

This book recounts Leonard's progression from a shy fourteen-year-old through family obligations which pushed him into a professional boxing career and superstardom.   (JHS)

376   Haskins, James. **Teen-age alcoholism.** Hawthorne, 1976.

A historical approach is used to discuss alcohol use and abuse, teenage drinking, the physiological and psychological effects of alcohol, and the treatment for alcoholism.   (BL)

377   Haskins, James. **Werewolves.** Watts, 1981.

A compendium of international folklore on werewolves is provided and the development of changes in social attitudes through the centuries is analyzed.   (SLJ)

378   Haskins, James. **Who are the handicapped?** Doubleday, 1978.

Here is a look at the position of the handicapped in our society, past and present attitudes, and types of handicaps with emphasis on handicapped children.   (JHS)

379   Haskins, James. **Winnie Mandela: life of struggle.** Putnam, 1988.

This partial biography traces the major events of Winnie Mandela's life to include her education, her relationship with her family, her marriage to Nelson, her imprisonment and bannings, as well as the victories and losses in her aspect of the struggle to abolish apartheid in South Africa.   (ALR)

380 Haskins, James. **Your rights, past and present; a guide for young people.** Hawthorne, 1975.

Here is a survey of the development and present status of the rights of youth in five areas—labor, school, justice, in the home, and in choosing a home. (JHS)

381 Hayden, Robert C. **Eight Black American inventors.** Addison-Wesley, 1972.

These biographical sketches emphasize the technological contributions rather than the personal lives of black inventors. Inventions include the gas mask, the three-way traffic signal, the truck refrigeration unit, and the shoe lasting machine. (BL)

382 Hayden, Robert C., ed. **Kaleidoscope; poems by American Negro poets.** HBJ, 1967.

This anthology includes several eighteenth- and nineteenth-century black poets, but the emphasis is on poets of the twentieth century. (BRD)

383 Hayden, Robert C. **Seven Black American scientists.** Addison-Wesley, 1970.

These biographical sketches emphasize the scientific contributions rather than the personal lives of Daniel Hale Williams, Benjamin Banneker, Charles H. Turner, Ernest Just, Matthew Henson, and George Washington Carver. (BL)

384 Hayden, Robert C. and Harris, Jacqueline, eds. **Nine Black American doctors.** Addison-Wesley, 1976.

Among the achievements of these doctors are the development of a vaccine for smallpox, testing techniques for syphilis, chemotherapy, methods for identifying sickle-cell anemia, and the effects of diet on the development and cure of disease. (CLW)

385 Haynes, Henry Louis. **Squarehead and me.** Illustrated by Len Epstein. Westminster, 1980.

David considered "Squarehead" Palmer as someone to avoid associating with, but when circumstances bring them together for a few days on a farm, David begins to understand his friend's special problem. (OCLC)

386   Hicks, Nancy. **The honorable Shirley Chisholm, congresswoman from Brooklyn.** Lion Press, 1971.

This is a biography of a schoolteacher who became the first black woman to be elected to the Congress of the United States. (LJ)

387   Hughes, Langston. **Don't you turn back.** Poems selected by Lee Bennett Hopkins and illustrated by Ann Grifalconi. Knopf, 1969.

For younger readers, these meaningful poems express the experiences of black people in the United States. (BL)

388   Hughes, Langston. **Dream keeper, and other poems.** Knopf, 1932.

This collection is designed to appeal to young readers who will find their favorites included here. (BRD)

389   Hughes, Langston. **Famous American Negroes.** Dodd, 1954.

Biographies of well-known and less well-known Black Americans are presented to young readers. (BRD)

390   Hughes, Langston. **Famous Negro heroes of America.** Illustrated by Gerald McCann. Dodd, 1958.

These biographical sketches of sixteen black men and women, written for young people, progresses from the sixteenth century. (BRD)

391   Hughes, Langston. **Famous Negro music makers.** Dodd, 1955.

These are short biographical sketches of Black Americans who have achieved fame or made a large contribution to music. Groups such as the Fisk Jubilee Singers are included. (BRD)

392   Hughes, Langston. **The first book of Africa.** Watts, 1960.

This introduction to the continent of Africa includes historical information about medieval black kingdoms and the Moslem influence, peoples and governments, and problems within certain countries. (BRD)

393   Hughes, Langston. **First book of jazz.** Illustrated by Cliff Roberts. Watts, 1954.

A history and analysis of jazz written for young readers includes relationships of old work songs, the jubilees, blues, and ragtime to their social eras. (BRD)

394   Hughes, Langston. **First book of Negroes.** Illustrated by Ursula Koering. Watts, 1952.

An introductory account of black people and their life and culture in Africa and North America is told in semifictional form through the experiences of a small boy who lives in New York. (BRD)

395   Hughes, Langston. **Jazz.** Updated and expanded by Sandford Brown. Watts, 1982.

This expansion of the 1976 edition includes Hughes's introduction to jazz, chapters on big bands and jazz singers, plus a revised conclusion that summarizes the place of jazz in this country's musical picture. (BL)

396   Hunter, Kristin. **Guests in the promised land.** Scribner, 1973.

Eleven short stories examine facets of the problems faced by a black child in a white world. (BCCB)

Winner: Coretta Scott King Honorable Mention Book, 1974.

397   Hunter, Kristin. **Lou in the limelight.** Scribner, 1981.

Sixteen-year-old Lou is determined to continue with her singing despite her mother's stern warnings about "the Devil's money." (BL)

Winner: Coretta Scott King Honorable Mention Book, 1982.

398   Hunter, Kristin. **The Soul Brothers and Sister Lou.** Scribner, 1968.

The very different values of black identity and militancy come into conflict among members of a newly formed neighborhood club when a white policeman kills an innocent fellow member. (LJ)

399   Jackson, Jesse. **Black in America; a fight for freedom.** By Jesse Jackson and Elaine Landau. Messner, 1973.

Here is a short history of the struggle of blacks in the United States from colonial times to the early 1970s. (CC)

400   Jackson, Jesse. **The fourteenth Cadillac.** Doubleday, 1972.

When two black adolescent boys try to find work in a south-

ern city in 1925, being an undertaker's helper is one possibil-
ity, but Stonewall fears the work and contends with his hypocritical tattletale of a brother. While his mother has high ambitions for him, his father feels that a seventeen-year-old boy has
a right to honest failure.   (EJ)

401   Jackson, Jesse. **Make a joyful noise unto the Lord! The life of Maha-
lia Jackson, queen of gospel singers.** Crowell, 1974.

From a choir girl in New Orleans to world-renowned artist,
she never let European music destroy her African-American
roots.   (CC)

402   Jackson, Jesse. **The sickest don't always die the quickest.** Doubleday, 1971.

This is a plotless series of incidents in the life of a twelve-year-
old boy who lives in a black community of Columbus, Ohio,
in 1920.   (BCCB)

403   Jackson, Jesse. **Tessie.** Illustrated by Harold L. James. Harper, 1968.

Tessie is the first black in an exclusive private school where
she adjusts, fights prejudice and snobbery, works to compen-
sate for a weak scholastic background, and finds time to recognize and nurture her individual self.   (BL)

404   Johnson, Brenda A. **Between the devil and the sea: the life of James
Forten.** Illustrated by Donald George Miller. HBJ, 1974.

Born of free parents in Philadelphia in 1776, Forten rose from
an apprentice to a well-to-do owner of a sail loft at age thirty-
four. He ran a station on the Underground Railroad, prevented
passage of racist laws in Pennsylvania, and subsidized the abolitionist newspaper *Liberator.*   (SLJ)

405   Johnson, James Weldon. **Lift every voice and sing: words and music.** Illustrated by Mozelle Thompson. Hawthorn, 1970.

The song known as the Negro National Anthem is presented
with words, piano arrangement, guitar chords, and pictures.
(BL)

406   Jordan, June. **Dry victories.** Holt, 1972.

This is a dialogue between two boys who discuss the Reconstruction and Civil Rights eras. Colloquial speech is printed in the style of a drama script. (BCCB)

407   Jordan, June. **His own where.** Crowell, 1971.

Free verse and black speech present the story of Buddy and Angela, black teenagers in distressed family situations, who find solace in the cemetery where they can be quiet and alone. (LJ)

408   Jordan, June, ed. **Soulscript: Afro-American poetry.** Doubleday, 1970.

Poems by more than sixty black poets show past history and present anger. (LJ)

409   Jordan, June. **Who look at me?** Crowell, 1969.

Poetry explains experiences, feelings, and shared past history of black people and implores readers of all ages and races to discover others—to look at and see. (LJ)

410   Killens, John Oliver. **Great gittin' up morning.** Doubleday, 1972.

This story describes the experiences of Vesey, a black man who lived in Charleston, South Carolina, in 1820. He led an unsuccessful plot to free the slaves and was hanged in 1822. (BRD)

411   King, Martin Luther. **Daddy King: an autobiography.** By Martin Luther King, Sr. with Clayton Riley. Morrow, 1980.

King describes his boyhood and rise in the ministry of the largest black congregation in Atlanta and in the community to become a fighter for the vote and other civil rights many years before his son emerged as a national leader. (BRD)

412   King, Martin Luther, Jr. **We shall live in peace: the teachings of Martin Luther King, Jr.** Edited by Deloris Harrison and illustrated by Ernest Crichlow. Hawthorne, 1968.

Excerpts from Dr. King's speeches are arranged in generally chronological order beginning with the Montgomery bus boycott and extending to his assassination. (BRD)

413   Lacy, Leslie Alexander. **Black Africa on the move.** Watts, 1969.

Research-based and personal experiences focus on political,

economic, and social conditions in Africa south of the Sahara.   (BL)

414   Lacy, Leslie Alexander. **Cheer the lonesome traveler: the life of W. E. B. Du Bois.** Dial, 1970.

This is a biography of a distinguished black leader.   (BL)

415   Lawrence, Jacob. **Harriet and the promised land.** Illustrated by Jacob Armstead Lawrence. Simon & Schuster, 1968.

The ballad-style text is incidental to the forceful, vividly colored painting which tells the story of Harriet Tubman. (DCPL)

416   Lester, Julius. **The tales of Uncle Remus: the adventures of Brer Rabbit.** Illustrated by Jerry Pinkney. Dial, 1987.

Forty-eight tales are told in a manner true to oral traditions but divorced from the Uncle Remus character whom some find offensive.   (BL)

Winner: Notable Children's Books (American Library Association), 1987.

417   Lester, Julius. **This strange new feeling.** Dial, 1982.

Here are three true or reality-based stories on the theme of slaves who long for freedom and of their love.   (BCCB)

Winner: Coretta Scott King Honorable Mention Book, 1983.

418   Lester, Julius. **To be a slave.** Illustrated by Tom Feelings. Dial, 1968.

The actual words of slaves reveal the anguish of their lives. (BL)

419   Lester, Julius. **Who I am.** Poems by Julius Lester, and photos by David Gahr. Dial, 1974.

Lester's poems and the accompanying photographs reflect upon the themes of identity, childhood, city life, country surroundings, and love.   (BRD)

420   Lincoln, C. Eric. **The Negro pilgrimage in America; the coming of the age of the Blackamericans,** rev. ed. Praeger, 1970.

This edition describes the achievements, contributions, and

heritage of Blackamericans from 1600 to publication date. The panorama unfolds through vignettes of men and women through the centuries.   (BRD)

421   McKissack, Patricia C. **Martin Luther King, Jr., a man to remember.** Childrens Pr., 1984.

This book addresses King's relationship with other black leaders, movements, politicians, and the FBI, as well as allegations of his Communist views.   (CC)

422   McKissack, Patricia C. **Mary McLeod Bethune: a great American educator.** Childrens Pr., 1985.

This biography of a black woman educator, leader, and advisor to many, including Franklin D. Roosevelt, provides a view of a slave's life before and after slaves were freed.   (SLJ)

423   McKissack, Patricia C. **Michael Jackson, superstar!** Illustrated. Childrens Pr., 1984.

The story of the public Michael as derived from newspapers, magazines, and books is presented here.   (BL)

424   McKissack, Patricia C. **Paul Laurence Dunbar, a poet to remember.** Childrens Pr., 1984.

This book presents a turn-of-the century black poet and novelist whose works were among the first to give an honest presentation of black life.   (CC)

425   Mathis, Sharon Bell. **Listen for the fig tree.** Viking, 1974.

A sixteen-year-old blind black girl lives with her widowed and alcoholic mother. When a neighbor attempts to attack her, other neighbors rescue, protect, and soothe her.   (BCCB)

426   Mathis, Sharon Bell. **Teacup full of roses.** Viking, 1972.

Joe promises his girlfriend that when they are married, they will live in a teacup full of roses, in a happy world unlike his conflict and despair of reality.   (BCCB)

427   Meriwether, Louise. **Don't ride the bus on Monday: The Rosa Parks story.** Illustrated by David Scott Brown. Prentice-Hall, 1973.

This picture-book biography of Parks's early life focuses on her 1955 refusal to give up her bus seat to a white man—an act which sparked the Montgomery, Alabama, bus boycott and intensified demonstrations among American blacks. (LJ)

428   Meriwether, Louise. **The freedom ship of Robert Smalls.** Illustrated by Lee Jack Morton. Prentice-Hall, 1971.

This book covers Smalls's childhood years and tells of his contribution as a black slave who sailed a confederate ship past the forts guarding Charleston Harbor and turned *The Planter* over to the Union forces. (BCCB)

429   Meriwether, Louise. **The heart man: Dr. Daniel Hale Williams.** Illustrated by Floyd Sowell. Prentice-Hall, 1982.

Daniel Hale Williams worked a succession of jobs— shoemaker, barber, telephone lineman—until he obtained his medical degree and opened his own hospital in 1891. There he performed the first successful open-heart surgery. (LJ)

430   Millender, Dharathula H. **Martin Luther King, Jr.: boy with a dream.** Illustrated by Al Fiorentino. Bobbs-Merrill, 1969.

The life story of the black minister, author, and civil rights leader is presented in this biography. (BCCB)

431   Moore, Carmen. **Somebody's angel child: the story of Bessie Smith.** Crowell, 1969.

This complete biography of the great blues singer includes a portrayal of her poverty-stricken childhood in the slums of Chattanooga, her fame, her alcoholic downslide, and her tragic death. (BRD)

432   Mountoussamy-Ashe, Jeanne. **Viewfinders: black women photographers.** Dodd, 1986.

This work describes the triumphs and struggles of various women photographers of different areas, focusing on those of the early twentieth-century. (DCPL)

433   Myers, Walter Dean. **Adventure in Grenada.** Penguin, 1985.

Teenage brothers enjoy an enviable life-style accompanying their mother, an anthropologist, to exotic locations. (BL)

434   Myers, Walter Dean. **Ambush in the Amazon.** Penguin, 1986.

While camping in the Amazon rain forest, Chris and his brother Ken try to save a tribal village from the attacks of what appears to be a reincarnated swamp monster. (NUC)

435   Myers, Walter Dean. **The black pearl and the ghost or one mystery after another.** Illustrated by Robert Quakenbush. Viking, 1980.

Slapstick humor and much action constitute two short stories—one a detective story and the other a ghost story. (BCCB)

436   Myers, Walter Dean. **Brainstorm.** Photos by Chuck Freeman. Watts, 1977.

This science fantasy designed for slow, older readers is set in 2076 when a series of storms causes people who are outdoors to revert to an infantile state. A spaceship crew of teenagers demolish the attack planet which is run by giant computers. (BCCB)

437   Myers, Walter Dean. **Crystal.** Viking, 1987.

A beautiful, black, sixteen-year-old girl is the envy of her friends in Harlem. She enters the glamorous world of modeling and meets Rowena, an experienced model who acts as a catalyst when Crystal must make an important decision. (PW)

438   Myers, Walter Dean. **Duel in the desert.** Penguin, 1986.

While camping in Morocco, Chris and his brother try to discover who stole a valuable silver chalice from a Moroccan palace. (NUC)

439   Myers, Walter Dean. **Fast Sam, Cool Clyde and Stuff.** Viking, 1975.

An eighteen-year-old male recalls when he was thirteen, hanging out on 116th Street and enjoying being part of a circle of friends. (BL)

Winner: Coretta Scott King Honorable Mention Book, 1976.

440   Myers, Walter Dean. **The hidden shrine.** Penguin, 1985.

When two brothers are with their mother, an anthropologist,

in Hong Kong, they learn of artifacts disappearing from area temples and investigate. (BL)

441   Myers, Walter Dean. **Hoops: a novel.** Delacorte, 1981.

Eighteen-year-old Lonnie has basketball talent, but is skeptical of authority and afraid of emotional commitments when a former professional player becomes his team's coach. (BL)

442   Myers, Walter Dean. **It ain't all for nothin'.** Viking, 1978.

Twelve-year-old Tippy tells of a crisis in his life when his beloved grandmother becomes unable to care for him and he must go to live with his father who is a drifter and a petty criminal. (BCCB)

443   Myers, Walter Dean. **The legend of Tarik.** Viking, 1981.

This medieval story set in North Africa tells of a black champion who frees oppressed peoples from a white tyrant. (BL)

444   Myers, Walter Dean. **Mojo and the Russians.** Viking, 1977.

An eighteen-year-old male reminisces about his life at thirteen, his friends, and their aspirations and adventures. (LA)

445   Myers, Walter Dean. **Motown and Didi: a love story.** Viking, 1984.

Didi is intent on escaping her stress-ridden life in Harlem by attending college across the country. (BL)

Winner: Coretta Scott King Award, 1985.

446   Myers, Walter Dean. **The Nicholas factor.** Viking, 1983.

A college student is convinced to join the Conservative Crusade Society. He later abandoned it and was pursued by its criminal leaders. (BCCB)

447   Myers, Walter Dean. **The outside shot.** Delacorte, 1984.

This is a sequel to *Hoops.* Lonnie has left Harlem and has arrived at a small Indiana college on a basketball scholarship. He encounters discrimination along with other aspects of adjustment to college life. (BCCB)

448   Myers, Walter Dean. **Scorpions.** Harper, 1988.

Twelve-year-old friends live in Harlem and are confronted

with the "choice" to join The Scorpions, a gang. Jamal, who is black, raises money for his imprisoned brother's legal fees by running crack for the gang. The gun which he inherits as gang leader is used by his Puerto Rican friend, Tito, to save Jamal's life. This story of a cold and frightening world has a barely comforting ending. (BCCB)

Winner: Notable Children's Books (American Library Association), 1988.

449   Myers, Walter Dean. **Social welfare.** Watts, 1976.

This is a simplified explanation of the origin of the welfare system during the Depression, how it operated, circumstances that might force a family into welfare, and the inequities that plague the system. (BL)

450   Myers, Walter Dean. **Tales of a dead king.** Morrow, 1983.

When John and Karen go to Egypt to work on a dig with an archaeologist, he is nowhere to be found because thieves are holding him captive. (BL)

451   Myers, Walter Dean. **Won't know till I get there.** Viking, 1982.

When Steve tries to impress his new foster brother by painting a name on the side of a subway car, he is caught and their gang must serve time working in an old-age home. (VOYA)

452   Myers, Walter Dean. **The world of work: a guide to choosing a career.** Bobbs-Merrill, 1975.

Basic information on approximately 180 occupations with listings of hundreds more are provided. This book discusses the nature of work, strategy for selecting a career, and instructions for preparing resumes. (LJ)

453   Myers, Walter Dean. **The young landlords.** Viking, 1979.

A gang acquires, by chance, a slum building and a member tells of the gang's efforts to improve the property and to put it on a sound financial basis. (BCCB)

Winner: Notable Children's Books (American Library Association), 1979; Coretta Scott King Award, 1980.

454   Owens, Jesse. **The Jesse Owens story.** By Jesse Owens with Paul G. Neimark. Putnam, 1970.

One of America's greatest Olympic stars tells of his childhood and sports competition in the 1930s. He treats his exploitation and discrimination without vindictiveness.   (BL)

455   Palmer, C. Everard. **Big Doc Bitteroot.** Bobbs-Merrill, 1971.

This story concerns Jamaican village life and the acceptance of a charlatan who plans to fleece the town and move on.   (LJ)

456   Palmer, C. Everard. **The cloud with the silver lining.** Illustrated by Laszio Acs. Pantheon, 1967.

When Grandpa, their guardian, is disabled, two brothers take over the small family farm in a Jamaican village.   (BL)

457   Palmer, C. Everard. **A dog called Houdini.** Illustrated by Maurice Wilson. Dutton, 1979.

A duel between an outlaw dog and the dogcatcher divides the town until the catcher's son rescues the drugged and injured animal.   (SLJ)

458   Palmer, C. Everard. **The sun salutes you.** Bobbs-Merrill, 1971.

Mike returns to his Jamaican town to discover several facts relating to a former resident's intent to defraud the people. (BCCB)

459   Palmer, C. Everard. **The wooing of Beppo Tate.** Andre Deutsch, 1972.

This story portrays life among West Indian villagers with eleven-year-old Beppo as the central character.   (TLS)

460   Patterson, Lillie. **Benjamin Banneker: genius of early America.** Illustrated by David Scott Brown. Abingdon, 1978.

This is a young reader's biography of the black scientist who demonstrated mathematical abilities and inventive genius. He designed and carved a wooden clock, and helped to design the city of Washington, D.C. He engaged in a self-directed, lifelong study that led to astronomy and authorship of an almanac, and stood boldly against slavery.   (BL)

Winner: Coretta Scott King Honorable Mention Book, 1979.

461 Patterson, Lillie. **Lumberjacks of the north woods.** Illustrated by Victor Mays. Garrard, 1967.

This book presents the romance, bravado, courage, and necessity of lumberjacks from 1850 to 1900 to search for great pines in the north woods of Minnesota, Michigan, and Wisconsin. Patterson explains the lumbering cycle, camps, cutting, and log floats down river to the sawmills. (NYTBR)

462 Patterson, Lillie. **Martin Luther King, Jr.: man of peace.** Garrard, 1969.

Emphasizing the personal determination of the civil rights activist who attracted world attention with nonviolent protests and boycotts, this biography tells the story of the man of peace. (BL)

Winner: Coretta Scott King Award, 1970.

463 Patterson, Lillie. **Meet Miss Liberty.** Macmillan, 1962.

This book covers the conception, design, and construction of the Statue of Liberty, and the raising of funds and its dedication. (BRD)

464 Patterson, Lillie. **Sequoyah: the Cherokee who captured words.** Illustrated by Herman B. Vestal. Garrard, 1975.

Fictionalized dialogue highlights this biography of Sequoyah's life. (SLJ)

465 Patterson, Lillie. **Sure hands, strong heart: the life of Daniel Hale Williams.** Illustrated by David Scott Brown. Abingdon, 1981.

This is the story of the life and work of the black surgeon who founded Chicago's Provident Hospital, transformed Freedmen's Hospital in Washington, D.C., from ill-managed to a reputable status, and trained others for medical careers. (BL)

466 Perry, Margaret. **Rainy day magic: the art of making sunshine on a stormy day.** M. Evans, 1970.

This make-it book features projects requiring inexpensive materials which are readily available. (LJ)

467 Petry, Ann. **Harriet Tubman, conductor on the Underground Railroad.** Crowell, 1955.

A black slave woman born in 1820 became famous and beloved as one of the conductors on the Underground Railroad. (BRD)

468   Petry, Ann. **Tituba of Salem Village.** Crowell, 1964.

In this reality-based historical fiction, a slave transported from the West Indies to puritanical New England is caught up in the Salem witch hunt in 1692. (BL)

469   Robeson, Susan. **The whole world in his hands: a pictorial biography of Paul Robeson.** Citadel, 1981.

Susan's biography of her grandfather is assembled from archival collections in addition to the written and spoken words of the gifted actor, singer, and athlete who also held a law degree. (BL)

470   Robinson, Jackie and Duckett, Alfred. **Breakthrough to the big league.** Harper, 1965.

The black baseball star discusses his entrance into the big league which was exclusive of black players before his arrival. He also shares many thoughts and details about the game. (LJ)

471   Rogers, J. A. **World's great men of color.** Edited by John Henrik Clarke. Macmillan, 1972.

Included in this work are short biographies of two hundred famous blacks from Imhotep to Joe Louis. It was originally published in 1946 and intended to provide success stories chiefly for black youth. (LJ)

472   Rollins, Charlemae Hill. **Black troubadour: Langston Hughes.** Rand McNally, 1970.

This biography includes dramatic works for which Hughes wrote the script or lyrics. (BCCB)

Winner: Coretta Scott King Award, 1971.

473   Rollins, Charlemae Hill. **Famous American Negro poets.** Dodd, 1965.

These are biographical sketches of twelve black poets whose poems are of interest to young people and whose works are summarized and occasionally analyzed with sample selections. (BL)

474   Rollins, Charlemae Hill. **Famous Negro entertainers of stage, screen, and TV.** Dodd, 1967.

Biographical sketches of sixteen black entertainers in various fields of the performing arts are presented.   (BL)

475   Schockley, Ann Allen. **Living Black American authors: a biographical directory.** By Ann Allen Schockley and Sue P. Chandler. Bowker, 1973.

The authors provide information on black authors, famous and less familiar, who have been omitted from standard biographical references about contemporary authors.   (BRD)

476   Shepard, Ray Anthony. **Sneakers.** Dutton, 1973.

A black boy and a white boy who are co-captains of their football team don't get along. The black boy's new sneakers, bought with family grocery money, are stolen by the white co-captain just before the big game. Nevertheless, the black boy makes the winning touchdown in his old sneakers.   (BCCB)

477   Sherlock, Philip. **The land and people of the West Indies.** Illustrated. Lippincott, 1967.

This survey of the Caribbean Archipelago stresses the political and cultural differences and the geographical similarities of the islands.   (HB)

478   Steptoe, John. **Marcia.** Illustrated by John Steptoe. Viking, 1976.

A fifteen-year-old girl tries to understand her ambivalence about sex as advice about birth control, female dependency, and solo child rearing is given. Societal ideals are also explored by the characters.   (BCCB)

479   Steptoe, John. **Uptown.** Illustrated by John Steptoe. Harper, 1970.

Two black boys walk through Harlem and provide a positive dialogue rather than a story as they talk about what they see.   (BCCB)

480   Tarry, Ellen. **Young Jim: the early years of James Weldon Johnson.** Dodd, 1967.

This book presents the boyhood and young manhood of a noted black poet, son of a poor minister in Jacksonville, Florida, who, by age thirty had practiced law, administered a school of one thousand pupils, edited and published a daily newspaper, and written poetry and librettos for musical plays. (BL)

481   Tate, Eleanora E. **The secret of Gumbo Grove.** Watts, 1987.

When a young black girl helps an elderly lady clean up a grave in the cemetery, history and controversy explode upon the townspeople near Myrtle Beach, South Carolina. (ED)

482   Taylor, Mildred D. **Let the circle be unbroken.** Dial, 1981.

This sequel to *Roll of Thunder, Hear My Cry* is the story of the black Logan family during the Depression years in rural Mississippi and black-white relations there. (BCCB)

Winner: Notable Children's Books (American Library Association), 1981; Coretta Scott King Award, 1982.

483   Taylor, Mildred D. **Roll of thunder, hear my cry.** Illustrated by Jerry Pinkney. Dial, 1976.

The Logan family exhibits black pride and love for each other and their land as they experience a bitter financial struggle and condescension by whites. (BCCB)

Winner: Coretta Scott King Honorable Mention Book, 1977; John Newbery Medal Award, 1977.

484   Teague, Bob. **Live and off-color: news biz.** A & W, 1982.

Bob Teague examines the fascinations and frustrations of his profession which he regards as a branch of show business. (BL)

485   Thomas, Joyce Carol. **The golden pasture.** Scholastic, 1986.

This is the growing-up story of a twelve-year-old boy of black and Cherokee heritage, and of his complex relationships with his black father and grandfather and a beautiful raindrop Appaloosa rodeo horse. (SLJ)

486   Thomas, Joyce Carol. **Journey.** Scholastic, 1988.

Nutmeg Alexander has an affinity with tarantula spiders—they share secrets with her and make her giggle. She is fifteen years old when she helps solve the mystery of friends who disappear and are later found dead. (ALR)

487   Thomas, Joyce Carol. **Marked by fire.** Avon, 1982.

This story mainly about women in a black, rural Oklahoma community focuses on one special child—the ritual of her birth in the cotton fields with the women all participating in the pain and the joy; her growth as the gifted, beautiful darling of the community; the horror of her rape at age 10, and her recovery and subsequent maturing. (SLJ)

Winner: American Book Award, 1983.

488   Thomas, Joyce Carol. **Water girl.** Avon, 1986.

In this novel, Amber, a black teenage girl, learns that she is adopted. Thomas's *Marked by Fire* is the story of Amber's mother. (BRD)

489   Turner, Glennette T. **The Underground Railroad in Du Page County, Illinois.** Newman Press, 1986.

This slim book explores some of the history of slavery through a discussion of an escape route for runaway slaves through a section of Illinois. (ED)

490   Turner, Glennette T. and Tilley, Phyllis Jones. **Make and keep family memories.** Newman Press, 1983.

The authors explain some procedures for tracing and maintaining your family's history. (ED)

491   Walter, Mildred Pitts. **Because we are.** Lothrop, 1983.

Emma, a black, bright, and beautiful high school student, experiences adjustments to a new school, parental divorce and biracial remarriage, and other adolescent social and academic pressures. (BCCB)

Winner: Coretta Scott King Honorable Mention Book, 1984.

492   Walter, Mildred Pitts. **The girl on the outside.** Lothrop, 1982.

This fictionalization of the 1957 integration of Little Rock's Central High School alternates third-person narratives which focus on the experiences of two girls—one black and the other white—during the few days before nine black students are to integrate the school. (BL)

493   Walter, Mildred Pitts. **Have a happy . . . : a novel.** Illustrated by Carole M. Byard. Lothrop, 1989.

Upset because his birthday falls on Christmas Day and will therefore be eclipsed as usual, and worried that there is less money because his father is out of work, eleven-year-old Christopher takes solace in the carvings he is preparing for Kwanzaa, the African-American celebration of their cultural heritage. (ED)

494   Walter, Mildred Pitts. **Justin and the best biscuits in the world.** Lothrop, 1986.

Justin can't seem to do anything right, so his widowed grandfather invites him for a visit and gently teaches him certain basic tasks formerly regarded as "women's work." (BL)

Winner: Coretta Scott King Award, 1987.

495   Walter, Mildred Pitts. **Lillie of Watts takes a giant step.** Illustrated by Helen Johnson. Doubleday, 1971.

Lillie Stevens enters junior high school filled with emotional crises, but she emerges with a definite self-identity which is helped by her membership in the African-American Culture Club. (PW)

496   Walter, Mildred Pitts. **Trouble's child.** Lothrop, 1985.

Martha, almost fifteen and considered marriageable, realizes that to get the education she desires, she must leave the remote Louisiana island and the herb-doctoring midwifery skills that gave her grandmother the community's respect. (BL)

497   Washington, Booker T. **Up from slavery: an autobiography.** Doubleday, 1963.

First published in 1901, this account of his early days as a slave and the means by which he acquired his education also relates to how he organized Tuskegee Institute to educate others in the hope of bringing freedom to his race. (JHS)

498   Webb, Sheyann and Nelson, Rachel West. **Selma, Lord Selma.** Edited by Frank Sikera. Univ. of Alabama Pr., 1980.

Webb and Nelson recount the tense days of their eighth and ninth year of life when they walked with Martin Luther King, Jr. on the March to Selma. (BCCB)

499 Wilkes, Alfred W. **Little boy black.** Illustrated by George Cephas Ford. Scribner, 1971.

This story centers around a nine-year-old black boy who lives with his parents in a small town in North Carolina. It involves his relations with white people and how he must come to terms with bigotry toward himself, his parents, and his friends. (LJ)

500 Wilkinson, Brenda Scott. **Ludell.** Harper, 1975.

This portrays Wilkinson's memories of almost fifteen years of childhood experiences in a black community in rural Georgia during the 1950s. (BCCB)

501 Wilkinson, Brenda Scott. **Ludell and Willie.** Harper, 1977.

This is a sequel to *Ludell*. When the grandmother with whom she lives dies, Ludell must move to New York just before her graduation and away from Willie, whom she loves. As a result, she is furious and resentful. (BCCB)

502 Wilkinson, Brenda Scott. **Ludell's New York time.** Harper, 1980.

In this third book about Ludell, she is living in New York with her domineering mother, working several jobs, making friends, coping with discrimination, and longing for Willie, now a serviceman whom she will soon marry. (BCCB)

503 Wilkinson, Brenda Scott. **Not separate, not equal.** Harper, 1987.

Six black students are chosen to desegregate a white high school in Georgia in 1965. This story portrays how the teenagers experience attacks by vicious dogs, exclusion from school activities at both black and white schools, blatant racial incidents, and the difficulty of maintaining boy- and girlfriends across the different experience. How they overcame these experiences is also explained. (WLB)

504 Wilson, Beth P. **Giants for justice: Bethune, Randolph, and King.** HBJ, 1978.

Three outstanding black leaders who paved the way toward dignity and freedom for black people in education, labor, and civil rights are biographically sketched. (OCLC)

505   Wilson, Beth P., reteller. **The great Minu.** Illustrated by Jerry Pinkney. Follett, 1974.

Based on a West African folktale, this is the story of a poor farmer who visits Accra and questions what he doesn't understand. The answer he gets is always "minu," which means "I do not understand." Because the poor farmer also doesn't understand, he concludes that minu is a person whose life he does not prefer after all.   (SLJ)

506   Wilson, Beth P. **Muhammad Ali.** Illustrated by Floyd Sowell. Putnam, 1974.

The prizefighter whose skill won him an Olympic gold medal and the world heavyweight championship is portrayed.   (OCLC)

507   Wilson, Beth P. **Stevie Wonder.** Illustrated by James Calvin. Putnam, 1979.

This biography for young readers portrays the blind composer, pianist, and singer whose musical ability, which was apparent from his childhood, has earned him numerous awards and tremendous popularity.   (OCLC)

508   Young, Bernice Elizabeth. **Harlem: the story of a changing community.** Messner, 1972.

Text, pictures, and drawings cover the Harlem area from the first Dutch settlements to the early 1970s and express hope for the improvement of the area.   (BL)

509   Young, Margaret Buckner. **Black American leaders.** Watts, 1969.

Leaders in civil rights, government, politics, and the international scene are each described on one or two pages. Each description also includes a photograph.   (BCCB)

510   Young, Margaret Buckner. **The first book of American Negroes.** Watts, 1966.

A factual account of the achievements of black people is provided against a background of the conditions under which they were accomplished.   (BL)

Chapter 3

Books for
Young Adult Readers

Readers at the senior high school level and above are entitled to be informed and sufficiently challenged. Therefore, the upper range of books represented in this chapter may also be appropriate for college preparatory or first-year college reading. The selections here should prove beneficial to individuals and teachers who wish to pursue deeper understandings of their own or their students' ethnic identity and history.

More representative in this chapter than in the previous ones are books which emphasize some aspect of blackness. Among the types of books represented here, poetry, fiction, drama, and history are predominant. Entries for award-winning books also feature a concluding identification of the name and year of the award.

511   Abdul-Jabbar, Kareem. **Giant steps.** By Kareem Abdul-Jabbar and Peter Knobler. Bantam, 1983.

The 7'2" basketball player for the Los Angeles Lakers (named Lew Alcindor before his conversion to orthodox Islam in 1968) recalls growing up in New York an unusually tall, only child in a tightly run, middle-class black family. This autobiography focuses on his feelings of racial, social, and religious alienation.   (BRD)

512   Adams, Russell L. **Negroes in our history.** Illustrated by Eugene Winslow. Afro-Am, 1964.

This is the visual education companion to Adams's *Great Negroes, past and present.*   (NUC)

513   Allen, Samuel, comp. **Poems from Africa.** Illustrated by Romare Bearden. Crowell, 1973.

A wide-ranging selection of poetry by West, South, and East Africans expresses a broad gamut of emotions on personal and general themes reflecting the essence of Africa.   (BL)

514   Anderson, Jervis. **A. Philip Randolph, a biographical portrait.** HBJ, 1973.

The book is a biography of the black founder and long-time president of the Brotherhood of Sleeping Car Porters.   (BRD)

515   Anderson, Jervis. **This was Harlem: a cultural portrait, 1900–1950.** Farrar, 1982.

This book chronicles fifty years of cultural history of a neighborhood which had been almost exclusively white until 1925 when it had an international reputation as the mecca of black life and culture.   (BRD)

516   Anderson, Marian. **My Lord what a morning.** Cresset Pr., 1957.

This is an autobiography of one of the world's leading contraltos who appeared in famous international concert halls.   (ED)

517   Andrews, Raymond. **Appalachee Red: a novel.** Illustrated by Benny Andrews. Dial, 1978.

The title reflects the name of a small town in Georgia and the son of its most influential white man and his married black maid. The story is about the son's efforts to avenge himself on his father.   (BRD)

518   Angelou, Maya. **And still I rise.** Random, 1978.

This poetry enlarges on themes from the author's autobiographical writings and earlier poetry.   (BRD)

519   Angelou, Maya. **Gather together in my name.** Random, 1974.

Here is the sequel to *I Know Why the Caged Bird Sings,* in which the author is an unmarried sixteen-year-old with a new baby to support.   (BRD)

520   Angelou, Maya. **The heart of a woman.** Random, 1981.

This fourth volume of the author's autobiography covers her life in the late 1950s and 1960s—a time of acute racial awareness for her.   (BRD)

521   Angelou, Maya. **I know why the caged bird sings.** Random, 1970.

An autobiography covering the childhood and adolescence of a black girl in rural Arkansas; St. Louis, Missouri; and San Francisco.   (BRD)

Winner: Coretta Scott King Honorable Mention Book, 1971.

522   Angelou, Maya. **Just give me a cool drink of water 'fore I d i i ie: the poetry of Maya Angelou.** Random, 1971.

Part one of this collection contains poetry of love, anguish, sharing, fear, affection, and loneliness. Part two features poems of racial confrontation—protest, anger, and irony.   (BRD)

523   Angelou, Maya. **Now Sheba sings the song.** Illustrated by Tom Feelings. Dial, 1987.

Drawings of black women of all ages from all over the world attempt to convey the beauty of women of color. They are unified by Angelou's poem which is the title.   (ED)

524   Angelou, Maya. **Oh pray my wings are gonna fit me well.** Random, 1975.

This collection includes poems of love and memory, racial confrontation, misplaced patriotism, and songs of the street and of the heart.   (BRD)

525   Angelou, Maya. **Shaker, why don't you sing?** Random, 1983.

Angelou's fourth collection is about the blues, of recovering from passion, of the smells and sounds of southern cities, of living life right on Saturday night.   (HB)

526   Angelou, Maya. **Singin' and swingin' and gettin' merry like Christmas.** Random, 1976.

A continuation of Angelou's autobiography tells of her unsuccessful marriage, her continual efforts to support her family, and the rise of her theatrical career.   (BRD)

527   Ashe, Arthur. **Portrait in motion.** With Frank Deford. Houghton, 1975.

This is a daily diary from Wimbledon 1973 to Wimbledon 1974.   (BRD)

528   Attaway, William. **Blood on the forge.** Doubleday, 1941.

Three black brothers leave their Kentucky farm during World War I to work in the western Pennsylvania steel mills.   (BRD)

529   Attaway, William. **Let me breathe thunder.** Doubleday, 1939.

Two hoboes roaming around the country are somewhat impeded by the adoption of a little Mexican boy who weaves himself into their lives and affections and brings something gentle to their attention.   (BRD)

530   Bailey, Pearl. **Hurry up, America, and spit.** HBJ, 1976.

The author calls upon fellow Americans to admit their errors, which, when repeated, ought not be excused. We must spit out what we cannot live on or by.   (BRD)

531   Bailey, Pearl. **Pearl's kitchen: an extraordinary cookbook.** HBJ, 1973.

Pearl provides anecdotes about her public and private life including approximately 100 recipes—some of which are from her friends.   (BRD)

532   Bailey, Pearl. **The raw Pearl.** HBJ, 1968.

The author describes her life and career as an entertainer, singer, and actress.   (BRD)

533   Bailey, Pearl. **Talking to myself.** HBJ, 1971.

The singer's thoughts, that were originally written in hotels, airplanes, and at home, range in variety from her relationship with God to her resentment of certain fans who crassly intrude upon her privacy. (BRD)

534   Baker, Houston A. **Singers of daybreak: studies in Black American literature.** Howard Univ. Pr., 1974.

This collection of essays includes pieces on writers whose works have served to illuminate the spirit of civilization: James Weldon Johnson, Richard Wright, Paul Laurence Dunbar, Gwendolyn Brooks, Jean Toomer, and George Cain. (BRD)

535   Baker, Josephine. **Josephine.** By Josephine Baker and Jo Bouillon; tr. from French by Mariana Fitzpatrick. Harper, 1977.

This book is a biography of the first black international star who had to emigrate to France before being accepted and becoming famous in show business. She was a humanitarian devoted to the many children she adopted. (BRD)

536   Baldwin, James. **Amen corner: a play.** Dial, 1966.

The story is of members of a Harlem storefront church and their spiritual leader, Sister Margaret, who distorted family values in order to answer what she believed was the Lord's call. (BRD)

537   Baldwin, James. **Blues for Mister Charlie: a play.** Dial, 1964.

Pivotal to this story is the murder of a young black male who had returned to a small town in the Deep South to recover from drug addiction and to rebuild his life. (BRD)

538   Baldwin, James. **A dialogue [by] James Baldwin [and] Nikki Giovanni.** Lippincott, 1973.

This conversation, taped in London for WNET, explores problems facing black and white Americans, as well as the troubles besetting the world. (BRD)

539   Baldwin, James. **The fire next time.** Dial, 1963.

An autobiographical and philosophical discussion of

Baldwin's belief that black and white people deeply need each other to become a nation and that racial separation is no more valid from Malcolm X than from Senator Byrd. (BRD)

540   Baldwin, James. **Go tell it on the mountain.** Knopf, 1953.

A story of religious experience among blacks in Harlem in which the account of a young man's conversion on his fourteenth birthday is set against the story of his forefathers and told in flashbacks. (BRD)

541   Baldwin, James. **Going to meet the man.** Dial, 1965.

This book is a first collection of the author's stories. (BRD)

542   Baldwin, James. **Nobody knows my name: more notes of a native son.** Dial, 1961.

Baldwin draws on his experiences and observations in the U.S. and Europe in these essays about relationships between blacks and whites and between the writer and society. (BRD)

543   Baldwin, James. **Notes of a native son.** Beacon, 1955.

Personal essays provide an account of Baldwin's life as a boy and a young man in Harlem. They also reflect an effort to retrieve blacks from the abstractions of the do-gooders and the no-gooders. (BRD)

544   Baldwin, James. **One day when I was lost: a scenario based on Alex Haley's The Autobiography of Malcolm X.** Dial, 1973.

Here is a film script which outlines the facts of Malcolm X's life. (BRD)

545   Baldwin, James. **Tell me how long the train's been gone.** Dial, 1968.

From his hospital bed, the narrator recalls his Harlem childhood, family, youthful struggles, love affair, and successful stage career. (BRD)

546   Bambara, Toni Cade, ed. **The black woman.** New Amer. Lib., 1970.

A collection of poems, stories, and essays that reveals thoughts and interests of black women in America. (ED)

547 Bambara, Toni Cade. **The salt eaters.** Random, 1980.

This book portrays the lives of two black women of different generations and life within the Claybourne Infirmary where old timers sometimes believed that it was safer to live with complaints, necessary to cooperate with grief, and all right to become an accomplice in self-ambush. (BRD)

548 Bambara, Toni Cade. **The seabirds are still alive: collected stories.** Random, 1977.

Ten stories deal primarily with the black experience. Each involves the recognition or solution of some personal problem or difficult situation on the part of the protagonist. (BRD)

549 Baraka, Imamu Amiri (Jones, Leroi), ed. **African congress: a documentary of the first modern Pan-African Congress.** Morrow, 1972.

This book chronicles the results of the first Congress of African People held in Atlanta in 1970, which brought together black cultural and political nationalists and sympathizers. (BRD)

550 Baraka, Imamu Amiri (Jones, Leroi). **In our terribleness: (some elements and meaning in black style).** Photographs by Fundi (Billy Abernathy). Bobbs-Merrill, 1971.

This poetic photographic essay re-creates and defines black life for the black reader. Title slang reverses the white standard. (BRD)

551 Baraka, Imamu Amiri (Jones, Leroi). **Raise, race, rays, raze: essays since 1965.** Random, 1971.

These essays expound a cultural black nationalism. (BRD)

552 Bates, Daisy. **The long shadow of Little Rock: a memoir.** McKay, 1962.

Bates relates her role in the Little Rock integration fight and states her belief that the incident shattered the faith in American democracy for many blacks and for others. (BRD)

553 Beckwourth, James P. **Life and adventures of James P. Beckwourth, mountaineer, scout, pioneer, and chief of the Crow nation of Indians.** Written from his own dictation, by T. D. Bonner, ed. Knopf, 1931.

This is a reprint of the autobiography of a mulatto fur trader-scout who became a Crow Indian tribe member and the hero of many western tall tales. (BRD)

554   Bennett, Lerone. **Before the Mayflower: a history of the Negro in America, 1619–1962.** Johnson, 1962.

This history of the Black American, whose ancestors arrived in Jamestown a year before the arrival of the Mayflower, begins in Africa and ends with Martin Luther King, Jr. (BRD)

555   Bennett, Lerone. **Black Power U.S.A.: the human side of Reconstruction, 1867–1877.** Johnson, 1967.

This book is a historical study of the years when black men were elected to the legislatures of every southern state. (BRD)

556   Bennett, Lerone. **Confrontation: black and white.** Johnson, 1965.

This book is an account of the struggle of Black Americans for justice, equality, and dignity. (BRD)

557   Bennett, Lerone. **The Negro mood, and other essays.** Johnson, 1964.

Five essays organized around the general theme expressed in the title reveal four different rebellions: against the conservative within and without, on the streets, and in the thoroughfares of the mind. (BRD)

558   Bennett, Lerone. **Wade in the water.** Johnson, 1979.

Fifteen dramatic episodes in the history of African Americans in the United States are reconstructed. (BRD)

559   Bennett, Lerone. **What manner of man: a biography of Martin Luther King, Jr.** Johnson, 1964.

A biography of the third black, the twelfth American, and the youngest person to receive the Nobel Peace Prize since its institution in 1895. (BRD)

560   Berry, Mary Frances. **Long memory: the black experience in America.** By Mary Frances Berry and John W. Blassingame. Oxford Univ. Pr., 1982.

This survey of African-American history focuses on such

themes and subjects as family and church, sex and racism, politics, economics, education, criminal justice, and black nationalism. (BRD)

561   Blassingame, John W. **The slave community: plantation life in the antebellum South.** Oxford Univ. Pr., 1972.

This book results from an examination of sources, including memoirs of former slaves, for the ways that blacks became enslaved, their process of acculturation in the American South, and their ties to African heritage. It explains how the slave was able to control parts of his own life while often wearing the mask of submissiveness required by the harsh realities of the plantation regime. (BRD)

562   Bogle, Donald. **Toms, coons, mulattoes, mammies, and bucks: an interpretive history of blacks in American films.** Viking, 1973.

This book traces the role of blacks in American fictional films from movies such as "Wooing and wedding of a coon" (1905) to latter-day opera such as "Shaft." (BRD)

563   Bontemps, Arna Wendell, ed. **American Negro poetry.** Hill & Wang, 1963.

Poems spanning a seventy-year period reflect the anguish of an oppressed people on universal themes of love, time, nature, and death. Biographical notes are provided for the fifty-six poets represented. (BRD)

564   Bontemps, Arna Wendell. **Black thunder.** Macmillan, 1936.

This fictionalized version of the Gabriel Insurrection of 1800 tells the story of a slave on a Virginia plantation who planned to seize the arsenal and capture Richmond but who was thwarted by an unprecedented rainstorm and betrayal. (BRD)

565   Bontemps, Arna Wendell. **Drums at dusk.** Macmillan, 1939.

A story of the black rising in Haiti during the French Revolution. The protagonist is a young Frenchman who is in sympathy with the blacks. (BRD)

566   Bontemps, Arna Wendell. **Free at last: the life of Frederick Douglass.** Dodd, 1971.

The major emphasis of this book is on the period following

Douglass' escape from slavery at about age twenty, and some earlier life episodes shown through flashbacks. (BRD)

567 Bontemps, Arna Wendell. **God sends Sunday.** HBJ, 1931.

This story chronicles the rise of little Angie, a tiny black jockey who won notoriety for his luck during the 1890s and of how he lost his luck and became a penniless wanderer. (BRD)

568 Bontemps, Arna Wendell, ed. **The Harlem Renaissance remembered: essays edited with a memoir.** Dodd, 1972.

The world of black writers who gravitated to New York and constituted the Harlem Renaissance is described and discussed in terms of the artists' themes, patterns, and approaches. (BRD)

569 Bontemps, Arna Wendell. **The old South: "A Summer Tragedy," and other stories of the thirties.** Dodd, 1973.

A portrait of southern life as experienced and understood by the author is told in twelve short stories which deal with black experiences. (BRD)

570 Bontemps, Arna Wendell. **We have tomorrow.** Houghton, 1945.

This book contains twelve fictionlike biographical accounts of success gained over obstacles by young blacks. Biographies of Hazel Scott, Benjamin Davis, Dean Dixon, Mildred E. Blount, and others are presented in these stories. (BRD)

571 Bontemps, Arna Wendell. **Young Booker: Booker T. Washington's early days.** Dodd, 1972.

This book is an account of Washington's life from his birth in 1856 to his Atlanta Compromise speech in 1895. (BRD)

572 Bontemps, Arna Wendell and Conroy, Jack. **Anyplace but here.** Hill & Wang, 1966.

Notes compiled from the WPA Writers' Project in Chicago during the 1940s are revised to explain black migrations in the United States. (BRD)

573 Bontemps, Arna Wendell and Conroy, Jack. **They seek a city.** Doubleday, 1945.

This study of black migration from the South to the North and

West, during a period of more than a century, begins with the flight of slaves from the antebellum South via the Underground Railroad. (BRD)

574 Booker, Simeon. **Black man's America.** Prentice-Hall, 1964.

The former White House correspondent for *Ebony* and *Jet* magazines reviews the Civil Rights movement. (BRD)

575 Braithwaite, William Stanley. **Lyrics of life and love.** H. B. Turner, 1904.

These poems of a rising young black poet reflect the gloom of life and its wildest joys. (BRD)

576 Braithwaite, William Stanley. **Selected poems.** Coward, 1948.

This selection of Braithwaite's works is on traditional subjects and in traditional form. (BRD)

577 Braithwaite, William Stanley. **The William Stanley Braithwaite reader.** Ed. by Philip Butcher. Univ. of Michigan Pr., 1972.

This collection of the works of a black critic, editor, and poet contains letters, criticisms, social protest writings, and autobiographical reminiscences. (BRD)

578 Brawley, Benjamin Griffith. **Africa and the war.** Duffield, 1918.

The author aims to present the striking features of a definite situation developed by the world conflict and to indicate its meaning for America. (BRD)

579 Brawley, Benjamin Griffith. **Early Negro American writers: selections with biographical and critical introductions.** Univ. of North Carolina Pr., 1935.

These selections are from the writings of Black Americans from about 1720 and 1730 to around Civil War times. (BRD)

580 Brawley, Benjamin Griffith. **Negro builders and heroes.** Univ. of North Carolina Pr., 1937.

This compilation contains biographical sketches of black leaders and also provides chapters on blacks in war times, in educational and religious work, in literature and art, and in science and invention. (BRD)

581   Brawley, Benjamin Griffith. **The Negro genius: a new appraisal of the achievement of the American Negro in literature and the fine arts.** Dodd, 1937.

This discourse gives attention to recent black authors and artists, especially musicians.   (BRD)

582   Brawley, Benjamin Griffith. **Negro in literature and art in the United States.** Duffield, 1918.

Brawley provides biographical sketches of the artists whose achievements in literature and the arts are discussed.   (BRD)

583   Brawley, Benjamin Griffith. **Paul Laurence Dunbar: poet of his people.** Univ. of North Carolina Pr., 1936.

This biography portrays Paul Laurence Dunbar who rose from an elevator operator to a position as the most celebrated of black writers and who died in 1906 at the age of thirty-four. (BRD)

584   Brawley, Benjamin Griffith. **Short history of the American Negro.** Macmillan, 1913.

This study written for the general reader aims to deal with the political, economic, social, religious, and cultural phases of black life in order to provide historical background for material published in magazines and newspapers.   (BRD)

585   Brawley, Benjamin Griffith. **Social history of the American Negro.** Macmillan, 1921.

Benjamin Brawley presents a historical progression of black life in its connection with the nation, including blacks coming to America, the Colonial era during which blacks passed from a condition of servitude into real slavery, and various phases up to the Civil War.   (BRD)

586   Brawley, Benjamin Griffith. **Your Negro neighbor.** Macmillan, 1918.

Brawley pleads for the black race by presenting evidence of their achievements, by emphasizing the incongruity of advocating democracy abroad while failing to practice it at home, and by pointing out that the U.S. race problem affects U.S. relations with our island dependencies and with Latin American countries.   (BWD)

587   Brewer, John Mason. **Word on the Brazos: Negro preacher tales from the Brazos bottoms of Texas.** Illustrated by Ralph White, Jr. Univ. of Texas Pr., 1953.

This collection of black preacher anecdotes, rather than stories or tales, shows his use of humor in religion.   (BRD)

588   Brooke, Edward W. **The challenge of change: crisis in our two-party system.** Little, 1966.

A former United States Attorney General declares that Republicans have veered too far from the ideals of Lincoln and Theodore Roosevelt, and offers recommendations for dealing with poverty, racial inequity, and urban problems.   (BRD)

589   Brooks, Gwendolyn. **Annie Allen.** Harper, 1949.

These poems portray through one woman's experiences in Bronzeville the universal implications of poverty, loneliness, brief fantasies of escape, loss, and the finality of death.   (BRD)

Winner: Pulitzer Prize, 1950.

590   Brooks, Gwendolyn. **In the Mecca: poems.** Harper, 1968.

The title poem portrays the lost and tragic lives of people living in a decayed apartment building.   (BRD)

591   Brooks, Gwendolyn. **Report from part one.** Broadside, 1972.

Brooks's autobiographical assemblage of personal memoirs, mental notations, interviews, letters, and photographs is a retrospection of growing up in Chicago and her involvements in the Black Arts movement.   (BRD)

592   Brown, Claude. **The children of Ham.** Stein & Day, 1976.

A group of black teenagers and adults lives together for survival in three apartments in an otherwise abandoned and deteriorated Harlem tenement. Each member or friend of the group explains the group's attraction and personal beliefs and philosophies.   (BRD)

593   Brown, Claude. **Manchild in the promised land.** Macmillan, 1965.

Realities of Brown's childhood and youth during the 1940s and 1950s accentuate the desolations and survivals of his contemporaries during the dark night of the black soul.   (NYTBR)

594   Brown, Frank London. **Trumbull Park.** Regnery, 1959.

This novel describes what happens when a small group of black families move out of the tenements in which they have spent their lives and into a new housing development where white families have settled and where anti-black feeling is very strong.   (BRD)

595   Brown, Sterling A. **The collected poems of Sterling A. Brown.** Harper, 1980.

Sonnets, prose, blues, dialect, and formal poems are found in this collection.   (BRD)

596   Brown, Sterling A. **Southern road: poems.** Illustrated by Elmer Simms Campbell. HBJ, 1932.

Some of these poems are in dialect, but most are on themes "dug from the deep mine of Negro folk poetry."   (BRD)

597   Brown, Sterling A.; Davis, Arthur Paul; and Lee, Ulysses Grant, eds. **Negro caravan: writings by American Negroes.** Dryden Pr., 1942.

This book contains poetry, short stories, excerpts from novels, folk literature, drama, biography, and essays by Black Americans from 1760 to 1942.   (BRD)

598   Bullins, Ed. **Five plays.** Bobbs-Merrill, 1969.

Goin' a Buffalo, In the Wine Time, A Son, Come Home, The Electronic Nigger, and *Clara's Ole Man* are five plays about Black American life.   (BRD)

Winner: Vernon Rice Drama Desk Award, 1986.

599   Bullins, Ed. **The reluctant rapist.** Harper, 1973.

This novel portrays the struggles of a young black man as he runs from a North Philadelphia ghetto where his friends face violence, destructive sexuality, and hopelessness.   (BRD)

600   Bullins, Ed. **The theme is blackness: "The Corner" and other plays.** Morrow, 1972.

Fifteen plays represent a cross section of Bullins's works. The introduction traces the development of black theater through the 1960s and into the 1970s.   (BRD)

601 Burroughs, Margaret G. **Africa, my Africa.** Illustrated by Margaret G. Burroughs. Du Sable Mus. Pr., 1970.

Eighteen poems begin with an African American's joyful arrival in Africa and portray that arrival as a fulfillment of identity. The theme of the African American as a stranger in African society introduces the complexity that reverberates throughout the volume—the African American is home, but not at home. (DLB)

602 Butcher, Margaret Just. **Negro in American culture.** Based on materials left by Alain Locke. Knopf, 1956.

This posthumous version details the black's role in American society and culture as slave, freedman, and citizen, and discusses his role in the arts and education. (BRD)

603 Carew, Jan. **Green winter, a novel.** Stein & Day, 1965.

A British Guiana scholarship student in Moscow discovers much about Soviet society, including its subtle and its more direct forms of racial prejudice. (BL)

604 Carew, Jan. **A touch of Midas.** Coward, 1958.

A British Guiana boy is sponsored by a wealthy white man, becomes educated, and leaves the confines of village life. His efforts to become the wealthiest prospector in the bush country are accompanied by thoughtless behavior that leads to poverty and a mine disaster. (BL)

605 Carmichael, Stokely. **Black Power: the politics of liberation in America.** By Stokely Carmichael and Charles V. Hamilton. Random, 1967.

The authors explain the origins, development, and goals of the Black Power movement and claim that black people have been misled by white and black leaders who have fostered the illusion that a democratic America would allow democracy for all people. (BRD)

606 Carter, Rubin "Hurricane." **The sixteenth round; from number 1 contender to #45472.** Viking, 1974.

Carter reached success in 1964 by challenging the middle-weight boxing crown, but three years later he stood accused and convicted of slaying three people. Here he states his innocence and pleads for help. (BRD)

607 Cayton, Horace R. **Long old road.** Simon & Schuster, 1964.

This is an autobiography of Cayton, a black sociologist and newspaperman. (BRD)

608 Cayton, Horace R. and Mitchell, George Sinclair. **Black workers and the new unions.** Univ. of North Carolina Pr., 1939.

This book studies the economic status and industrial position of blacks as industrial laborers and their participation in labor unions. (BRD)

609 Chalk, Ocania. **Black college sport.** Dodd, 1976.

This is the story of blacks in American college sports from the beginning of intercollegiate competition until World War II. (BRD)

610 Chamberlain, Wilt and Shaw, David. **Wilt: just like any other 7-foot black millionaire who lives next door.** Macmillan, 1973.

The basketball star writes about his professional career, people he met, places of travel, exploitation, and coaches, among other topics. (BRD)

611 Chestnutt, Charles Waddell. **Colonel's dream.** Doubleday, 1905.

The story of an ex-Confederate officer who seeks his postwar fortune in New York and returns to the South after twenty years. (BRD)

612 Childress, Alice, ed. **Black scenes.** Doubleday, 1971.

This collection of brief scenes from plays about blacks by Black American writers is gathered because of the lack of such material for use in auditions and classrooms. (BRD)

613 Childress, Alice. **A short walk.** Coward, 1979.

Cora James's short walk through life carries her from birth through marriage, her flight to Harlem, and love with a childhood sweetheart who is involved with the Marcus Garvey movement. (BRD)

614 Childress, Alice. **Those other people.** Putnam, 1989.

> The characters in this story tell their own dramatic stories which involve a student and school employees in a small town, sexual confusion, homosexuality, child abuse, and brave honesty. The student, seventeen-year-old Jonathan Barnett, emerges with his self-assurance intact. (ALR)

615 Chisholm, Shirley. **The good fight.** Harper, 1973.

> A congresswoman from New York City describes how, as a black woman, she ran as a candidate for the presidency, and her continuing struggle for the reform of American politics. (BRD)

616 Chisholm, Shirley. **Unbought and unbossed.** Houghton, 1970.

> Chisholm describes her life, career, opinions of the U.S. political scene, and her thoughts on some major issues of our time. (BRD)

> **Winner:** Coretta Scott King Honorable Mention Book, 1971.

617 Christian, Barbara. **Black women novelists: the development of a tradition, 1892–1976.** Greenwood, 1980.

> This survey explores the images of black women in black fiction by early and contemporary novelists. The future of black women's writing is also considered. (BRD)

618 Clark, Kenneth B. **Dark ghetto: dilemmas of social power.** Harper, 1964.

> The former chief consultant to Harlem Youth Opportunities Unlimited (HARYOU) analyzes the poverty, crime, low aspirations, family instability, and exploitation of the degraded humans who are social victims of a world for which they are not responsible. (BRD)

619 Clark, Kenneth B. **The Negro protest: James Baldwin, Malcolm X, Martin Luther King talk with Kenneth B. Clark.** Beacon, 1964.

> These interviews were originally recorded for the National Educational Television and Radio Center. Prefatory notes are given for each personality. (BRD)

620   Clark, Kenneth B. **Prejudice and your child.** Beacon, 1955.

A psychology professor considers prejudices from a racial and minority group aspect and provides a program of action for churches, schools, social agencies, and parents.   (BRD)

621   Clarke, John Henrik, ed. **American Negro short stories.** Hill & Wang, 1966.

This collection of thirty-one short stories with short biographical sketches of authors includes Du Bois, Chestnutt, Leroi Jones, Baldwin, Killins, and Paule Marshall.   (BRD)

622   Clarke, John Henrik, ed. **Malcolm X: the man and his times.** Macmillan, 1969.

This collection of essays by people who either knew Malcolm X personally or deeply felt his impact also includes some of Malcolm's speeches and a recorded conversation with the FBI in 1964 shortly after his break with Elijah Muhammad. (BRD)

623   Clarke, John Henrik. **Marcus Garvey and the vision of Africa.** Random, 1974.

This selection of writings by and about Garvey examines his thinking and action.   (BRD)

624   Clarke, John Henrik, ed. **William Styron's Nat Turner: ten black writers respond.** Beacon, 1968.

The editor's introduction and nine essays attack a distortion of historical fact regarding the life of Nat Turner, the leader of a slave rebellion in Virginia in 1831.   (BRD)

625   Cleaver, Eldridge. **Eldridge Cleaver: post-prison writings and speeches.** Edited with an appraisal by Robert Scheer. Random, 1969.

This book supplements Cleaver's autobiography *Soul on Ice* and discusses key events in his life since his release on parole from prison. It also reviews his situation in light of current events and developments.   (BRD)

626   Cleaver, Eldridge. **Soul on ice.** McGraw-Hill, 1968.

This collection of essays and open letters about the forces

which shaped Cleaver's life was written in California's Folsom State Prison.   (BRD)

627   Clifton, Lucille. **Generations: a memoir.** Random, 1976.

Clifton traces her family back to her great, great grandmother who was born free in Africa and died free in America, but who was sold into slavery and separated from her mother when she was eight years old.   (BRD)

628   Clifton, Lucille. **Good news about the earth: new poems.** Random, 1972.

Forty-five poems about black identity in the urban world are written by a lyric poet confident of her own time and place. (BRD)

629   Clifton, Lucille. **Two-headed woman.** Univ. of Massachusetts Pr., 1980.

Clifton celebrates the body and mourns blindness, the loss of loved ones, and human failures.   (LJ)

Winner: Juniper Prize for Poetry, 1980.

630   Cone, James H. **The spirituals and the blues: an interpretation.** Seabury, 1972.

This examination of spirituals and blues as cultural expressions of the black community argues that black music must be lived before it can be understood.   (BRD)

631   Conyers, James E. **Black elected officials: a study of Black Americans holding governmental office.** By James E. Conyers and Walter L. Wallace. Russell Sage Foundation, 1976.

This report analyzed the results of a mail survey to all black elected officials at state, county, and local levels regarding their political beliefs, office-seeking motivations, personal background, party affiliations, sources of support, impacts, expectations, and election district characteristics.   (BRD)

632   Cornish, Sam. **Sam's world.** Decatur Hse., 1978.

These poems chronicle a witness to the legacy of dirt-poor slaves and a celebration of American blackness inclusive of guts, endurance, and blues transcendence.   (LJ)

633   Cornish, Sam and Dixon, Lucian W. **Chicory: young voices from the black ghetto.** Association Pr., 1969.

A wide variety of poems provide insight into the ghetto and are written in the language of the people who live there.   (LJ)

634   Counter, S. Allen. **I sought my brother: an Afro-American reunion.** By S. Allen Counter and David L. Evans. MIT Press, 1981.

This book accounts the reunion of two African Americans who made seven trips to the Surinam rain forest in South America to live with the descendants of African slaves who fled Guiana in the seventeenth century.   (BRD)

635   Cruse, Harold. **The crisis of the Negro intellectual.** Morrow, 1967.

Cruse contends that the failure of the black intellectual derives from the Harlem Renaissance when black artists and intellectuals failed to combine their cultural nationalism with comparable political and economic movements—an error that persists to this day.   (BRD)

636   Cruse, Harold. **Rebellion or revolution?** Morrow, 1968.

This collection of essays written since 1950 discusses the present racial impasse in America and examines the impact and relevance of thinkers, writers, and performers.   (BRD)

637   Cullen, Countee. **Ballad of the Brown girl: an old ballad retold.** Harper, 1927.

This old ballad is a narrative poem of Lord Thomas and the two who loved him, Fair London and the Brown girl.   (BRD)

638   Cullen, Countee. **Black Christ, and other poems.** Harper, 1929.

The title poem tells the story of a young black who is lynched for the sin of another man and who, Christlike, dies and lives again.   (BRD)

639   Cullen, Countee. **Caroling dusk.** Illustrated by Aaron Douglas. Harper, 1927.

This anthology of the work of black poets presents some new voices from the early 1920s.   (BRD)

640   Cullen, Countee. **Color.** Harper, 1925.

These are poems in which the color of the poet's people is often the theme. (BRD)

641   Cullen, Countee. **Copper sun.** Harper, 1927.

This is Cullen's second volume of lyric poems. (BRD)

642   Cullen, Countee. **The Medea [of Euripides: a new version] and some poems.** Harper, 1935.

Some of Cullen's lyrics and his version of "The Medea" written for Rose McClendon, the star of "In Abraham's Bosom" are included in this collection. (BRD)

643   Cullen, Countee. **On these I stand.** Harper, 1947.

This collection of poems selected by Cullen shortly before his death represents his choice of his best verses. (BRD)

644   Cullen, Countee. **One way to heaven.** Harper, 1932.

This first novel pictures two widely different phases of black life portrayed through the experiences of a servant girl and her employer in her circle of Harlem sophisticates. (BRD)

645   Daniels, Douglas Henry. **Pioneer urbanites: a social and cultural history of black San Francisco.** Temple Univ. Pr., 1980.

The focus is on black migrants to San Francisco between 1850 and 1940 to show how their character and resourcefulness enabled them to take advantage of a variety of economic opportunities on the West Coast. (BRD)

646   Danner, Margaret Esse. **The down of a thistle: selected poems, prose poems and songs.** Illustrated by Fred L. Weinman. Country Beautiful, 1976.

Textures, colors, sounds, flora, fauna, and people forged by and found in the African matrix and the American milieu constitute these poems. (BRD)

647   Davis, Angela. **Angela Davis—an autobiography.** Random, 1974.

Davis tells of her childhood, family life, and education; her political development; her fight for her UCLA job teaching philosophy; and her 1972 trial on charges of murder, kidnapping, and conspiracy.   (LJ)

648   Davis, Angela, et al. **If they come in the morning: voices of resistance.** Third World Press, 1971.

The central argument is that most persons confined in jails, lockups, reformatories, houses of detention, and penitentiaries in our country are political prisoners, the victims of political oppression. The title is from the concluding sentence of James Baldwin's "Open Letter to Angela Davis:" "If they take you in the morning, they will be coming for us that night." (SR)

649   Davis, Angela. **Women, race and class.** Random, 1982.

Thirteen essays cover the period from slavery to the present and explore the sporadic alliance between the black liberation and the women's rights movements.   (N)

650   Davis, Arthur P. **From the dark tower: Afro-American writers 1900–1960.** Howard Univ. Pr., 1974.

Social and literary backgrounds of the New Negro Renaissance (1900–1948) and the mainstream (1940–1960) attempt to provide facts concerning writers' lives which enhance appreciation of their works.   (BRD)

651   Davis, Frank Marshall. **Black man's verse.** Black Cat, 1935.

Davis's first volume of verse brings a western note to black expression.   (N)

652   Davis, Sammy. **Yes, I can: the story of Sammy Davis, Jr.** By Sammy Davis, Jr. and Jane and Burt Boyar. Farrar, 1965.

Beginning with his childhood in vaudeville where he learned his craft, Davis tells of the conflicts and events which shaped his life.   (BRD)

653   Delany, Samuel R. **The jewel-hinged jaw: notes on the language of science fiction.** Dragon Publishing Corp., 1977.

This collection of reprinted critical essays explores a variety of analytical topics in an attempt to generate a vocabulary, or language, for the critical evaluation of the genre.   (C)

654   Demby, William. **Beetlecreek.** Rinehart (Holt), 1950.

Life for an elderly white man who has lived fifteen solitary years in a black section of a rural southern town changes negatively when a black from Pittsburgh visits him and introduces him to the people nearby.   (BRD)

655   De Veaux, Alexis. **Don't explain: a song of Billie Holiday.** Illustrated by Alexis De Veaux. Harper, 1980.

This prose poem, a fictionalized biography of Billie Holiday, tells of her struggle to be respected and of her losing battle against heroin. Information about her life is scanty or not provided.   (SLJ)

Winner: Coretta Scott King Honorable Mention Book, 1981.

656   De Veaux, Alexis. **Spirits in the street.** Illustrated by author. Anchor Books, 1973.

This collection of De Veaux's poems include narrative, lyrics, and dialogue for which the unifying theme is the struggle of the spirit in the vortex of ghetto life.   (LJ)

657   Dodson, Owen. **Powerful long ladder.** Farrar, 1946.

A first volume of poems, some of which are purely personal and others of more general interest, is formed as sonnets, songs, and verse drama.   (BRD)

658   Douglass, Frederick. **Narrative of the life of Frederick Douglass, an American slave.** Written by Frederick Douglass and edited by Benjamin Quarles. Harvard Univ. Pr., 1960.

This is one of three autobiographical works by the self-taught slave. It is the story of his life up to his escape to freedom with denunciations of the principle of man owning man.   (PLC)

659   Drake, St Clair and Cayton, Horace R. **Black metropolis: a study of Negro life in a northern city.** HBJ, 1945.

This sociological study of black life in Chicago began as investigations of general social conditions surrounding the problem of juvenile delinquency on Chicago's South Side.   (BRD)

660   Du Bois, Shirley Graham. **His day is marching on: a memoir of W. E. B. Du Bois.** Lippincott, 1971.

The author describes life with her husband, the biographee,

from their introduction, their work together for the NAACP in New York, the injustices of the 1940s and 1950s, and his work in world peace efforts which led the United States government to suspect him of being a communist. (BL)

661   Du Bois, William Edward Burghardt. **Dark princess: a romance.** HBJ, 1928.

Outraged by the discrimination against him at a New York medical college, a black man of brilliant promise leaves for Berlin where he joins a movement of dark people whose high priestess is an Indian princess. (BRD)

662   Du Bois, William Edward Burghardt. **Quest of the silver fleece.** McClurg, 1911.

White fields of cotton, the silver fleece which black labor and northern capital transmute into gold, blend with the story of a young black girl from the country who comes to school with a burning desire to learn. (BRD)

663   Dumas, Henry. **Ark of bones, and other stories.** Edited by Eugene B. Redmond for Henry Dumas posthumously. Random, 1974.

These nine stories are primarily about people who are fairly young. All are about very poor people and all are in the speech of black men and women. (BRD)

664   Dumas, Henry. **Play ebony, play ivory.** Edited by Eugene B. Redmond for Henry Dumas posthumously. Random, 1974.

This is a collection of poems by a poet and fiction writer who was killed by a policeman in Harlem. (BRD)

665   Dunbar, Ernest, ed. **The black expatriates: a study of American Negroes in exile.** Dutton, 1968.

Interviews of sixteen Black Americans who for various reasons decided to leave America to live elsewhere, such as Africa, Western Europe, and Scandinavia. (BRD)

666   Dunbar, Paul Laurence. **Howdy, honey, howdy.** Dodd, 1905.

This is a collection of Dunbar's verse in dialect. (BRD)

667   Dunbar, Paul Laurence. **Joggin' erlong.** Dodd, 1906.

Here are other dialect poems by Dunbar. (BRD)

668   Dunbar, Paul Laurence. **Lyrics of sunshine and shadow.** Dodd, 1905.

About eighty poems, some of which are in black dialect, range from the grave to the gay. (BRD)

669   Dunham, Katherine. **Island possessed.** Doubleday, 1969.

This sequel to the autobiography *A Touch of Innocence* is about Haiti's rigid social structure, its great natural beauty, its leaders, and the native culture built on ancient customs and traditions of black Africa. (BRD)

670   Dunham, Katherine. **Journey to Accompong.** Illustrated by Ted Cook. Holt, 1947.

A dancer and anthropologist travel to the mountains of Jamaica to study native dances from the Maroons, a remnant people descended from African slaves who rebelled against the Spaniards in the sixteenth century. (BRD)

671   Edet, Edna Smith, comp. **The griot sings: songs from the black world.** Publishing Center for Cultural Resources, 1978.

This collection of 115 songs from various parts of Africa, the Caribbean, Latin America, and the United States also includes children's games, dances, work songs, and songs of social commentary. (IBCB)

672   Edmonds, Randolph. **Land of cotton, and other plays.** Assoc. Pubs., 1942.

One four-act play and four one-act plays about blacks are intended primarily for black audiences. (BRD)

673   Edwards, Harry. **The revolt of the black athlete.** Free Pr., 1969.

Edwards, who directed the boycott (the Olympic Project for Human Rights) during the 1968 games in Mexico City, reveals the trials and tribulations encountered by black athletes in sporting endeavors. He explodes the myth that athletics is the one sure road to racial equality—prejudices and hypocritical attitudes prevail on and off the field. (BRD)

674   Edwards, Harry. **Sociology of sports.** Dorsey Pr., 1973.

Three parts establish the focus and limit the scope to its institutionalized form, treat the relationships of the sports institution and society at large, and evaluate the future of sports as it is relevant to social change.   (BRD)

675   Edwards, Harry. **The struggle that must be: an autobiography.** Macmillan, 1980.

Edwards, who organized the 1968 Olympic black athletes' protest, traces his life from poverty in East St. Louis to his sociology professorship at Berkeley.   (BRD)

676   Edwards, Junius. **If we must die.** Doubleday, 1963.

A black veteran of the Korean War is followed through a troubled day in a small southern town where he attempts to register to vote and loses his job as a result.   (BRD)

677   Ellison, Ralph. **Invisible man.** Random, 1952.

This is the story of a black man who moves from youthful affirmation in a small southern town to total rejection after a Harlem race riot, and who must contend with whites and powerful blacks.   (BRD)

678   Ellison, Ralph. **Shadow and act.** Random, 1964.

These essays concern literature and folklore, the black musical expression—especially jazz and the blues—and the complex relationship between the Black American subculture and North American culture as a whole.   (BRD)

679   Emanuel, James A. **Dark symphony: Negro literature in America.** Edited by James A. Emanuel and Theodore L. Gross. Free Pr., 1968.

Stories, poems, memories, essays, and scholarly studies by thirty-four Black American writers are compiled in this volume of black literature.   (CSM)

680   Fair, Ronald. **Hog butcher.** HBJ, 1966.

After two young black boys in Chicago witness the accidental shooting of a local sports hero, one boy is especially troubled by the example of an attempted police department cover-up, a small riot, pressure to change his testimony, and the example of adults who switch their stories.   (BRD)

681   Fair, Ronald. **Many thousand gone: an American fable.** HBJ, 1965.

In 1836, fictive Jacobs County is geographically and socially isolated with successive generations of blacks existing in virtual servitude to successive generations of Jacobses, until in 1838, an aged and beloved black woman cracks the feudal domain.   (BRD)

682   Fair, Ronald. **We can't breathe.** Harper, 1972.

This autobiographical novel concerns a black person growing up in Chicago's slums during the 1930s and 1940s, and begins with the writer as the seven-year-old narrator.   (BRD)

683   Fair, Ronald. **World of nothing: two novellas.** Harper, 1971.

The title novella tells of a young black man in Chicago who is becoming a wino and shares an apartment with a man who is also bound to the street and the bottle.   (BRD)

684   Fax, Elton C. **Black artists of the new generation.** Illustrated by John Thomas Biggers. Dodd, 1971.

Personal experiences of seventeen leading Black American artists form the basis of the commentary revealed by their creations in painting, sculpture, and photography.   (DCPL)

685   Fax, Elton C. **Garvey: the story of a pioneer black nationalist.** Illustrated by Elton Clay Fax. Dodd, 1972.

This derivative study, from Amy Garvey's writings on her husband, is of the nature of Garvey's career and his impact as a radical black liberationist leader.   (BL)

686   Fax, Elton C. **Seventeen black artists.** Illustrated. Dodd, 1971.

These biographies are of well-known and less well-known contemporary black artists. Explanations are provided of the social and family background that produced each artist and set their work in the context of time and place, delineating the black experience as it affects creativity.   (LJ)

Winner: Coretta Scott King Award, 1972.

687   Fisher, Rudolph. **Conjure-man dies: a mystery tale of dark Harlem.** Covici, 1932.

A black detective solves a crime mystery.   (BRD)

688   Fisher, Rudolph. **Walls of Jericho.** Knopf, 1928.

This story portrays stormy relationships among groups within the Harlem society as reflected through the encounters of a young piano mover with a pretty housemaid who teaches him the truth about himself.   (BRD)

689   Franklin, John Hope. **The Emancipation Proclamation.** Doubleday, 1963.

Franklin deals with the principal outlines of the history of the document and indicates its general significance to contemporary and future generations.   (BRD)

690   Franklin, John Hope. **From slavery to freedom.** Knopf, 1947.

This book traces the history of blacks in America, from the beginnings in Africa to the present by including important economic, political, social, and cultural trends.   (BRD)

691   Gaines, Ernest J. **Autobiography of Miss Jane Pittman.** Dial, 1971.

This novel is in the guise of the tape-recorded recollections of a 110-year-old black woman who has witnessed both slavery and the black militancy of the 1960s.   (BRD)

692   Gaines. Ernest J. **Bloodline.** Dial, 1968.

Five stories of black life in the rural south are contained in this book.   (BRD)

693   Gaines, Ernest J. **Of love and lust.** Dial, 1967.

When young Marcus is bonded out of jail where he has been awaiting trial after killing another black in a roadhouse fight, he is sent to the Hebert plantation to work in the fields. (BRD)

694   Giovanni, Nikki. **Cotton candy on a rainy day: poems.** Morrow, 1978.

These poems show an introspective response to a shifting world with abstract images.   (BL)

695 Giovanni, Nikki. **My house: poems.** Morrow, 1972.

> Thirty-six poems reflect a sense of black pride, strong passion, and rage in a mood gentler than her earlier volume. (BL)

696 Giovanni, Nikki. **A poetic equation: conversations between Nikki Giovanni and Margaret Walker.** Howard Univ. Pr., 1974.

> This dialogue between two black female poets includes topics on Vietnam, the racial struggle and its future, sex roles, and their attitudes toward violence. (BRD)

697 Glass, Frankcina. **Marvin and Tige.** St. Martin's, 1977.

> A middle-aged, white alcoholic and former advertising executive takes as an adopted son an eleven-year-old black con artist, and a comical alliance is formed. (BL)

698 Gordone, Charles. **No place to be somebody: a black comedy in three acts.** Bobbs-Merrill, 1961.

> Through action set in a black-owned bar in New York's West Village, the play portrays the lives and confrontations of blacks and whites. (BRD)

699 Goss, Clay. **Homecookin': five plays.** Howard Univ. Pr., 1975.

> Five one-act plays focus on people and their struggle to get together in reality which is sad, funny, and powerful. (LJ)

700 Greenlee, Sam. **The spook who sat by the door.** Barron, 1969.

> This novel concerns the first black C.I.A. agent and his attempts to use his training to organize a Chicago ghetto gang into a guerilla force. (LJ)

701 Gregory, Dick (Richard Claxton). **Dick Gregory's natural diet for folks who eat: cooking with Mother Nature.** Edited by James R. McGraw with Alvenia M. Fulton. Harper, 1973.

> This introduction to natural foods also suggests diets for putting on and taking off weight. (BRD)

702 Gregory, Dick (Richard Claxton). **Dick Gregory's political primer.** Edited by James R. McGraw. Harper, 1971.

> Gregory, a black activist, offers his interpretation of American

history, politics, and politicians, and comments on party plat-forms, techniques of persuasion, citizen surveillance by gov-ernment agencies, and the requisite qualifications of candi-dates for a public office. (BRD)

703   Gregory, Dick (Richard Claxton). **Nigger: an autobiography.** By Dick Gregory with Robert Lipsyte. Dutton, 1964.

Gregory's intention is to take that bludgeon of a word and do what he can to end its power to maim. (BRD)

704   Gregory, Dick (Richard Claxton). **No more lies: the myth and the reality of American history.** Edited by James R. McGraw. Harper, 1971.

Gregory examines American history and declares that many of the accepted models are myths which have been assimilated to produce a profound national sickness which, unless cured, will bring destruction from the inside. (CHR)

705   Gregory, Dick (Richard Claxton). **The shadow that scares me.** Edited by James R. McGraw. Doubleday, 1968.

In ten articles, Gregory explores his attitudes toward life in America and writes about the black man in a white society with primary attention to the morality of right and wrong actions. (BRD)

706   Gregory, Dick (Richard Claxton). **Up from Nigger.** With James R. McGraw. Stein & Day, 1976.

This addendum to Gregory's autobiography, *Nigger,* covers eleven years during which he became known more for politi-cal actions than for his comedy. It is also a compilation of political battlegrounds of the period—Selma, Watts, Chicago, and Vietnam. (LJ)

707   Grier, William H. **Black rage.** By William H. Grier and Price M. Cobbs. Basic Books, 1968.

Two professors of psychiatry describe the plight of the Black American who, in essence, has been violated from the time of enslavement to the present. They also define the depression, listlessness, and apathy which they believe to be the underly-ing life tone of Black Americans. (BRD)

708   Grier, William H. **The Jesus bag.** By William H. Grier and Price M. Cobbs. McGraw-Hill, 1971.

The theses here are that Christianity was forced on blacks as a pacifier, blacks believed it more than whites did, blacks are now the only true practicing Christians, and the morality which they developed for Christianity must be adopted by this nation if it is to survive.   (BRD)

709   Guy, Rosa. **The disappearance: a novel.** Delacorte, 1979.

A streetwise black adolescent is acquitted of murder and is taken in by a do-gooder whose eight-year-old daughter disappears two days later.   (BL)

710   Guy Rosa. **A measure of time.** Holt, 1983.

A young black woman leaves her home and family in the South for the high life of Harlem in the 1920s.   (BL)

711   Guy, Rosa. **My love, my love, or the peasant girl.** Holt, 1985.

Based on Hans Christian Andersen's "Little Mermaid," this story is of the ill-fated love of a poor girl for a rich young mulatto whom she rescues from a near-fatal car crash.   (BL)

Winner: Other Award, 1987.

712   Guy, Rosa. **Ruby.** Viking, 1976.

This sequel to *The Friends* portrays a stern father and two motherless girls who move from Trinidad to New York and strive to adjust socially.   (BCCB)

713   Gwaltney, John Langston. **The dissenters: voices from contemporary America.** Random, 1986.

This is a collection of twenty-seven interviews with people believed to represent a willingness to take risks for unpopular causes and convictions. The "principled dissenters" range from a white Quaker grandmother to a black Buddhist who worked for the Veteran's Administration.   (BRD)

714   Gwaltney, John Langston. **Drylongso: a self-portrait of Black America.** Random, 1980.

This series of statements by ordinary black people resulted

from field research in the early 1970s by a black anthropologist from Columbia University. (BRD)

715   Haley, Alex. **Roots.** Doubleday, 1976.

Haley tracked his ancestry seven generations back to a small village in The Gambia, western Africa, where his Mandinkan antecedent, Kunta Kinte, was abducted in the eighteenth century and shipped to slavery in America. It accounts Kinte's life and that of his children down to Haley's birth in Ithaca, New York. (BRD)

716   Hamilton, Charles V. **The bench and the ballot: southern federal judges and black voters.** Oxford Univ. Pr., 1973.

Using fifteen cases brought into four southern federal courts during 1957–1965, the author discusses the black voter registration struggle and concentrates on the courts' achievements and failures. (LJ)

717   Hamilton, Charles V. **The black experience in American politics.** Putnam, 1973.

Writings of selected black spokesmen from Booker T. Washington to Eldridge Cleaver outline major themes of black political thought in twentieth-century America. (BRD)

718   Hamilton, Charles V. **The black preacher in America.** Morrow, 1972.

From material collected in interviews with ministers from around the country, Hamilton discusses preachers' roles, activities, and major areas of criticism from various sources within the black community. He charges that the ministry is materialistic, nonintellectual, authoritarian, and politically uninvolved. (BRD)

719   Hamilton, Virginia. **Anthony Burns: the defeat and triumph of a fugitive slave.** Knopf, 1988.

This is the story of a slave who, after escaping to Boston, is recaptured by his southern master and returned to Virginia by the power of the Fugitive Slave Act. It tells of abolitionists' attempts to resist the law, a judge's fateful decision, and a black minister's determined and successful efforts to buy Burns's freedom. Selections from the Fugitive Slave Act of

1850 are also included.   (BCCB)

Winner: Notable Children's Books (American Library Association), 1988; Boston Globe-Horn Book Award, 1988; Jefferson Cup Award, 1989; School Library Journal "Best Books of the Year," 1988.

720   Hamilton, Virginia. **Magical adventures of Pretty Pearl.** Harper, 1983.

A god child from Mount Highness takes it upon herself to go down and render assistance to poor, misguided humans. (VOYA)

Winner: Notable Children's Books (American Library Association), 1983; Coretta Scott King Honorable Mention Book, 1984.

721   Hamilton, Virginia. **Paul Robeson: the life and times of a free black man.** Harper, 1974.

The son of an ex-slave, this gifted athlete and scholar worked his way through Columbia Law School, was branded as a communist sympathizer, was denounced by black leaders for harming the cause of his own people, had his passport canceled, and was unable to perform in public for ten years. (BRD)

722   Hamilton, Virginia. **A white romance.** Philomel Bks., 1987.

As her all-black high school becomes more racially mixed, Talley befriends a white girl who shares her enthusiasm for running and who becomes romantically involved with a drug dealer.   (SLJ)

723   Handy, William Christopher, ed. **Blues: an anthology.** Illustrated by Miguel Covarrubias. Boni, 1926.

This anthology of blues includes music.   (BRD)

724   Handy, William Christopher. **Father of the blues: an autobiography.** Edited by Arna Bontemps. Macmillan, 1941.

This is an autobiography of a black writer of popular songs who is particularly famous for his "Memphis Blues" and "St. Louis Blues."   (BRD)

725   Handy, William Christopher, ed. **Treasury of the blues.** Boni, 1949.

This edition of a book first published in 1926 provides complete words and music for sixty-seven great songs from "Memphis Blues" to the present, including historical and critical text. (BRD)

726   Handy, William Christopher, ed. **Unsung Americans sung.** Handy Bros. Music Co., 1944.

Black writers and composers pay tribute to twenty outstanding blacks with articles pertinent to black culture and history, and with songs, many of which are arranged for part singing. (BRD)

727   Harding, Vincent. **The other American revolution.** UCLA Center for Afro-American Studies; Institute of the Black World, 1980.

This is an interpretive survey of black struggle in America from its African roots to the assassination of Martin Luther King, Jr., and Harding's reflections on that struggle.   (LJ)

728   Harding, Vincent. **There is a river: the black struggle for freedom in America.** HBJ, 1981.

This first volume of a trilogy focuses on slave rebellions and the use of force by northern blacks to prevent enforcement of fugitive slave laws.   (NR)

729   Harper, Michael S. **Dear John, dear Coltrane: poems.** Univ. of Pittsburgh Pr., 1970.

This collection of poems is concerned with forms of nature and the black experience.   (BRD)

730   Harper, Michael S. **Debridement.** Doubleday, 1973.

This trio of poetic sequences represents three eras in U.S. history and explores the life of a key figure in the black man's valiant struggle to achieve identity in America.   (BRD)

731   Harper, Michael S. **Images of kin: new and selected poems.** Univ. of Illinois Pr., 1977.

This collection includes fourteen new poems with some others from the poet's previous works.   (BRD)

732   Harper, Michael S. **Nightmare begins responsibility.** Univ. of Illinois Pr., 1975.

This collection of verse is Harper's sixth volume of poetry. (BRD)

733   Harper, Michael S. and Stepto, Robert B. **Chant of saints: a gathering of Afro-American literature, art, and scholarship.** Univ. of Illinois Pr., 1979.

This anthology is the work of thirty contemporary black writers, visual artists, and essayists and includes reproductions of artwork, interviews, scholarly essays, fiction, and poetry. (BRD)

734   Harris, Abram Lincoln. **The Negro as capitalist: a study of banking and business among American Negroes.** American Acad. of Pol. & Soc. Sciences, 1936.

The subtitle explains the focus of this work.   (BRD)

735   Harris, Joseph E. **The African presence in Asia: consequences of the East African slave trade.** Northwestern Univ. Pr., 1971.

This exploratory study of the dispersion of Africans to Asia was researched through oral testimonies and archival documents in England, Iran, India and Ethiopia.   (BRD)

736   Harrison, Deloris. **Journey all alone.** Dial, 1971.

A teenage black girl is confronted with the dismal reality of her world and begins to withdraw into fantasy when her father deserts the family.   (NUC)

737   Haskins, James. **Andrew Young, man with a mission.** Lothrop, 1979.

This biography of Andrew Young ranges from a comfortable childhood in New Orleans to his position as United States Ambassador to the United Nations.   (SHS)

Winner: Coretta Scott King Honorable Mention Book, 1980.

738   Haskins, James. **Black theater in America.** Crowell, 1982.

The evolution of black theater in America from pre-Civil War days to modern ventures lends insights into difficulties experienced by black writers and performers who struggled to be accepted and to overcome character stereotypes. (SHS)

739   Haskins, James. **Pele: a biography.** Doubleday, 1976.

The biography of Erdson Arantes Do Nascimento (Pele), the Brazilian soccer player who became an international star, includes an explanatory section about the game. (SHS)

740   Haskins, James. **Real estate careers.** Watts, 1978.

An introduction to a variety of real estate jobs emphasizes the qualities needed for success. (BL)

741   Haskins, James. **Scott Joplin.** By James Haskins with Kathleen Benson. Stein & Day, 1980.

Here is the life story of Scott Joplin, the black, ragtime musician from Texas who gained an unusual education for his time and wrote an astounding number of innovative "rags" and opera before his death at 49 in an asylum. (SHS)

742   Haskins, James. **Witchcraft, mysticism and magic in the black world.** Doubleday, 1974.

This book traces the magic and religion of blacks from Africa, through adaptations during slavery to the present. (SHS)

743   Hayden, Robert. **Angle of ascent: new and selected poems.** Liveright, 1975.

With a new mixture of modes, the poet takes up, celebrates, and contends with the history of his people. (BRD)

744   Hayden, Robert. **Selected poems.** October House, 1967.

Hayden's first collection to be published in the United States celebrates the quiet moments of personal life and his impressions of Mexico, among other themes. (BRD)

745   Hedgeman, Anna Arnold. **The gift of chaos: decades of American discontent.** Oxford Univ. Pr., 1977.

This account of the Civil Rights movement is Hedgeman's search for actuality after encountering the chaos imposed upon blacks by American society. (BRD)

746   Hedgeman, Anna Arnold. **The trumpet sounds: a memoir of Negro leadership.** Holt, 1964.

This memoir, although not precisely autobiographical, is of Hedgeman's years as a leader from 1922 through the 1963 Freedom March on Washington.   (BRD)

747   Henderson, David. **De mayor of Harlem: the poetry of David Henderson.** Dutton, 1970.

These poems are predominantly about city life and incorporate folk tradition and everyday idioms.   (BRD)

748   Henderson, David. **Jimi Hendrix, voodoo child of the Aquarian age.** Doubleday, 1978.

This book examines the late rock musician's personality, life, politics, and music.   (BRD)

749   Henderson, Stephen. **Understanding the new black poetry; black speech and black music as poetic references.** Morrow, 1973.

This introduction to black poetry includes an anthology whose poems provide working models of the author's observations. The book also explains modern black poetry as a mode and presents the criteria by which it must be judged. (BRD)

750   Henri, Florette. **Black migration: movement North, 1900–1920.** Doubleday, 1975.

This work surveys the causes and processes of black migration and resulting life in northern cities. It also discusses black economic status, black leaders and their goals, racist ideas of the time, and black participation in World War I.   (LJ)

751   Hercules, Frank. **I want a black doll.** Simon & Schuster, 1978.

This story portrays the unsuccessful attempt of a biracial couple to find marital happiness in America during a period of social bitterness.   (BRD)

752   Higginbotham, A. Leon. **In the matter of color: race and the American legal process, the colonial period.** Oxford Univ. Pr., 1978.

A judge uses six cases to compare and contrast among the

states demonstrating the diversity, and yet, common use of the law to protect, extend, and deepen the economic exploitation and social degradation of blacks. (NYTBR)

753   Himes, Chester B. **Black on black: Baby Sister and selected writings.** Doubleday, 1972.

This collection of the author's works spans four decades and runs the genre gamut of seventeen short stories, five essays, and one full-length movie scenario. (BRD)

754   Himes, Chester B. **Blind man with a pistol.** Morrow, 1969.

Two detectives from *Cotton Comes to Harlem* search through the mad world of brotherhood marches, Black Power, Black Muslims, and loud-mouthed soul leaders for the elusive murderer of a white homosexual film producer. (BRD)

755   Himes, Chester B. **Cast the first stone.** Coward, 1952.

This is a realistic, psychological portrayal of imprisoned men in which the chief character tells his story of the early years of his twenty-year prison term. (BRD)

756   Himes, Chester B. **Cotton comes to Harlem.** Putnam, 1965.

Black detectives Grave Digger Jones and Coffin Ed Johnson are heroes in this careening search by white hijackers, a fake neo-Marcus Garvey, and the detectives for $87,000 swindled from Harlem residents in a back-to-Africa scheme. (BRD)

757   Himes, Chester B. **If he hollers let him go.** Doubleday, 1945.

A young, educated black man narrates his wartime experiences in Los Angeles when the joys of a responsible job and reciprocal love did not shield him from the constant barrage of racial prejudices. (BRD)

758   Himes, Chester B. **Lonely crusade.** Knopf, 1947.

This is a story about a thoughtful young black who becomes a union organizer at a West Coast airplane factory during wartime. (BRD)

759   Himes, Chester B. **Pinktoes: a novel.** Stein & Day, 1965.

While a black woman's existence centers around the presence

of influential whites at her Harlem gatherings, those she pursues also have personal agendas to fulfill. (BRD)

760   Himes, Chester B. **The quality of hurt, the autobiography of Chester Himes.** Doubleday, 1971.

Himes's theme is the peculiar anguish of the intelligent Black American. (BRD)

761   Himes, Chester B. **Run man run.** Putnam, 1966.

A drunken white detective accidently kills a black porter, and, to destroy evidence against him, kills a second and seriously wounds a third person whose story is not believed. (BRD)

762   Himes, Chester B. **Third generation.** World, 1954.

This is the story of three generations of a black family from their early days of freedom from slavery, through years of rising to a position of comfort, to a final tragedy. (BRD)

763   Hodges, Willis Augustus. **Free man of color: the autobiography of Willis Augustus Hodges.** Edited by Willard B. Gatewood, Jr. Univ. of Tennessee Pr., 1982.

Hodges was a free black, born in Virginia, active in New York abolitionist and temperance circles. He briefly edited an antislavery newspaper (*The Ram's Horn*, 1847–1848), and after the Civil War, was a Republican politician in Virginia and served in the Constitutional Convention of 1867–1868. (BRD)

764   Holder, Geoffrey. **Caribbean cookbook.** Illustrated by Geoffrey Holder. Viking, 1973.

This collection of recipes from Trinidad, Jamaica, Guadeloupe, and other Caribbean islands covers fish, poultry, meat, vegetables and rice, breads, desserts, and drinks. (BRD)

765   Holder, Geoffrey and Harshman, Tom. **Black gods, green islands.** Illustrated by Geoffrey Holder. Doubleday, 1959.

These five tales taken from black peoples of Caribbean islands are presumably African in origin. (BRD)

766   Huggins, Nathan Irvin. **Black odyssey: the Afro-American ordeal in slavery.** Pantheon, 1977.

Huggins is a history professor who sees oppression, not freedom, as the major theme in the fabric of American social history. This interpretive story of slavery in America is told from the slaves' perspectives. (BRD)

767   Huggins, Nathan Irvin. **Harlem Renaissance.** Oxford Univ. Pr., 1971.

This story attempts to show the cultural diversity in Harlem during the 1920s and the effect of political figures, writers, and jazzmen. (BRD)

768   Huggins, Nathan Irvin. **Protestants against poverty: Boston's charities, 1870–1900.** Greenwood, 1971.

This study attempts to trace the impact of industrial and social change on Boston charities in the late nineteenth century. (BRD)

769   Huggins, Nathan Irvin. **Slave and citizen: the life of Frederick Douglass.** Edited by Oscar Handlin. Little, 1980.

This is a biography of the nineteenth-century black leader who was born a slave, escaped to freedom, and became the most prominent black speaker in the abolitionist movement. (NR)

770   Hughes, Langston. **African treasury.** Crown, 1960.

This miscellany of more than forty pieces represents contemporary writings by African poets and authors. (BRD)

771   Hughes, Langston. **Ask your mama: 12 moods for jazz.** Knopf, 1961.

This book contains twelve poems that are to be read aloud to jazz music, using the Hesitation Blues as leitmotif. (BRD)

772   Hughes, Langston, ed. **The best short stories by Negro writers: an anthology from 1899 to the present.** Little, 1967.

Forty-seven stories are collected in this volume, fourteen of which are first publications. (BRD)

773   Hughes, Langston. **The big sea: an autobiography.** Knopf, 1940.

The poet, novelist, and playwright recounts his life story up to age twenty-seven, including a freighter trip to Africa, his struggles to make a living in Paris during the 1920s, and his part in the Harlem Renaissance. (BRD)

774   Hughes, Langston. **Black misery.** Illustrated by Arouni. Eriksson, 1969.

Short statements with a simple picture explain black misery to nonblacks. Example: "Misery is when you learn that you are not supposed to like watermelon but you do." (LJ)

775   Hughes, Langston. **Fields of wonder.** Knopf, 1947.

This book is a collection of lyric poems. (BRD)

776   Hughes, Langston. **Fight for freedom: the story of the NAACP.** Norton, 1962.

The accomplishments of this organization and its leaders over half a century since its founding are presented with particular attention to its legal victories. (BRD)

777   Hughes, Langston. **Fine clothes to the Jew.** Knopf, 1927.

In this poetic procession of people given in brief, revealing glimpses, Hughes divines the aspirations and tragic frustrations of black people. (BRD)

778   Hughes, Langston. **Good morning revolution: uncollected social protest writings.** Edited by Faith Berry. Hill & Wang, 1973.

Economic conditions of the 1930s and the racism which affected the author are reflected in these poems, essays, and one short story. (BRD)

779   Hughes, Langston. **I wonder as I wander: an autobiographical journey.** Rinehart (Holt), 1956.

This installment of the autobiography begun in *The Big Sea* contains accounts of journeys through Russia, Spain, China, and Japan. (BRD)

780   Hughes, Langston. **Laughing to keep from crying.** Holt, 1952.

Twenty-four short prose pieces concern the black and other minority groups in relationships among themselves and among dominant whites. (BRD)

781   Hughes, Langston. **Montage of a dream deferred.** Holt, 1951.

Kaleidoscopic flashes make a poem on Harlem of the early 1950s. (BRD)

782   Hughes, Langston, ed. **New Negro poets U.S.A.** Indiana Univ. Pr., 1964.

This selection of poems by thirty-seven black poets includes the lyrical and protest poems, personal and general descriptions, and reflective statements.   (BRD)

783   Hughes, Langston. **Not without laughter.** Knopf, 1930.

Sandy's family includes relatives whose aspirations range from pretense behavior to singing the blues, but he aspires toward formal education and a contribution to the race.   (BRD)

784   Hughes, Langston. **One-way ticket.** Illustrated by Jacob Armstead Lawrence. Knopf, 1949.

This collection of poems on black subjects is variously presented as lyrics, dirges, and dramatic soliloquies.   (BRD)

785   Hughes, Langston. **The panther and the lash: poems of our times.** Knopf, 1967.

Here is a collection of Hughes's writings.   (BRD)

786   Hughes, Langston. **Pictorial history of the Negro in America.** Third revision edited by C. Eric Lincoln and Milton Meltzer. Crown, 1968.

An inviting volume is appropriately illustrated with prints, posters, and woodcuts.   (BL)

787   Hughes, Langston, ed. **Poems from black Africa, Ethiopia [and other countries].** Indiana Univ. Pr., 1962.

This volume contains poetry by African poets from Congo, Ethiopia, Gabon, Ghana, Ivory Coast, Kenya, Liberia, Madagascar, Mozambique, Nigeria, Nyasaland, Senegal, Sierra Leone, South Africa, and Southern Rhodesia.   (BRD)

788   Hughes, Langston. **Reader.** Braziller, 1958.

This volume contains selected short stories, plays, poems, and excerpts from novels, essays, and speeches written by Langston Hughes.   (BRD)

789   Hughes, Langston. **Selected poems.** Illustrated by E. McKnight Kauffer. Knopf, 1959.

This potpourri spans the career of Hughes from 1926 to 1958.   (BRD)

790   Hughes, Langston. **Shakespeare in Harlem [and other poems].** Illustrated by E. McKnight Kauffer. Knopf, 1942.

This book of light verse presents African Americana in the blues mood.   (BRD)

791   Hughes, Langston. **Simple speaks his mind.** Simon & Schuster, 1950.

Simple expresses his views on many subjects, but always from the point of view of his race.   (BRD)

792   Hughes, Langston. **Simple stakes a claim.** Rinehart (Holt), 1957.

Simple gives his opinion on things which include his native state of Virginia and the black vote.   (BRD)

793   Hughes, Langston. **Simple takes a wife.** Simon & Schuster, 1953.

Stories of black life in Harlem are told through conversations between Hughes and Mr. Jesse B. Semple (better known as Simple).   (BRD)

794   Hughes, Langston. **The sweet flypaper of life.** Photos by Roy De Carava. Simon & Schuster, 1956.

This fictional document of life in Harlem is told in the words of an elderly black woman and is seen with a corresponding truth through her old, bright eyes.   (BRD)

795   Hughes, Langston. **Tambourines to glory.** Day, 1959.

This novel describes two women who decide to start a church of their own. Essie is a good, honest woman. Too honest, according to Laura, whose motives are simply to make money and live it up.   (BRD)

796   Hughes, Langston. **Ways of white folks.** Knopf, 1934.

These short stories describe relations between white and black people from the black point of view.   (BRD)

797   Hughes, Langston. **Weary blues.** Knopf, 1926.

Poems reflect the heavy heritage of slavery, the dim racial memories of Africa, and fears in modern America. (BRD)

798   Hughes, Langston and Bontemps, Arna Wendell, eds. **Book of Negro folklore.** Dodd, 1958.

"From Brer Rabbit to Jesse B. Semple" might be the subtitle of this book which presents the black folk saga in America through folk expression mined out of racial experience. (BRD)

799   Hughes, Langston and Bontemps, Arna Wendell, eds. **Poetry of the Negro, 1746–1949: an anthology.** Doubleday, 1949.

An anthology in three sections presents black poets of the United States, tributary poems by nonblacks, and the Caribbean. (BRD)

800   Hughes, Langston and Bontemps, Arna Wendell, eds. **The poetry of the Negro, 1746–1970: an anthology.** Doubleday, 1968.

Works of one hundred sixty-three poets from prerevolutionary times to publication date are represented. (BRD)

801   Hughes, Langston and Meltzer, Milton. **Black magic: a pictorial history of the Negro in American entertainment.** Prentice-Hall, 1967.

This history traces the saga of the black singer, dancer, actor, writer, and composer from the slave days to this publication date. (BRD)

802   Hunter, Kristin. **God bless the child.** Scribner, 1964.

In her determination to get ahead, a young black girl works two jobs, begins to gamble, makes money and goes hopelessly into debt because of her desperate response. (BRD)

803   Hunter, Kristin. **The landlord.** Scribner, 1966.

The psychotic son of a ruthless multimillionaire businessman buys a dilapidated apartment house filled with nonpaying mostly black tenants and seeks to prove his self-worth. (BRD)

804   Hunter, Kristin. **The survivors.** Scribner, 1975.

A lonely black woman in the hostile city interprets a crippled boy's ingratiating behavior as a nuisance, then as a danger before she softens her attitude and accepts him as her foster child. (LJ)

805 Hurston, Zora Neale. **Dust tracks on a road: an autobiography.** Lippincott, 1942.

This book portrays the black female anthropologist and folk song writer who was born in the all-black town of Eatonville, Florida, and who completed studies at Barnard in order to begin her lifework. (BRD)

806 Hurston, Zora Neale. **I love myself when I am laughing: and then again when I am looking mean and impressive.** Edited by Alice Walker. Feminist Press, 1979.

The problems of love are thematically dominant in these selections from Hurston's biographical works, collections of Black American and West Indian folklore, essays, and fiction. (C)

807 Hurston, Zora Neale. **Jonah's gourd vine.** Lippincott, 1934.

This story of black life in the South is told in dialect and concerns a big, lovable, fair-complexioned black preacher with great talent for emotionalism and a powerful fascination for women. (BRD)

808 Hurston, Zora Neale. **Moses, man of the mountain.** Lippincott, 1939.

A novel based on the life of the biblical character is written in modern colloquial terms and emphasizes those aspects which show Moses as the great magician and voodoo man. (BRD)

809 Hurston, Zora Neale. **Mules and men.** Illustrated by Miguel Covarrubias. Lippincott, 1935.

The first part contains a collection of black folktales. The second part describes voodoo practices carried on by blacks in the South. (BRD)

810 Hurston, Zora Neale. **Seraph on the Suwanee.** Scribner, 1948.

This novel of western Florida, the "cracker" region, at the beginning of the century describes a family's life in a vernacular tongue. (BRD)

811   Hurston, Zora Neale. **Tell my horse.** Lippincott, 1938.

Hurston recounts in popular style the results of her investigations of the folklore and the voodoo culture of Haiti and Jamaica where she researched with help from a Guggenheim fellowship. (BRD)

812   Hurston, Zora Neale. **Their eyes were watching God.** Lippincott, 1937.

In this picture of life among blacks in Florida, the heroine is a lovely quadroon and the story is of her three marriages. (BRD)

813   Jackson, Jesse. **Anchor man.** Illustrated by Doris Spiegel. Harper, 1947.

This sequel to *Call Me Charley* uses the theme of racial understanding at Arlington High where Charley, the only black student, is happy and accepted until an influx of black students arrives from another part of town.   (BRD)

814   Jackson, Jesse. **Call me Charley.** Illustrated by Doris Spiegel. Harper, 1945.

This is the story of a black boy in a previously all-white neighborhood, and his friendships and problems in the local public school.   (BRD)

815   Jackson, Jesse. **Charley starts from scratch.** Harper, 1958.

Charley Moss leaves home for a summer job, starts training for track, and accepts good and bad experiences in his efforts to become a track star.   (ED)

816   Jackson, Mae. **Can I poet with you?** Black Dialogue Pr., 1969.

Jackson's work reflects serious intents about the growth processes and direction of black people who must evolve to where they should be—living in each other.   (ND)

817   Johnson, James Weldon. **Along this way.** Viking, 1933.

This autobiography narrates the social, political, and cultural adventures of James Weldon Johnson, a lawyer, poet, musical comedy composer, diplomatic official, author, editor, orator, and educator.   (BRD)

818   Johnson, James Weldon. **Autobiography of an ex-colored man.** Knopf, 1927.

First published anonymously, this story reads more like the composite autobiography of the black race in the United States. (BRD)

819   Johnson, James Weldon. **Fifty years, and other poems.** Cornhill Co., 1918.

These poems reflect Johnson's observations and life experiences in North and South America. (BRD)

820   Johnson, James Weldon. **God's trombones.** Illustrated by Aaron Douglas. Viking, 1927.

Seven Negro sermons in verse were inspired by memories of sermons by black preachers heard in Johnson's childhood. (BRD)

821   Johnson, James Weldon. **Negro Americans, what now?** Viking, 1934.

Here are expressions of concern with the status of black citizens in the United States and of the basis upon which their continued existence as an important part of the population should be carried. (BRD)

822   Johnson, James Weldon. **Saint Peter relates an incident: selected poems.** Viking, 1935.

This is a collection of lyrics and dialect poems, many of which are from the volume *Fifty Years and Other Poems.* (BRD)

823   Jones, Leroi (Baraka, Imamu Amiri). **Black magic: sabotage, target study, black art; collected poetry, 1961–1967.** Bobbs-Merrill, 1970.

This collection of poems ranges from statements of beauty and love to an articulation of the extent of black rage at white society. (BRD)

824   Jones, Leroi (Baraka, Imamu Amiri). **Black music.** Morrow, 1968.

This collection of record reviews, liner notes, interviews, articles, and comments has appeared in other music-oriented publications. (BRD)

825 Jones, Leroi (Baraka, Imamu Amiri). **Blues people: Negro music in white America.** Morrow, 1963.

Jones views the slaves' path to citizenship and makes an analogy through the music most closely associated with them—blues and jazz. (BRD)

826 Jones, Leroi (Baraka, Imamu Amiri). **Four black revolutionary plays: all praises to the black man.** Bobbs-Merrill, 1970.

These plays are about the destruction of white people who are responsible for a corrupt society destructive to black people. (BRD)

827 Jones, Leroi (Baraka, Imamu Amiri). **Home: social essays.** Morrow, 1966.

Twenty-four essays written since 1960 on various subjects, including politics, racism, literature, foreign policy, sex, and semantics. (BRD)

828 Jones, Leroi (Baraka, Imamu Amiri). **The system of Dante's hell.** Grove, 1965.

Three scenarios include childhood and adolescence in the black slums of Newark, the experiences of a northern black in a small southern town where the Air Force has sent him, and glimpses of life in New York. (BRD)

829 Jones, Leroi (Baraka, Imamu Amiri). **Tales.** Grove, 1967.

This collection of Jones's short stories is largely personal, autobiographical revelations. (BRD)

830 Jones, Leroi (Baraka, Imamu Amiri) and Neal, Larry, eds. **Black fire: an anthology of Afro-American writing.** Morrow, 1968.

Essays, poems, short stories, and plays by more than seventy black writers are contained in this anthology.

831 Jordan, June. **Some changes.** R. W. Baron, 1970.

This book celebrates the community of black people with poems invested with deeply private despair and warmth. (PW)

832 Kelly, William Melvin. **Dancers on the shore.** Doubleday, 1964.

Blacks are the major participants in this collection of sixteen short stories.

833   Kelly, William Melvin. **Dem.** Doubleday, 1967.

A Madison Avenue advertising executive and his wife become parents to fraternal twins—one white and one black. This novel portrays the executive's subsequent encounter with the black part of the city.   (BRD)

834   Kelly, William Melvin. **A different drummer.** Doubleday, 1962.

In a mythical state bounded by Alabama, Tennessee, Mississippi, and the Gulf of Mexico, a lone black male decides to heed his conscience and refuse to participate in a society based upon inequality.   (BRD)

835   Kelly, William Melvin. **A drop of patience.** Doubleday, 1965.

This novel is of a twice-handicapped man—he is black and blind—who is an immensely gifted jazz musician distrustful of the white world.   (BRD)

836   Kelly, William Melvin. **Dunfords travels everywheres.** Doubleday, 1970.

The first of three sections is about a Black American filtering through a fictitious country in Europe with a group of white Americans. The remaining sections show the episodes of a con-man in Harlem, New York, and some of the author's creative prose discussions.   (BRD)

837   Killens, John Oliver. **And then we heard the thunder.** Knopf, 1962.

This is a novel about a black amphibious regiment in World War II and the pressures of Jim Crow which led ultimately to a bloody race riot.   (BRD)

838   Killens, John Oliver. **Black man's burden.** Trident, 1965.

A commentary on the image white legend has imposed on blacks and which is accepted by many of them.   (BRD)

839   Killens, John Oliver. **The cotillion: or one good bull is worth half the herd.** Trident, 1970.

This story depicts the efforts of a West Indian woman of mixed parentage to install her daughter in the upper echelons of the black bourgeoisie by means of an annual debutante ball sponsored by an organization of middle-class black women. (BRD)

840   Killens, John Oliver. **Youngblood.** Dial, 1954.

This first novel by Killens tells the story of a black family in Georgia during the early 1920s.   (BRD)

841   King, Anita, ed. and comp. **Quotations in black.** Greenwood, 1981.

This book contains more than eleven hundred quotations from over two hundred black people, and more than four hundred proverbs from over forty countries. Biographical notes are provided for each person quoted.   (BRD)

842   King, Coretta Scott. **My life with Martin Luther King, Jr.** Holt, 1969.

The widow tells of their life together from their marriage in 1953 to his assassination in 1968 in Memphis, Tennessee. (BRD)

843   King, Martin Luther, Jr. **Strength to love.** Harper, 1963.

Seventeen of King's sermons are collected in this volume.

844   King, Martin Luther, Jr. **Stride toward freedom: the Montgomery story.** Harper, 1958.

The story of the black boycott of Montgomery's Jim Crow bus lines is told by the young minister who became a well-known spokesman for oppressed people.   (BRD)

845   King, Martin Luther, Jr. **Where do we go from here: chaos or community?** Harper, 1967.

The civil rights leader discusses the next steps to achieve equality, which include wide coalitions and continuous efforts to influence the political process.   (BRD)

846   King, Martin Luther, Jr. **Why we can't wait.** Harper, 1964.

In this story of the Birmingham demonstrations and the March on Washington by Black Americans, Dr. King spells out the reasons for black demonstrations, the why of Freedom Now, and the frustration that breeds impatience.   (BRD)

847   King, Woodie, ed. **BlackSpirits: a festival of new black poets in America.** Random, 1972.

Black identity is the dominant theme in this anthology of thirty contemporary black poets which includes Imamu Baraka, Sonia Sanchez, Don Lee, and David Henderson. (C)

848   Knight, Etheridge. **Black voices from prison.** Pathfinder, 1970.

This collection of essays, poems, and stories was done by Knight and fellow inmates at the Indiana State Prison. They proclaim their status as the classic end product of a segregated society and demonstrate that prisons are housing educated militants. (C)

849   Lacy, Leslie. **Native daughter.** Macmillan, 1974.

This personal narrative describes Lacy's summer experiences as a teacher in a poverty program for black, unwed mothers in Bedford-Stuyvesant. (LJ)

850   Lacy, Leslie Alexander. **The rise and fall of a proper Negro: an autobiography.** Macmillan, 1970.

Lacy tells why he became a nonviolent activist and a militant nationalist who settled in Ghana and became a pivotal figure in the influential African-American community around Nkrumah. He describes the coup d'etat and Nkrumah's downfall. (BRD)

851   Ladner, Joyce A., ed. **The death of white sociology.** Random, 1973.

The thesis of these essays is that blacks must take charge and examine the black scene themselves, and present both the positive and negative aspects of the black experience, instead of dwelling on the pathology of the black condition or faulting blacks for not being white. (LJ)

852   Ladner, Joyce A. **Tomorrow's tomorrow: the black woman.** Doubleday, 1971.

In this sociological study of black girls growing up in a St. Louis housing project, Ladner examines their life chances, expectations, middle-class aspirations, and feelings about pregnancy, child rearing, marriage, boyfriends, and parents. She concludes that there is much in the black life-style that is worth emulation by the white middle class. (LJ)

853   Lee, Don L. **Directionscore: selected and new poems.** Broadside, 1971.

This revolutionary poet has blended new and previously published poems. (BRD)

854   Lester, Julius. **All is well.** Morrow, 1976.

Lester describes his family relationships and those with other friends and fellow workers in the Civil Rights movement. He also reflects on the Beat Generation, SNCC, Black Power during the 1960s, and shares his journeys to Cuba and Vietnam.   (LJ)

855   Lester, Julius. **Long journey home: stories from black history.** Dial, 1972.

Six pieces of historical fiction capture the movement and emotion of a southern serfdom in the 1920s. Former slaves and freedmen react to their condition through interviews and footnotes.   (BRD)

856   Lester, Julius. **Look out, Whitey! Black Power's gon' get your mama!** Dial, 1968.

In this history and explication of the Black Power movement, Lester reads into the earlier period of the Civil Rights movement the anger of its present mood and sees that anger as one with the black reaction to oppression from American slavery's earliest days.   (LJ)

857   Lester, Julius. **Revolutionary notes.** R. W. Baron, 1969.

Here are essays and articles, some previously published, which consider the peace movement, the death of Che Guevara, the International War Crimes Tribunal, and the revolutionary.   (BRD)

858   Lester, Julius. **Search for a new land: history as a subjective experience.** Dial, 1969.

Lester shares his beliefs and private feelings about how lawmaking affects everyone and the power that laws and lawmaking bodies have over every individual.   (WLB)

859   Lester, Julius. **Two love stories.** Dial, 1972.

This book contains two low-keyed yet emotional novellas on the painful experiences of young love.   (BL)

860 Lewis, David L. **District of Columbia: a bicentennial history.** American Association for State and Local History. Norton, 1976.

This book surveys the early history of the district, presents a largely demographic portrait, and discusses the struggle for home rule and the continuing problems of an increasingly black city ringed by white suburbs. (BRD)

861 Lewis, David L. **King: a critical biography.** Praeger, 1970.

Lewis emphasizes King's intellectual and public life with the thesis that King was a man of ability made great by a particular confluence of circumstances. King's successes and failures are analyzed for their causes and effects on the man and on the national course of events. (LJ)

862 Lewis, David L. **When Harlem was in vogue.** Knopf, 1981.

Starting in 1905 when white Harlem began changing, Lewis plots the dark trek uptown. Continuing to the March 19, 1935 riot, he concentrates on the 1920s. (LJ)

863 Lewis, Samella Sanders. **Black artists on art,** Volume 2 [by] Samella Sanders Lewis and Ruth G. Waddy. Illustrated by Samella Lewis. Contemporary Books, 1971.

Photographs of black artists of varying experiences and their definitions of black art today are arranged with plates of their work displayed. Some works speak for themselves while others are explained by the responsible artist. (BRD)

864 Lightfoot, Claude M. **Ghetto rebellion to black liberation.** International Publishers, 1968.

Lightfoot maintains that black liberation cannot be attained in the United States without changing the nation's economic and political system. He presents his views on the black revolt against racism, criticizes black separatist trends, probes the nature of white racism, and supports the right of black people to armed self-defense. (BRD)

865   Lincoln, C. Eric. **The Black Muslims in America.** Beacon, 1961.

Sociologist C. Eric Lincoln explains the Black Muslim move-ment in the United States by describing the forerunners, ori-gins, doctrines, organization, and leaders of the group. He contends that the organization will expand as long as racial tension flourishes.   (BL)

866   Lincoln, C. Eric, ed. **Martin Luther King, Jr.: a profile.** Hill & Wang, 1970.

These essays by thirteen writers are part biography and part social and cultural history.   (BRD)

867   Lincoln, C. Eric. **My face is black.** Beacon, 1964.

This minister-teacher-author analyzes the new mood among Black Americans and defines the willingness to be black and the willingness to damn anyone who is not. The mood tends to reject the American dream, the white man's religion, and the concept of nonviolence. Lincoln sees the church as the only institution which can bring black and white together. (BRD)

868   Lincoln, C. Eric. **Sounds of the struggle: persons and perspectives in civil rights.** Morrow, 1967.

In this collection of eighteen prepublished pieces, the minister-author traces the civil rights struggle during the past seven years.   (BRD)

869   Locke, Alain Le Roy. **The Negro in art.** Associates in Negro Folk Educ., 1941.

This is a pictorial record of black artists and the black theme in art. The first and largest section is devoted to illustrations of works from the days of slave apprentices to the Federal Arts Projects. Part three portrays the ancestral arts as they appeared in Africa and their influence in painting and sculpture.   (BRD)

870   Locke, Alain Le Roy. **New Negro: an interpretation.** Boni, 1925.

Included in this compilation are works by every young Black American who has achieved literary distinction by this publi-cation date. Some established writers are also represented. (BRD)

871   Locke, Alain Le Roy, ed. **When peoples meet: a study in race and culture contacts.** Edited by Alain Le Roy Locke and Bernhard J. Stern. Progressive Educ. Assoc., 1942.

A study of what happens when dominant and minority groups meet—everywhere in the world, past and present—is analyzed by such authors as Ruth Benedict, Franz Boas, Charles Darwin, Margaret Mead, Robert Redfield, and Clark Wissler. (SS)

872   Locke, Alain Le Roy and Gregory, Montgomery. **Plays of Negro life: a source-book of Native American drama.** Illustrated by Aaron Douglas. Harper, 1927.

This collection of twenty plays is about black life written by black and white authors. Included are a chronology of black theater and a bibliography of black drama. (BRD)

873   Logan, Rayford Whittingham, ed. **The attitude of the southern white press toward Negro suffrage, 1932–1940.** Foundation Pubs., 1940.

Here are the results of an assessment of editorials, news, and letters to the editor from thirty-six newspapers in twelve southern states. (BRD)

874   Logan, Rayford Whittingham. **The diplomatic relations of the United States with Haiti, 1776–1891.** Univ. of North Carolina Pr., 1941.

Here is a study of the policy of the United States toward the black republic of Haiti which was set up in America on French foundations. The history of the nation is also sketched. (BRD)

875   Logan, Rayford Whittingham. **Negro in American life and thought: the nadir, 1877–1901.** Dial, 1954.

This is a study of the political, social, and economic aspects of the "Negro problem" during the last quarter of the nineteenth century. (BRD)

876   Logan, Rayford Whittingham, ed. **What the Negro wants.** Univ. of North Carolina Pr., 1944.

Fourteen prominent blacks are of one mind that blacks want to take part, without arbitrarily imposed handicaps, in the duties and benefits of the society they live in; to be counted as human beings when white Christians and democrats say "all men are brothers" and "all men are created equal." (BRD)

877   Logan, Rayford Whittingham and Winston, Michael R., ed. **The dictionary of American Negro biography.** Norton, 1983.

This is a collection of more than seven hundred biographical sketches of Black Americans who were major influences in their region or local community. Living persons are excluded and the cut-off date was January 1, 1970.   (BRD)

878   Lomax, Louis E. **The Negro revolt.** Harper, 1962.

Included here is a short history of race relations from the American Revolution to present; a sociological and psychological history of the black race; some reasons why the current revolt began when it did; and discussions of the NAACP, the sit-ins, the Freedom Rides, and Black Muslims.   (N)

879   Lomax, Louis E. **The reluctant African.** Harper, 1960.

A journalist describes his 1960 journey to Cairo, East and South Africa, meeting insurgent leaders, and recording their philosophies and methods.   (BRD)

880   Lomax, Louis E. **When the word is given . . . : a report on Elijah Muhammad, Malcolm X, and the Black Muslim world.** World, 1963.

This account is based on newspaper articles and interviews with Black Muslims over a period of time. The second part is comprised of speeches by Elijah Muhammad and Malcolm X.   (BRD)

881   Long, Charles H. **Alpha, the myths of creation.** Braziller, 1964.

Actual texts of myths from a wide range of cultures are included in this discussion of the general character of various kinds of creation myths.   (BRD)

882   Lorde, Audre. **The black unicorn: poems.** Norton, 1978.

In poems, some of which were published previously, Lorde expresses her identity as a black woman in Africa and in America.   (BRD)

883   Lorde, Audre. **Chosen poems, old and new.** Norton, 1982.

This selection of poems is set mainly in New York City, span a thirty-year period, and focus on lore and rage.   (BRD)

884   Lorde, Audre. **Coal.** Norton, 1976.

The title means "the total black," the word being spoken from the earth's inside. Coal becomes a knot of flame, then a diamond.   (BRD)

885   Lorde, Audre. **The New York head shop and museum.** Broadside, 1975.

Lorde writes about the experiences of a modern black woman.   (BRD)

886   Lorde, Audre. **Zami: a new spelling of my name.** Persephone Pr., 1982.

Lorde calls this autobiography a "biomythography." She was the youngest child in an insulated West Indian immigrant family in late-Depression Harlem, and one of the few black students at a public high school for academically gifted girls. She left home at 17, worked her way through college, and traveled to Mexico where she felt visible and affirmed.   (MS)

887   Lucas, Curtis. **Flour is dusty.** Dorrance, 1944.

This novel concerns the experience of an ambitious young black in the South who, after a bad start, came North to further struggles.   (BRD)

888   Lucas, Curtis. **Third ward, Newark.** Ziff-Davis, 1946.

This is the story of a young girl (blighted by her psychological reaction to the brutal murder of her childhood friend by a white man) and her patient, ambitious husband who rise to happiness and fall to tragedy as the result of the continual struggle between blacks and whites.   (BRD)

889   McKay, Claude. **Banana bottom.** Harper, 1933.

When a Jamaican girl is adopted by missionaries and sent to England to be educated, she returns to conflict between English life-styles and her black ancestry.   (BRD)

890   McKay, Claude. **Banjo.** Harper, 1929.

This story depicts the life of a roving black longshoreman on the swarming waterfront of Marseilles.   (BRD)

891   McKay, Claude. **Gingertown.** Harper, 1932.

Twelve stories of black life in Harlem and in the West Indies portray men and women who are dominated by bitterness and humility, bewilderment and passion.   (BRD)

892   McKay, Claude. **Harlem: Negro metropolis.** Dutton, 1940.

This sober and rounded account of the black section of Harlem includes history, businesses, amusements, politics, and personalities such as Father Divine, Marcus Garvey, and Sufi Abdul Hamid.   (BRD)

893   McKay, Claude. **Harlem shadows.** HBJ, 1922.

These poems by a Jamaican-born American are love lyrics, but none are in dialect.   (BRD)

894   McKay, Claude. **Home to Harlem.** Harper, 1928.

Jake Brown drifts home to Harlem from France via England. (BRD)

895   McKay, Claude. **A long way from home.** Furman, 1937.

Here is an autobiography of a Jamaican-born Black American poet.   (BRD)

896   McKay, Claude. **The passion of Claude McKay: selected poetry and prose, 1912–1948.** Edited by Wayne F. Cooper. Schocken, 1973.

This collection includes McKay's essays and personal letters from his expatriate years, 1925–1932.   (BRD)

897   McKay, Claude. **Selected poems.** Bookman, 1953.

This collection contains religious poems and poems of Harlem, Jamaica, and the faraway places of his lonely wanderings.   (BRD)

898   McKissick, Floyd. **Three-fifths of a man.** Macmillan, 1969.

McKissick, former national director for the Congress of Racial

Equality, presents proposals for solving our nation's racial crisis through honest application of the United States Constitution and through black economic power.   (BRD)

899   McPherson, James Alan. **Hue and cry: short stories.** Little, 1969.

Here are ten stories about blacks who are pullman porters, students, intellectuals, jazz musicians, and Black Power leaders. Whites are the focus of some stories.   (BRD)

900   Major, Clarence. **The dark and feeling: Black American writers and their work.** Third World Press, 1974.

This collection of essays, book reviews, biographical sketches, and interviews about contemporary Black American authors is written for blacks by a black novelist-poet critic.   (LJ)

901   Major, Clarence. **Dictionary of Afro-American slang.** International Publishers, 1970.

More than 2,500 expressions that have been used characteristically or exclusively by blacks are defined with the period of their vogue specified for many of the expressions.   (BRD)

902   Major, Clarence. **The new black poetry.** International Publishers, 1969.

These single poems by seventy-six black poets, many of them under age thirty, express the crisis and drama of the late 1960s.   (BRD)

903   Major, Clarence. **Swallow the lake.** Wesleyan Univ. Pr., 1970.

The title refers to Lake Michigan, and "I couldn't swallow it," Major says. These poems are about the broken civilization, the loves and nightmares of a sensitive man.   (BRD)

904   Major, Gerri. **Gerri Major's black society.** With Doris E. Saunders. Johnson, 1977.

A society page editor chronicles the changing values, challenges, and societal restrictions of free blacks from the later colonial period to the third quarter of the twentieth century. Also discussed are various organized protests and supportive activities, and the creation of societies designed to bring about social and economic betterment.   (BL)

905   Malcolm X. **The autobiography of Malcolm X.** With the assistance
       of Alex Haley. Grove, 1965.

       Shortly before his assassination, Malcolm X dictated to a jour-
       nalist friend his metamorphosis from Malcolm Little (straight-A
       student of Lansing, Michigan) to Detroit Red (Harlem pimp,
       thief, and drug-pusher) to Malcolm X (Elijah Muhammad's
       right-hand man) to El-Hajj Malik El-Shabazz (African-American
       Muslim and pilgrim to Mecca). (BRD)

906   Malcolm X. **By any means necessary: speeches, interviews and a
       letter.** Edited by George Breitman. Pathfinder, 1970.

       This volume reflects Malcolm X's interest in the underdevel-
       oped nations and what he believed was a common bond be-
       tween the black people oppressed in America and the op-
       pressed of Asia and Africa. (LJ)

907   Malcolm X. **Malcolm X speaks: selected speeches and statements.**
       Edited by George Breitman. Merit Pub., 1965.

       This book begins with Malcolm X speaking as a Black Muslim
       leader to a black conference in Detroit in 1963 and continues
       up to a radio debate three nights before his murder. (BRD)

908   Malcolm X. **The speeches of Malcolm X at Harvard.** Edited by
       Archie Epps. Morrow, 1969.

       These talks, given in 1961 and 1964, express Malcolm X's
       views of black nationalism. (LJ)

909   Mapp, Edward. **Blacks in American films: today and yesterday.**
       Scarecrow, 1972.

       The history of black performers in American films is traced
       from one of the earliest silent films ("The wooing and wed-
       ding of a coon" [1905]) to "Cotton comes to Harlem"
       (1970). (C)

910   Mapp, Edward, ed. **Puerto Rican perspectives.** Scarecrow, 1974.

       Eighteen essays focus on the plight and successes of the
       Puerto Rican in the United States in areas of education, the
       arts, the community, and the individual. (TCR)

911   Marshall, Paule. **Brown girl, brownstones.** Random, 1959.

       Selina and her family from Barbados move into a brownstone,

once a socially desirable home in Brooklyn, New York, and become initiated into their new life. (BRD)

912 Marshall, Paule. **The chosen place, the timeless people.** HBJ, 1969.

The place is at the remote end of a West Indian island and the timeless people are its inhabitants who experience the arrival of an advance team for a large American research development project directed by a Jew. Complex relationships evolve as confrontations of black and white, and haves and have-nots take place. (BRD)

913 Marshall, Paule. **Praisesong for the widow.** Putnam, 1983.

The black central character realizes that the familiar rituals of affluent widowhood are unbearable; she leaves her cruise in Grenada and meets an old man who influences her to order her memories and to reconsider her future. (BRD)

914 Marshall, Paule. **Soul clap hands and sing.** Atheneum, 1961.

Included here are four short stories, each describing how an aging and dying man attempts to face up to the decline of his virile powers. (NYHT)

915 Mayfield, Julian. **The grand parade.** Vanguard, 1961.

A school segregation crisis places a reform mayor in the predicament of having to expose corruption of old friends and associates who made his career possible. (BRD)

916 Mayfield, Julian. **The hit.** Vanguard, 1957.

This first novel is the story of a middle-aged man who determines to escape the frustrations of Harlem and his wife and go West to start anew. His plans fail. (BRD)

917 Mayfield, Julian. **Long night.** Vanguard, 1958.

A ten-year-old boy takes seriously his mother's half-serious warning, and when gang members steal his money, he spends the long night trying to earn, borrow, and finally steal to get an equal amount of money back. (BRD)

918 Mays, Benjamin E. **Born to rebel: an autobiography.** Scribner, 1971.

Mays, president of Morehouse College for twenty-seven years, tells of his life as a rebel who resisted humiliation and frustration and, with courage, helped to bring about change. Although morally brave, the great sadness in his life was his failure to comprehend the motives of black radicals who challenged his authority at Morehouse.   (BRD)

919   Mays, Benjamin E. **The Negro's God, as reflected in his literature.** Illustrated by James L. Wells. Chapman & Grimes, 1938.

This work traces the historical development of the idea of God in black literature from 1760 to 1937.   (BRD)

920   Mays, Benjamin E. and Nicholson, Joseph W. **Negro's church.** Institute of Soc. & Relig. Research, 1933.

This report is based upon a study of 609 urban and 185 rural churches in twelve cities and four country areas. The study covers the training and message of ministers; number, size, and distribution of the churches; methods of increasing membership; financial methods and conditions; and religious and social programs in the city and country.   (BRD)

921   Mebane, Mary. **Mary.** Viking, 1981.

Mebane writes of her childhood near Durham, North Carolina, where she suffered through poverty of money and family love to obtain advanced degrees from the University of North Carolina.   (LJ)

Winner: Coretta Scott King Honorable Mention Book, 1988.

922   Mebane, Mary. **Mary, wayfarer.** Viking, 1983.

In this continuation of her autobiography, Mebane tells about her life as an ambitious and educated black woman in North Carolina in the 1950s.   (LJ)

923   Meriwether, Louise. **Daddy was a number runner.** Prentice-Hall, 1970.

In addition to the usual adolescent crises, twelve-year-old Francine, whose dad is a number runner, experiences the disintegration of her family as a result of the economic and social pressures of ghetto living.   (LJ)

924   Metcalf, George R. **Black profiles.** McGraw-Hill, 1968.

Contained here are summaries of the life and work of the

following moderates: Martin Luther King, Jr.; W. E. B. Du Bois; Roy Wilkins; Thurgood Marshall; Jackie Robinson; Harriet Tubman; Medgar Evers; James Meredith; Rosa Parks; and Whitney Young, Jr. (BRD)

925   Metcalf, George R. **Up from within: today's new black leaders.** McGraw-Hill, 1971.

A former New York state senator has compiled biographies of eight black leaders: John Conyers, Jr.; Kenneth Gibson; Clifton Wharton, Jr.; Shirley Chisholm; Julian Bond; John Mackey; Alvin Poussaint; and Andrew F. Brimmer. (BRD)

926   Miller, Kelly. **Appeal to conscience: America's code of caste a disgrace to democracy.** Macmillan, 1918.

This is an appeal against lawlessness and segregation, and is in favor of true democracy and justice to blacks. (BRD)

927   Miller, Kelly. **Out of the house of bondage.** Neale Watson, 1914.

Miller considers the extent to which blacks have acquired the capacity to become partakers of the life, spirit, and power of that civilization of which they would constitute a part. He concludes that fifty years of liberty is too short a time in which to pass any final verdict upon a people. (N)

928   Miller, Kelly. **Race adjustment: essays on the Negro in America.** Neale Watson, 1908.

Nineteen essays discuss various phases of the dilemma about blacks and the questions that enter into a complete resolution. (BRD)

929   Mitchell, Henry H. **Black belief: folk beliefs of blacks in America and West Africa.** Harper, 1975.

Mitchell contends that Black American Christianity is not simply an European-American version of the faith taught to slaves. He seeks to prove an African-American linkage. (CHR)

930   Moody, Anne. **Coming of age in Mississippi.** Dial, 1968.

Moody tells of growing up in Mississippi's black belt as a sharecropper's daughter who would be the first to go to college. This autobiography covers Moody's life up to her college graduation and the Canton, Mississippi, Freedom Day March in 1964. (BRD)

931   Morgan, Kathryn L. **Children of strangers: the stories of a black family.** Temple Univ. Pr., 1980.

This autobiographical memoir of six generations of a black family extends from the time of the Civil War to publication date and seeks to explain how black parents help their children cope with a racist society. (C)

932   Morrison, Toni. **Beloved.** Knopf, 1987.

This story of Sethe, a runaway slave woman, includes portrayal of her violation, determined escape, and the horrifying consequences. She is alienated from the black community by gossip which also drives her two sons away from home and sends her remaining daughter into her own form of exile. Sethe is also haunted by a murdered girl called Beloved. (BL)

933   Morrison, Toni. **The bluest eye: a novel.** Holt, 1970.

A black, ugly, and poor woman spends the first year of her womanhood living in a storefront where she shares a bedroom with her brother, crippled mother, and drunken father. Pregnant by her father, she goes to a man who believes himself to possess holy powers. What she wants are blue eyes. (NYTBR)

934   Morrison, Toni. **Song of Solomon.** Knopf, 1977.

Macon Dead, the central character, had money, women, prestige in black middle-class circles, and a soft job collecting his slumlord father's rents. At thirty-two, he went to the South searching for lost gold and the adventure turned into a quest for his roots. (BRD)

935   Morrison, Toni. **Sula.** Knopf, 1974.

Two young black women in the colored section of Medallion, Ohio, share the focus of this story which spans forty years. Nel marries young and has a family. Sula leaves Medallion, goes to college, and lives as a vamp in the West before returning home where she ultimately sleeps with all of the black husbands of the town—including Nel's husband. When Sula dies alone, Nel is her only mourner. (BRD)

936 Morrison, Toni. **Tar baby.** Knopf, 1981.

The household of a rich retired businessman and his wife is disrupted sharply when the wife discovers a primitive man hiding in her closet, a fugitive on the run who falls in love with the couple's niece, an educated Paris model. (BRD)

937 Morrow, E. Frederic. **Black man in the White House: a diary of the Eisenhower years by the administrative officer for special projects, the White House, 1955–1961.** Coward, 1963.

This diary concerns three aspects of Morrow's life in the 1950s—daily activities, social events, and travel; his views of the administration and the Republican party on civil rights issues; and his increasing race militancy in tune with the rising tide of black pressure for true citizenship. (NYTBR)

938 Morrow, E. Frederic. **Forty years a guinea pig.** Pilgrim Press, 1980.

The first black presidential executive assistant updates his autobiography as he emphasizes his political experience and documents difficulties he faced as a spokesman for civil rights in the Eisenhower administration. (BRD)

939 Motley, Willard. **The diaries of Willard Motley.** Edited by Jerome Klinkowitz. Iowa State Univ. Pr., 1979.

This biography was culled from twenty-eight diaries kept by the novelist from 1926 through 1943, the year he completed his first novel. It shows that the origin of his preference to write about white characters was his conflict with his racial identity. (BRD)

940 Motley, Willard. **Knock on any door.** Appleton, 1947.

This realistic story is of an Italian boy in Chicago whose early tendencies towards decency were beaten down by his contacts with life along Chicago's streets. He turned killer and died in the electric chair. (BRD)

941 Motley, Willard. **Let no man write my epitaph.** Random, 1958.

The plot revolves around the young son of the crook executed at the end of Motley's *Knock on Any Door* and his mother who wants him out of the slums for a better chance than his father had. She becomes an addict but Nick is surrounded by a small community of people who want him to rise above that society. (BRD)

942   Motley, Willard. **Let noon be fair: a novel.** Putnam, 1966.

This story of a Mexican fishing village is told from the time it was an untouched Garden of Eden inhabited solely by artists and bronze noble savages, to the days when it was overtaken by phonies and American tourists with corrupting dollars. (SR)

943   Motley, Willard. **We fished all night.** Appleton, 1951.

This story tells about three young men in Chicago politics and labor circles before and after World War II. (BRD)

944   Moton, Robert Russa. **Finding a way out: an autobiography.** Doubleday, 1920.

The head of Tuskegee Institute wrote in the hope that telling his story would serve a useful purpose to clarify the hopes and aspirations of blacks and the difficulties they have had to overcome in making the progress realized over the fifty years of freedom from slavery—"the most remarkable of any race in so short a time." (BRD)

945   Moton, Robert Russa. **What the Negro thinks.** Doubleday, 1929.

The principal of Tuskegee Institute considers what blacks think of racial discrimination and of the experiences to which they are subjected because of their color.   (BRD)

946   Muhammad, Elijah. **Message to the black man in America.** Muhammad Mosque of Islam, No. 2, 1965.

This is a compendium of the doctrines and attitudes that Malcolm X assimilated during his stay in prison, and studied and preached on his release. These speeches and writings cover a thirty-year period. (SR)

947   Murphy, Beatrice M., ed. **Today's Negro voices: an anthology by young Negro poets.** Messner, 1970.

Here is a gathering of poems by Black American poets under thirty years old who have in common a fierce consciousness of race and a passionate emotion that is often proud, militant, and hate-filled. (BRD)

948 Murray, Albert. **The omni-Americans: new perspectives on black experience and American culture.** Outerbridge & Dienstfrey, 1970.

Murray argues that black life is no less complex than that of any other group; indeed it has produced the most complicated culture, and therefore the most complicated sensibility in the modern world. This book contests the oversimplification of black tribulations. (BRD)

949 Murray, Albert. **South to a very old place.** McGraw-Hill, 1971.

Murray concludes from sought-out opinions of white southern thinkers that the southern experience transcended the factors of race in shaping that unique being, the southerner. He defends Lyndon Johnson and Jews who have supported the black movement and ridicules blacks who have turned to Africa for their identity. (BRD)

950 Murray, Albert. **Stomping the blues.** McGraw-Hill, 1976.

In this examination of the blues spirit and blues as a cultured art form, the critic and novelist author views the music not as a primitive musical expression of black suffering but as an antidote to the bad times—active good-time music to be danced to because of its substance and talented exponents. (BRD)

951 Murray, Albert. **Train whistle guitar.** McGraw-Hill, 1974.

The protagonist is a young black boy growing up in Alabama in the 1920s who idolizes two blues players who pass through town occasionally. The boy runs away from home and is sent back, only to discover his concealed true parentage. (BRD)

952 Murray, Pauli. **Proud shoes: the story of an American family.** Harper, 1956.

This biography is of Murray's grandfather—an Irish-African descendant, a northern mulatto, and one of the few black soldiers in the Union Army—who chose to come South after the Civil War and start a school for newly freed blacks in Durham, North Carolina. (BRD)

953 Myers, Walter Dean. **Fallen angels.** Scholastic, 1988.

Seventeen-year-old Richie Perry is on his way to Vietnam in

1967, thinking that this is the time to get himself ready for college and becoming a writer. The horrors of war and death are forcefully articulated while he keeps his Harlem roots and family in focus.   (ALR)

Winner: Coretta Scott King Award, 1989; School Library Journal "Best Books of the Year" Award, 1988.

954   Myers, Walter Dean. **Sweet illusions.** Teachers and Writers Coll., 1987.

This novel features several girls from varying backgrounds who are together at a pregnancy counseling center. It focuses on their relationships with each other and with the boys who fathered their children.   (SLJ)

955   Naylor, Gloria. **Linden Hills.** Ticknor & Fields, 1985.

In this novel of black suburban life, the spokesman is an embittered undertaker who developed the posh black enclave to be a blister to the community. Generations later, two young street-smart boys stumble onto an awful secret and the true meaning of Linden Hills.   (LJ)

956   Naylor, Gloria. **Mama Day.** Ticknor & Fields, 1988.

On the black-owned and inhabited sea island off the southeast coast of the United States, Miranda Day is the elderly matriarch and direct descendant of a slave owner and his slave. This is the love story of her beloved great niece, Cocoa, who left the island and married an urban northerner.   (ED)

957   Naylor, Gloria. **The women of Brewster Place.** Viking, 1982.

Brewster Place was once the home of poor Irish and Italian immigrants, but is now a rotting tenement on a dead-end street which shelters black families. The novel portrays the courage, fear, and anguish of some of the women there who hold their families together while trying to make a home. (BRD)

958   Noble, Jeanne. **Beautiful, also, are the souls of my black sisters: a history of the black woman in America.** Prentice-Hall, 1978.

This study of the black woman traces her historical, sociological, and feminist experiences from her African beginnings to her current place in American society.   (LJ)

959   Owens, Jesse. **Blackthink: my life as black man and white man.** [By] Jesse Owens with Paul G. Neimark. Morrow, 1970.

The running-jumping hero of the 1936 Olympic Games in Berlin tells his reasons for believing that black militants are a malignant growth in this country. (ATL)

960   Owens, Jesse. **I have changed.** [By] Jesse Owens with Paul Neimark. Morrow, 1972.

This black athlete discusses how he has changed personally and politically, how he has come to greater self-knowledge, and how he has grown into militancy. (BRD)

961   Painter, Nell Irvin. **Exoduster: black migration to Kansas after Reconstruction.** Knopf, 1977.

This study is of the movement of blacks from Mississippi, Louisiana, Texas, and Tennessee into Kansas in 1879. (LJ)

962   Painter, Nell Irvin. **The narrative of Hosea Hudson: his life as a Negro Communist in the South.** Harvard Univ. Pr., 1979.

A steel mill worker in Alabama during the 1930s and 1940s recalls the history of the Communist party in the South as an almost exclusively black political movement. (LJ)

963   Palmer, C. Everard. **My father, Sun-Sun Johnson.** Andre Deutsch, 1974.

A young Jamaican boy cherishes the warmth of life, impoverished but filled with affection. However, his father is too kind to the neighbors and they eventually exploit away his home and possessions, and cause the break-up of his family. Rami is loyal to his father who temporarily accepts the disgrace and discomfort of his misfortune. (TLS)

964   Parks, Gordon. **Born black.** Illustrated by Gordon Parks. Lippincott, 1971.

Parks's observations of several black leaders are portrayed through commissioned articles and other original writing. Nine essays bear witness to the way a man's destiny can be controlled simply by his being born black. (BRD)

965   Parks, Gordon. **A choice of weapons.** Harper, 1966.

The photographer-journalist for *Life* magazine records autobiographically his battle against poverty and racism. This story concludes in 1944 when Parks learns suddenly that a special overseas assignment had been countermanded. (BRD)

966   Parks, Gordon. **Flavio.** Norton, 1978.

The photographer-author of the 1961 *Life* magazine photoessay on Rio de Janeiro slums writes in greater detail about the dying boy he found there and his efforts to discover what has happened since. (BRD)

967   Parks, Gordon. **Gordon Parks: a poet and his camera.** Viking, 1968.

In this collection of photographs, some are matched with poems on subjects which include love, birth, life, fear of death, and the condition of man. (H)

968   Parks, Gordon. **Gordon Parks: whispers of intimate things.** Illustrated by Gordon Parks. Viking, 1971.

This book of poems and color photographs reflects deep personal perceptions. (BRD)

969   Parks, Gordon. **The learning tree.** Harper, 1973.

A black family in a small Kansas town during the 1920s provides background for the story of the young son, Newt Winger, as he grows from childhood through his first love, tangles with the town tough, and experiences the awe of death. (ED)

970   Parks, Gordon. **To smile in autumn: a memoir.** Norton, 1979.

This third installment of a continuing autobiography covers 1944 to 1978 in the life of a photographer, composer, poet, movie producer, and director and displays heavy emphasis on the social turmoil of the 1960s. (SLJ)

971   Patterson, Lindsay, comp. **Black theater: a 20th century collection of the works of its best playwrights.** Dodd, 1971.

This anthology of plays expresses something about that specific moment when a black discovers that he is a "nigger" and how his mentality shifts gears in order to begin the long, uphill climb to bring psychological order out of chaos. (LJ)

972   Perry, Margaret. **Silence to the drums: a survey of the literature of the Harlem Renaissance.** Greenwood, 1976.

This biographical and critical study surveys the black writers of the 1920s and 1930s who formed the Harlem Renaissance and for whom negritude emerged as the focus of their writing in their real and spiritual home—Harlem.   (BRD)

973   Petry, Ann. **Country place.** Houghton, 1947.

Among a group of people living in a New England town, a returned soldier discovers facts of his wife's unfaithful behavior.   (BRD)

974   Petry, Ann. **Miss Muriel and other stories.** Houghton, 1971.

Short stories and novellas among which is the title story about the lifestyle of a black druggist and his family in an otherwise white town on Long Island, as seen through the eyes of the precocious young daughter.   (BRD)

975   Petry, Ann. **The narrows.** Houghton, 1953.

Link, a black boy, grows up in a small Connecticut town, graduates from Dartmouth Phi Beta Kappa and all-around athlete. His luck begins to fail when people discover that the girl he loves is white.   (BRD)

976   Petry, Ann. **The street.** Houghton, 1946.

The story is of a black woman and her struggles to retain her moral integrity and guard her young son from evil in a tiny, dark apartment in Harlem.   (BRD)

977   Pharr, Robert Deane. **The book of numbers.** Doubleday, 1969.

In a southern city during the 1930s, two itinerant black waiters become rich through a thriving numbers bank in the ghetto, during which time power and respectability are gained and lost.   (BRD)

978   Pharr, Robert Deane. **S.R.O.** Doubleday, 1971.

The Logan, a single-room occupancy hotel in Harlem, is a condensed version of the city where representatives of every element of lowlife reside. The narrator-hero checks in here after an epic three-week period of inebriation.   (BRD)

979 Pickens, William. **American Aesop: Negro and other humor.** William Pickens, 1926.

About two hundred stories are grouped as black stories, Jew stories, Irish stories, and cosmopolite stories with more than one-half classified as black stories. (BRD)

980 Plumpp, Sterling D. **The mojo hands call, I must go.** Thunder's Mouth Press, 1982.

Poems chronicle the struggle of a young man from rural Mississippi trying to come to terms with life in Chicago. (LJ)

981 Plumpp, Sterling D. **Somehow we survive, an anthology of South African writing.** Illustrated by Dumile Feni. Thunder's Mouth Press, 1982.

Sixty-seven poems and two short stories by radical South African poets within the country and in exile indicate an indictment of apartheid. (BRD)

982 Polite, Charlene Hatcher. **The flagellants.** Farrar, 1967.

A girl and a young poet live in a Greenwich Village apartment where they flagellate each other with their states of being, and sometimes physically, as well. (BRD)

983 Porter, James Amos. **Modern Negro art.** Dryden Pr., 1943.

This study of art produced by Black American painters and sculptors from the last quarter of the eighteenth century to publication date represents more than forty artists with eighty-five halftones of works. (BRD)

984 Portier, Sidney. **This life.** Knopf, 1979.

This autobiography portrays Sidney's life from his childhood on Cat Island in the Bahamas to his arrival in Miami at age sixteen and in New York City a year later with three dollars and total naivete, to his becoming an actor almost on a dare, and emergence as a star and an Oscar winner. (ED)

Winner: Coretta Scott King Award, 1981.

985 Powell, Adam Clayton. **Adam by Adam: the autobiography of Adam Clayton Powell.** Dial, 1971.

Powell, a congressman from Harlem between 1945–1970, de-

scribes his personal life, marriages, trial for income tax eva-
sion, ministry, and efforts to aid civil rights legislation.   (BRD)

986   Powell, Adam Clayton. **Keep the faith, baby!** Simon & Schuster,
       1967.

       The congressman and preacher offers a collection of sermons,
       meditations, and speeches he delivered at his Harlem
       church.   (BRD)

987   Powell, Adam Clayton. **Marching blacks: an interpretative history
       of the rise of the black common man.** Dial, 1946.

       The minister reviews the black struggle for economic and so-
       cial equality. He outlines the techniques of nonviolent but
       direct social action by which such progress has been achieved
       and by which he believes blacks can gain full rights in a free
       country.   (BRD)

988   Powell, Adam Clayton. **Riots and ruins.** R. R. Smith, 1945.

       This document expresses the outrage of a black leader who
       has had more than an ordinary insight into black and white
       feelings, and who has reported his fear of what he sees.
       (BRD)

989   Quarles, Benjamin. **Allies for freedom: blacks and John Brown.**
       Oxford Univ. Pr., 1974.

       Quarles seeks to delineate the relationships between Brown
       and the black community during Brown's life and the persis-
       tent interest in him by blacks.   (C)

990   Quarles, Benjamin. **Black abolitionists.** Oxford Univ. Pr., 1969.

       This professor-author seeks to show the extent to which blacks
       were involved in the crusade against slavery. He deals with
       black preachers, black agitators abroad, underground railroad
       operators, and the effects of the Fugitive Slave Law and John
       Brown's raid on black opinion.   (BRD)

991   Quarles, Benjamin, ed. **Blacks on John Brown.** Univ. of Illinois Pr.,
       1972.

       Included are various black writers' views of John Brown's
       meaning to black people. The variety of qualities admired in

Brown and the different ways they expressed their admiration are featured.   (C)

992   Quarles, Benjamin. **Lincoln and the Negro.** Oxford Univ. Pr., 1962.

A history professor explores many aspects of Lincoln's attitude toward blacks and their attitudes toward him that generally are not known. The change in the blacks' attitude toward Lincoln came with the abolition of slavery in the District of Columbia and the issuance of the Emancipation Proclamation.   (BRD)

993   Quarles, Benjamin. **The Negro in the American Revolution.** Univ. of North Carolina Pr., 1961.

This study deals with black soldiers in the continental armies and navies, in the militia of the states, under the British flag, and in labor and construction battalions. The writer finds that almost everywhere, black services were utilized only when the pressure of expediency made it absolutely necessary.   (BRD)

994   Quarles, Benjamin. **Negro in the Civil War.** Little, 1953.

This general survey of blacks in the Civil War describes their roles in military and behind the line activities.   (BRD)

995   Redding, Jay Saunders. **An American in India: a personal report on the Indian dilemma and the nature of her conflicts.** Bobbs-Merrill, 1954.

This book documents Redding's experiences in India where he was sent in 1952 by the Truman administration to present the American way of life to the Indian people.   (BRD)

996   Redding, Jay Saunders. **Lonesome road: the story of the Negro's part in America.** Doubleday, 1958.

Through the lives of twelve black men and one woman, the difficult struggle from slavery to equal rights is traced by the (then) head of the English Department at Hampton Institute, Virginia.   (BRD)

997   Redding, Jay Saunders. **The Negro.** Potomac Bks., 1966.

Here is summarized the history of blacks in the United States from 1619 to 1967 and outlines of the effects on Black Americans of major social, economic, and political events.   (BRD)

998   Redding, Jay Saunders. **No day of triumph.** Harper, 1942.

Something of this college professor's autobiography is combined with his findings from a study of southern black life which was funded by the Rockefeller Foundation. (BRD)

999   Redding, Jay Saunders. **On being Negro in America.** Bobbs-Merrill, 1951.

Redding combines comment and personal recollection in summing up the difficulty of being black in America. (BRD)

1000   Redding, Jay Saunders. **Stranger and alone.** HBJ, 1950.

This story follows a man of biracial heritage who hates his black heritage and wants to become someone of importance. (BRD)

1001   Redding, Jay Saunders. **They came in chains: Americans from Africa.** Lippincott, 1950.

Redding expounds that if all Americans understood some of the economic and historical causes of the present status of blacks, the "problem" might not be so much of a problem. (BRD)

1002   Redding, Jay Saunders. **To make a poet black.** Univ. of North Carolina Pr., 1939.

An appraisal of black literature from the indigenous perspective is interpreted in the light of the time in which the writers lived. (BRD)

1003   Reed, Ishmael, ed. **Calafia: the California poetry.** Y'Bird Bks., 1979.

This multicultural anthology of American poetry by more than two hundred poets covers a variety of techniques including ballads, stories, folktales, songs, and free verse. (BRD)

1004   Reed, Ishmael. **Chattanooga poems.** Random, 1973.

Here is a collection of Reed's verses. (BRD)

1005   Reed, Ishmael. **Conjure: selected poems, 1963–1970.** Univ. of Massachusetts Pr., 1972.

This collection of black-oriented poems represents a conscious production of an exclusively black aesthetic for Black Americans. (BRD)

1006   Reed, Ishmael. **Flight to Canada.** Random, 1976.

During the Civil War, a slave runs away from his master, hides out in Emancipation City, and eventually reaches Canada. Until his owner is dead and buried, however, he must remain a fugitive because of the resolve to capture him. (BRD)

1007   Reed, Ishmael. **The free-lance pallbearers.** Doubleday, 1967.

This novel is set in a country called HARRY SAM run by a leader of the same name. (BRD)

1008   Reed, Ishmael. **The last days of Louisiana Red.** Random, 1974.

An international organization of bad guys is trying to take over the manufacture of gumbo, a mysterious product with healing properties developed through black magic and voodoo. To defeat its opposition, the Solid Gumbo Works Corporation brings in renowned occult detective Papa LaBas, hero of Reed's *Mumbo Jumbo.* (BRD)

1009   Reed, Ishmael. **Mumbo Jumbo.** Doubleday, 1972.

Atonism is the rationalist, monotheistic, militarist creed dedicated to the suppression of animism, the natural magic figured in music, dance, and generative rhythms. The military arm of Atonism is the Wallflower Order—dedicated to the proposition that "Lord, if I can't dance, no one shall." This tyrannical order struggles against the jazz craze from New Orleans which threatens serious American civilization with the flapperization of all its children. (BRD)

1010   Reed, Ishmael, ed. **19 necromancers from now.** Doubleday, 1975.

This sampling of new, little-known novels and plays is predominantly by African-American, Indian-American, and Chinese-American writers. (BRD)

1011   Reed, Ishmael. **Shrovetide in old New Orleans.** Doubleday, 1978.

This collection of essays, interviews, book reviews, personal polemics, and reminiscences reveals Reed's distinctive view of all aspects of the African-American culture. (BRD)

1012   Reed, Ishmael. **The terrible twos.** St. Martin's, 1982.

America is observed from 1980 to 1990 in which cities and the economy are collapsing, radical Catholic clergy do battle with Moral Majoritarians, and a top male model elected to front for wealthy western businessmen turns into a compassionate neo-socialist. So also does Santa Claus.   (SR)

1013   Reed, Ishmael. **Yellow Back Radio broke-down.** Doubleday, 1969.

Into Yellow Back Radio, a pioneer town set in an apparent time-warp between 10,000 B.C. and 1970, rides the Loop Garoo Kid—a black cowboy, ornery desperado, and voodoo worker with a cleft foot.   (BRD)

1014   Reynolds, Barbara A. **Jesse Jackson: the man, the movement, the myth.** Nelson-Hall, 1975.

This account acknowledges Jackson's personal magnetism but also criticizes him because he has spread himself too thin in his attempt to replace Martin Luther King, Jr., and because he has failed to produce tangible results for most black Chicagoans.   (LJ)

1015   Roberts, J. Deotis. **Roots of a black future: family and church.** Westminster, 1980.

The black family and the church are brought together from a theological point of view as Roberts examines their unique relationship in the black experience. He seeks a theological understanding of the church and its mission in the black tradition and relates the African extended family concept to the Christian gospel of hope.   (BRD)

1016   Robeson, Eslanda Cardoza. **African journey.** Day, 1945.

The anthropologist and wife of Paul Robeson traveled through parts of South Africa with her young son in 1936 to learn something of the predicament of native inhabitants in her ancestral land. This is her account of the journey.   (BRD)

1017   Robeson, Eslanda Cardoza and Buck, Pearl. **American argument.** Day, 1949.

Personal conversations between the authors compare growing up in the United States as a black child in a white society and growing up in China as a white child among colored people. No subject is taboo as sex, marriage, women, children, education, politics, labor, and inequality of opportunity are discussed. (LJ)

1018   Robeson, Eslanda Cardoza. **Paul Robeson, Negro.** Harper, 1930.

This biography written by Robeson's wife acknowledges that when he graduated from Rutgers College in 1919, he was a football hero, a four-letter man in athletics, and had won the Phi Beta Kappa key. He later became famous on two continents as an actor and a singer. (BRD)

1019   Robeson, Paul. **Paul Robeson speaks: writings, speeches, interviews, 1918–1974.** Edited by Philip S. Foner. Brunner-Mazel, 1978.

This collection is an attempt to show the breadth and depth of Robeson's insight through his writings and speeches from the time he was twenty years old until his last public statement at age seventy-five. (BRD)

1020   Robinson, Jackie. **I never had it made.** As told to Al Duckett. Putnam, 1972.

Jackie Robinson accounts his rise from a poor southern family to become the first black baseball player in the major leagues, a member of the Hall of Fame, a successful businessman, a civil rights spokesman, and a political advisor. (LJ)

Winner: Coretta Scott King Award, 1973.

1021   Robinson, William H. **Phillis Wheatley in the Black American beginnings.** Broadside, 1975.

To refute the critics who accuse her of being imitative, unresponsive to the plight of slaves, impersonal, and obsequious, Robinson examined numerous letters and poems and points to Wheatley's piety and to the censorship by white printers. He contends that given her circumstances, Wheatley did what she could do to cope with and proclaim her blackness. (BRD)

1022   Rodgers, Carolyn M. **The heart as ever green: poems.** Anchor Books, 1978.

Themes within this collection of poems include love, black consciousness, feminism, and Christianity. (BRD)

1023 Rodgers, Carolyn M. **How I got ovah: new and selected poems.** Doubleday, 1975.

Autobiographical poems written in black English reveal Rodgers's transformation from a church-mocking militant black to a woman intensely concerned with God, traditional family values, and her private self. (BRD)

1024 Rollins, Charlemae Hill. **They showed the way: forty American Negro leaders.** Crowell, 1964.

Biographical accounts are presented of blacks successful in a wide variety of careers, ranging from the creative arts to the professions of law and medicine, exploration and invention, publishing, and religion. (BRD)

1025 Rowan, Carl Thomas. **Go South to sorrow.** Random, 1957.

Based on personal talks and observations during a trip to the South in 1956, Rowan reports on the conditions which persist since he wrote *South of Freedom* at the beginning of the decade. (BRD)

1026 Rowan, Carl Thomas. **The pitiful and the proud.** Random, 1956.

This report on India, Indonesia, and other uncommitted nations of Southeast Asia is of what the reporter saw, did, and said as a lecturer for the International Educational Exchange Program in 1954. (BRD)

1027 Rowan, Carl Thomas. **South of freedom.** Knopf, 1952.

This book reports the findings of a young black journalist who went South on assignment in 1951 to see if anything had changed in the condition of blacks since he left his native town in 1943. (BRD)

1028 Rowan, Carl Thomas. **Wait till next year.** [The life story of Jackie Robinson by Carl Thomas Rowan] with Jackie Robinson. Random, 1960.

The dramatic rise to fame of the first black in organized baseball is told describing spectacular plays, the hazards and indignities of the trial years, and the efforts of a few people in improving race relations in the sports world. (BK)

1029   Russell, Bill. **Go up for glory.** By Bill Russell as told to William McSweeney. Coward, 1966.

The thirty-year-old outstanding basketball athlete tells the story of his struggle to achieve success as a professional basketball player.   (BRD)

1030   Rustin, Bayard. **Down the line: [the] collected writings of Bayard Rustin.** Quadrangle Bks., 1971.

These essays, written over a thirty-year period, express Rustin's philosophy and program for action. His economic program calls for a distribution of wealth; his political program calls for a coalition of minorities.   (LJ)

1031   Rustin, Bayard. **Strategies for freedom: the changing patterns of black protest.** Columbia Univ. Pr., 1976.

Three lectures review the black struggle in this century and argue for the principles of integration, nonviolence, and coalition politics. Rustin is convinced that his race suffered when it followed the call of separation—only a concern for the class and racial bases of inequality can produce long-lasting effects.   (NY)

1032   Sampson, Henry T. **Blacks in black and white: a source book on black films.** Scarecrow, 1977.

This sourcebook presents relatively little-known facts concerning all-black cast films that were independently produced between 1910 and 1950. It also lists 384 all-black films which were independently produced.   (BRD)

1033   Sampson, Henry T. **Blacks in blackface: a source book on early black musical shows.** Scarecrow, 1980.

African Americans who pioneered as composers, performers, producers, and entertainers in a period when society operated against them are remembered here. Sampson documents their contributions to American life and culture during the nineteenth and twentieth centuries.   (BRD)

1034   Sanchez, Sister Sonia. **A blues book for blue black magical women.** Broadside, 1974.

These poems seek to assert the writer's identity as a black, as a female, as a Muslim, and as a keeper of society. They are aimed at increasing the self-esteem and self-awareness of Black American women. (C)

1035   Sanchez, Sonia. **It's a new day: poems for young brothas and sistuhs.** Broadside, 1971.

Here are poems especially for blacks which include songs and chants intended to stimulate black pride and concern. (P)

1036   Sanchez, Sonia. **We a badd d d d people.** Broadside, 1970.

Poems reflect an insistence upon dignity on black peoples' terms and upon revolution as an added component to the history, haunted memories, despair, and self-criticism that have been part of the black consciousness. (LJ)

1037   Savage, William Sherman. **Blacks in the West.** Greenwood, 1977.

This study covers the period from 1830 to 1890 and looks at the Black American's contribution to the development of the West. It examines why blacks chose to leave the East, where they settled, what jobs they took, and what political and social challenges they faced. (BRD)

1038   Sayers, Gayle. **I am third.** [By] Gayle Sayers with Al Silverman. Viking, 1970.

This autobiography is of the football running back whom many people considered to be the most spectacular in the game during his time. It covers Sayers' early childhood, public school and college days, his life as a professional player, and the events surrounding his knee injury sustained in 1968. (BRD)

1039   Schuyler, George S. **Black and conservative: the autobiography of George S. Schuyler.** Arlington, 1966.

Schuyler explains his association with conservativism in American life and politics. He states his preference for gradualism to civil disobedience, and that he is a foe of Communism and Socialism particularly as they affect the black American community. (LJ)

1040   Schuyler, George S. **Black no more: being the account of the strange and wonderful working of science in the land of the free, A.D. 1933–1940.** Macaulay, 1931.

This is a satire on the subject of color and race prejudice in the United States. A black physician discovers a depigmentation process whereby a black man could become blonde overnight. Soon, everyone is blonde and the special preferred skin color is dark. (BRD)

1041   Schuyler, George S. **Slaves today: a story of Liberia.** HBJ, 1931.

In this story based on the condition of slavery in the form of forced labor which Schuyler found existing in Liberia, an exposé of conditions recalls the horrors of the Belgian Congo. (BRD)

1042   Schuyler, Philippa. **Who killed the Congo?** Devin-Adair, 1962.

This book is Philippa Schuyler's explanation of the Congo in terms of its topography, history, customs, and politics, and her efforts to show all sides of the Congo picture and the roots of the drama. (LJ)

1043   Seale, Bobby. **A lonely rage: the autobiography of Bobby Seale.** Time-Life, 1978.

This is the autobiography of the co-founder of the Black Panther party, who was also a member of the Chicago Seven and a political activist. (BRD)

1044   Seale, Bobby. **Seize the time: the story of the Black Panther party and Huey P. Newton.** Random, 1970.

Seale was chairman of the Black Panther party and this book, part autobiography and history, attempts to clear up the notion that Panthers are ideologically anti-white and committed to the murder of policemen. (BRD)

1045   Shange, Ntozake. **Betsey Brown.** St. Martin's, 1985.

This is the story of thirteen-year-old Betsey who is poised between adolescence and adulthood. (EPL)

1046   Shange, Ntozake. **For colored girls who have considered suicide/ when the rainbow is enuf: a choreopoem.** Macmillan, 1977.

In this printed edition of a Broadway production that blends dance, music, and poetry, the poems represent different black women, each telling a tale of her own private terror, love, dreams, and despair. (C)

1047   Shange, Ntozake. **Nappy edges.** St. Martin's, 1978.

Here is a collection of poems by the author of *For Colored Girls Who Have Considered Suicide/When the Rainbow Is Enuf.* (BRD)

1048   Simmons, Herbert A. **Corner boy.** Houghton, 1957.

This is the story of an extremely intelligent eighteen-year-old peddler who has a potential denied fruition by society. (BRD)

1049   Sims, Naomi. **How to be a top model.** Illustrated by Mona Marks. Doubleday, 1979.

Sims deals with the physical requirements, makeup, exercise, diet, different types of modeling, procedures for breaking into a chosen field, male modeling, and the problems of being a black model. (VOYA)

1050   Smith, Vern E. **The Jones men.** Regnery, 1974.

This is the story of a ruinous subculture in which the men of the title are drug dealers whose places of operation are a shooting gallery and rented apartments in abandoned buildings. (BRD)

1051   Smith, William Gardner. **Anger at innocence.** Farrar, 1950.

Set in a South Philadelphia destitute neighborhood is this story of a tragic love affair between a shy and sensitive man whose life is blighted by marriage to a woman whom he does not love and who will not free him from the marriage. (NYTBR)

1052   Smith, William Gardner. **Last of the conquerors.** Farrar, 1948.

The story of Black American occupation troops in Germany focuses on the love relationship of a black private and a German girl. (BRD)

1053   Smith, William Gardner. **Return to Black America.** Prentice-Hall, 1970.

As a young Black American, Smith expatriated himself in the early 1950s, took up residence in Paris, and later traveled around Europe and Africa. He returned to the United States in 1967 as a television newsman from Ghana on assignment for firsthand information on the black evolution in the United States. This book presents his findings.   (BRD)

1054   Smith, William Gardner. **South Street.** Farrar, 1954.

Figures in a black community in Philadelphia emerge in this story of antagonistic relationships, love, and pressures that are imposed upon a biracial married couple who live there.   (BRD)

1055   Smythe, Mabel M., ed. **The Black American reference book.** Prentice-Hall, 1976.

Each of the thirty chapters in this book treats an aspect of black society in the United States. Topics treated include politics, legal status, education, employment, black religion, art, music, sports, literature, and theater.   (BRD)

1056   Snowden, Frank M. **Before color prejudice: the ancient view of blacks.** Harvard Univ. Pr., 1983.

This account of race relations from the middle of the third millennium B.C. until the sixth century A.D. emphasizes that color differences, important as they were in descriptive imagery, did not then have the pejorative association with inferiority, cultural distance, or other prejudicial aspects as those developed during the past several centuries.   (C)

1057   Snowden, Frank M. **Blacks in antiquity: Ethiopians in the Greco-Roman experience.** Harvard Univ. Pr., 1970.

A professor of classics gives a review of what was known and thought of dark- and black-skinned peoples of Africa in the ancient world—they were not uncommon in white cultures; there was no feeling of superiority based on color, no censure of miscegenation; there was emphasis on the equality of all men before God.   (LJ)

1058   Southerland, Ellease. **Let the lion eat straw.** Scribner, 1979.

A five-year-old black girl is taken from her foster home in

North Carolina to live with her real mother in New York City. She adjusts to life-styles, environment, people, and experiences which fortify her growth.   (BRD)

Winner: Coretta Scott King Honorable Mention Book, 1980.

1059   Southern, Eileen. **Biographical dictionary of Afro-American and African musicians.** Greenwood, 1982.

This volume covers more than fifteen hundred musicians of African descent born from about 1640 up to 1950 and native to the United States, Africa, Canada, Europe, Central America, and South America.   (BRD)

1060   Sowell, Thomas. **Black education: myths and tragedies.** McKay, 1972.

Sowell's personal experiences in black and white schools as both student and teacher constitute part one. Part two deals with black students in white colleges. Part three discusses black colleges, public schools, and race as it relates to intelligence. Part four contains some proposals for the improvement of black education.   (BRD)

1061   Sowell, Thomas. **The economics and politics of race: an international perspective.** Morrow, 1983.

Sowell's thesis is that cultural differences are consequential for economic performance and political stability. Tossing money (foreign aid, welfare, even education) at the social problems of certain peoples may satisfy various political needs, but it cannot produce any positive results as long as peoples' cultural behavior remains nonproductive or counterproductive.   (C)

1062   Sowell, Thomas. **Ethnic America: a history.** Basic Books, 1981.

Interrelated chapters trace the historical experience of nine of the largest ethnic groups in America—Irish, German, Jewish, Italian, Chinese, Japanese, Black, Puerto Rican, and Mexican. The author holds that there are no minorities because there is no majority.   (BRD)

1063   Sowell, Thomas. **Markets and minorities.** Basic Books, 1981.

Sowell's key question concerns the extent to which differences in the economic conditions of various groups are the result of discrimination. The scientific method is employed in using economic theory to analyze emotionally charged social phenomena concerning the conditions and treatment of minorities.   (BRD)

1064   Sowell, Thomas. **Race and economics.** McKay, 1975.

The author contends that race makes a difference in economic transactions as in other areas of life. Economics of race is considered in market transactions and in economic activities controlled or directed by the government.   (BRD)

1065   Spellman, A. B. **Four lives in the bebop business.** Pantheon, 1966.

In biographical sketches, four black jazzmen speak for themselves and provide the perspective of men practicing an art that is not regarded seriously or even as an art by those who set the cultural norms for this society.   (BRD)

1066   Spero, Sterling Denhard and Harris, Abram Lincoln. **Black worker: the Negro and the labor movement.** Columbia Univ. Pr., 1931.

This study of the status of blacks as workers in industry from the conditions of slavery to present in relation to the whole of the labor movement shows an interaction of race prejudice, trade union politics and structures, conditions of the labor market, etc.   (BRD)

1067   Stetson, Erlene, ed. **Black sister: poetry by Black American women, 1746–1980.** Indiana Univ. Pr., 1981.

Through this anthology, Stetson argues that despite differences in tone and centuries that separate them, black women poets are sisters who share autobiographical consciousness and an appreciation of their troubled history as blacks and as women.   (BRD)

1068   Tarry, Ellen. **Third door: the autobiography of an American Negro woman.** McKay, 1955.

A black Catholic writer describes her experiences in New York and in Alabama. During the Depression, she worked in Harlem with the founder of the interracial Friendship House, and later founded a similar institution in Chicago.   (BRD)

1069   Teague, Bob. **Letters to a black boy.** Walker & Co., 1968.

The NBC-TV news broadcaster writes a series of letters to his two-year-old son to read at age thirteen. He discusses being black in a white society, with views on religion, sex, and politics.   (LJ)

1070   Terrell, Mary Church. **A colored woman in a white world.** Ransdell, 1940.

Terrell was educated at Oberlin and in Paris and Berlin. She taught Latin and German, lectured and worked for the advancement of blacks, and married a lawyer who was appointed a judge by President Theodore Roosevelt.   (BRD)

1071   Thomas, Joyce Carol. **Bright shadow.** Avon, 1983.

In this sequel to *Marked by Fire,* Abyssinia is a young woman tempered by her childhood experiences and falling in love with an aspiring attorney, when tragedy once more enters her life.   (BL)

Winner: Coretta Scott King Honorable Mention Book, 1984.

1072   Thompson, Era Bell. **Africa, land of my fathers.** Doubleday, 1954.

A former editor of *Ebony* magazine provides an account of her tour of Africa where she visited or briefly saw eighteen countries.   (BRD)

1073   Thompson, Era Bell. **American daughter.** Univ. of Chicago Pr., 1946.

This autobiography of a black woman who became the senior interviewer with the United States employment service discusses her rise from a poverty-stricken childhood.   (BRD)

1074   Thorpe, Earl E. **Black historians: a critique.** Morrow, 1971.

In this revision of *Negro Historians in the United States* (1958), Thorpe presents a chronological look at his subject from 1800 to 1960, and discusses laymen as historians. (BRD)

1075   Thurman, Howard. **Deep river, an interpretation of Negro spirituals.** Howard Thurman, 1946.

This is a discussion of the backgrounds of Negro spirituals

and their religious concepts. It also includes essays and meditations based upon spirituals.   (BRD)

1076   Thurman, Howard. **Jesus and the disinherited.** Abingdon, 1949.

Jesus' words were directed to a disinherited people. Thurman analyzes these words with regard to blacks, Jews, and other minorities, and proposes the Christian solution to the problem. (BRD)

1077   Thurman, Howard. **The Negro spiritual speaks of life and death.** Harper, 1947.

In this lecture, Thurman reexamines spirituals to discover their contribution to man's thought on immortality. He concludes that the slave singers can rightfully take their place along side the great creative religious thinkers because they make "a worthless life worth living." (LJ)

1078   Thurman, Howard. **With head and heart: the autobiography of Howard Thurman.** HBJ, 1979.

Among the highlights of his life, Thurman was founder of San Francisco's interdenominational Fellowship Church and was Dean of the chapel and professor at Boston University. (BRD)

1079   Thurman, Wallace Henry. **The blacker the berry, a novel of Negro life.** Macaulay, 1929.

A young woman's black skin was an embarrassment to her among her lighter-hued family and acquaintances at home and in college. She later found it to be no different in Harlem. (BRD)

1080   Tolson, Melvin Beaunorus. **Caviar and cabbage: selected columns by the author from the Washington Tribune, 1932–1944.** Univ. of Missouri Pr., 1982.

This collection of essays by Melvin Tolson, poet and journalist, reflects political and religious views on ethnicity and social class, contemporary fiction and films, among other topics. (BRD)

1081   Tolson, Melvin Beaunorus. **Libretto for the Republic of Liberia.** Twayne, 1953.

Composed for the Liberian Centennial and International Exposition, this book celebrates the new, emergent status of black people throughout the world, particularly in Africa; the rediscovery of ancient wisdom and human value; the reassertion of freedom and equality principles; and the cultural sophistication of the modern intellectual life. (USQ)

1082   Tolson, Melvin Beaunorus. **Rendezvous with America.** Dodd, 1944.

This collection of short poems unveils some of the problems of our society and gives expression to the spirit of America as men of vision dare to hope for. (BRD)

1083   Toomer, Jean. **Cane.** Liveright, 1923.

A southern miscellany of short stories and sketches center about the emotional life of blacks with emphasis on the sensual. (BRD)

1084   Toppin, Edgar A. **A biographical history of blacks in America since 1528.** McKay, 1971.

This is a narrative history of African Americans from prehistoric times to 1971 and a biographical dictionary consisting of 145 biographies. The chapters were originally scripts for educational television and newspaper articles. (C)

1085   Turner, Lorenze. **Africanisms in the Gullah dialect.** Univ. of Chicago Pr., 1949.

The Gullah dialect is the language of blacks on the coastal islands off the Carolinas and Georgia. In a first intensive study of this dialect, Turner demonstrates the activity of a large element of West African language within it. (BRD)

1086   Turner, Rufus P. **Radio test instruments.** Ziff-Davis, 1945.

This extremely practical book explains the workings of various meters, checkers, bridges, frequency measuring devices for radio and audio frequencies, signal tracers, and miscellaneous test equipment. (LJ)

1087   Turpin, Waters Edward. **O Canaan!** Doubleday, 1939.

The title refers to Chicago and the story is of the black migration from Mississippi in 1916 and later. It focuses on the Joe

Benson family which prospers and provides every advantage to the children until the stock market crash brought bank failures and hard times.   (BRD)

1088   Turpin, Waters Edward. **These low grounds.** Harper, 1937.

In this novel which spans four generations of blacks, the hero is a college-bred boy who has great plans for the education of his people.   (BRD)

1089   Tuttle, William M. **Race riot: Chicago in the red summer of 1919.** Atheneum, 1970.

Here is an attempt to explain the origins of the riot between black and white Chicagoans in July 1919. Recorded testimonies of workers from both groups are used to focus on individual grievances and to show the increasing racial tensions in the factories and stockyards.   (BRD)

1090   Tuttle, William M. **W. E. B. Du Bois.** Prentice-Hall, 1973.

In three sections, William Tuttle provides selections from Du Bois' writings, articles by Du Bois' contemporaries which demonstrate the reactions that he provoked, and recent commentators who provide a historical perspective on Du Bois' life and work.   (BRD)

1091   Vroman, Mary Elizabeth. **Harlem summer.** Illustrated by John Martinez. Putnam, 1967.

A black youth from the deep South works in Harlem one summer and experiences the complexities of life in the North as he broadens his understanding of his race and his world.   (OCLC)

1092   Walker, Alice. **The color purple: a novel.** HBJ, 1982.

The story begins in the American South in the early 20th century as a fourteen-year-old girl is repeatedly raped by the man she believes to be her father. Continued abuse is somewhat relieved through her letters to God and then to her sister in Africa. Joy and beauty are discovered by the story's end.   (BRD)

1093   Walker, Alice. **Good night, Willie Lee. I'll see you in the morning: poems.** Dial, 1979.

This is another collection of Walker's poems which combine

feminist anger and determination with a black viewpoint. (BRD)

1094 Walker, Alice. **In love and trouble: stories of black women.** HBJ, 1973.

The protagonists are black women of differing ages and classes and their stories portray them as fighters who respond assertively to changes going on in their world. (LJ)

1095 Walker, Alice. **In search of our mother's gardens: womanist prose.** HBJ, 1983.

Walker defines a womanist as a "black feminist of color" and derives the word from the folk expression "you acting womanish." These writings span sixteen years of activism and growing awareness. (BRD)

1096 Walker, Alice. **Meridian.** HBJ, 1976.

A black civil rights worker turned New York artist returns to a town in the South to find his friend who has moved back to work among the poor blacks she was supposed to kill for. As they talk, their lives are retraced and her struggle to reconcile the gap between the intellectual language of politics and the emotional language of people's lives becomes the book's focus. (NW)

1097 Walker, Alice. **Once: poems.** HBJ, 1968.

In this first book of Walker's poems, many deal with the civil rights conflicts in the South. Other poems are from her experience of living in Africa. (BRD)

1098 Walker, Alice. **Revolutionary petunias and other poems.** HBJ, 1973.

These poems are about revolutionaries and lovers, about the loss of compassion and trust, and about those few who remain committed to beauty and to love even while facing the firing squad. (BRD)

1099 Walker, Alice. **The third life of Grange Copeland.** HBJ, 1970.

Grange Copeland abandons his wife and son in Georgia, goes North, and returns after years of confusing disappointment to find that his son has grown up, is satanic, brutalizes his wife, and is eventually imprisoned. For a while, life mellows, but tragedy erupts when the son is released.   (BW)

1100   Walker, Margaret. **For my people.** Yale Univ. Pr., 1942.

Diverse poetry is divided into three sharply contrasting sections—a series of public poems speaking directly to blacks; folk ballads written in black dialect and drawing heavily on folklore for subject matter; and sonnets, mostly personal and in the English tradition.   (BRD)

Winner: Yale Series of Younger Poets, 1942.

1101   Walker, Margaret. **Jubilee.** Houghton, 1966.

To Vyry, a slave since her birth and daughter of a slave, the first murmurings of freedom meant little. This story of Walker's great-grandmother unfolds with her dreams of possibilities of an education for her children.   (BRD)

Winner: Houghton-Mifflin Literary Fellowship Award, 1966.

1102   Wallace, Michele. **Black macho and the myth of the superwoman.** Dial, 1979.

The radical politics of the 1960s are discussed from the perspective of the black woman. Wallace contends that the aim of the black political movement became the pursuit of black manhood and the open denigration of black women was its corollary.   (N)

1103   Walrond, Eric. **Topic death.** Liveright, 1926.

This collection of short stories illumines the life of blacks in the American tropics. It ranges over the islands of Jamaica and Barbados, depicts the multitudes that helped to build the Panama Canal, and goes into Honduras and the jungles of South America.   (BRD)

1104   Walton, Hanes. **Black Republicans: the politics of the black and tan.** Scarecrow, 1975.

Walton studies black Republicans, particularly the faction that became known in the late nineteenth-century South after the emergence of and in opposition to the "lily-white" Republicans. This study of the black and tan Republicans covers the period from 1854–1972.   (JAMHIS)

1105 Walton, Hanes. **The political philosophy of Martin Luther King, Jr.** Greenwood, 1971.

In tracing King's intellectual development, Walton shows that his theory of nonviolent social change came from Jesus, Thoreau, and Gandhi. He learned that Christianity must deal with the spiritual and man's everyday socio-economic life from Rauschenbusch. Niebuhr gave him an understanding of collective sin and the complexities of individual and group behavior. His idealogy could not provide fundamental answers although his movement gained limited successes. (LJ)

1106 Walton, Ortiz. **Music: black, white & blue; a sociological survey of the use and misuse of Afro-American music.** Morrow, 1972.

Walton's basic thesis is that the creative genius of African-American music from ragtime to rock has been exploited and abused by an insensitive, avaricious, and racist white majority. (C)

1107 Washington, Booker T. **The Booker T. Washington papers; 2 volumes.** Edited by Louis R. Harlan. Univ. of Illinois Pr., 1972.

These gathered and annotated documents include letters, speeches, articles, and other writings from shortly after Washington's birth in 1856 to the death of his second wife in 1889. (BRD)

1108 Washington, Booker T. **Frederick Douglass.** Jacobs, 1907.

This study reveals Douglass as the personification of the historical events that marked the transition from slavery to citizenship. (BRD)

1109 Washington, Booker T. **Man farthest down: a record of observation and study in Europe.** By Booker T. Washington with the collaboration of Robert E. Park. Doubleday, 1912.

This work analyzes the results of Washington's study of the conditions of the poor and working classes in England and on the continent that would prove of value in his work at the Tuskegee Institute. (BRD)

1110 Washington, Booker T. **My larger education.** Doubleday, 1911.

Here continues the autobiographical narrative begun in *Up from Slavery.* (BRD)

1111   Washington, Booker T. **Negro in business.** Hertel, Jenkins & Co., 1907.

This book furnishes some record of the businesses awakening among blacks in the United States.   (BRD)

1112   Washington, Booker T. **Putting the most into life.** Crowell, 1906.

A series of Sunday evening talks recast and enlarged for the general public include aspects of the physical, mental, spiritual, and racial.   (BRD)

1113   Washington, Booker T. **Story of the Negro.** Doubleday, 1909.

The story of what black people have accomplished and attained is presented in three parts.   (BRD)

1114   Washington, Booker T., ed. **Tuskegee and its people: their ideals and achievements.** Appleton, 1905.

The contents, prepared by officers and former students of the normal and industrial institute at Tuskegee, address the problem of black education and include autobiographical sketches by some of its graduates.   (BRD)

1115   Washington, Booker T., and Du Bois, W. E. B., eds. **Negro in the South; his economic progress in relation to his moral and religious development; being the William Levi Bull lectures for the year 1907.** Jacobs, 1907.

An objective study of the influence of slavery is presented in two lectures—one by each of the editors.   (BRD)

1116   Washington, Joseph R. **Black and white power subreption.** Beacon, 1969.

A professor of religious studies seeks an understanding of Black Power's means and ends, and sources and resources, through an examination of its anatomy. He sees it as a pluralistic thrust with long roots in the past, coming as a result of the failure of white power.   (LJ)

1117   Washington, Joseph R. **Black religion: the Negro and Christianity in the United States.** Beacon, 1964.

"No" is the answer in four essays which respond to the question "Are Black American churches Christian?" Washington asserts that black church life has centered not on the cross and resurrection of Christ, but on the drive for freedom, rights, and opportunity. (BRD)

1118   Washington, Joseph R. **Black sects and cults.** Doubleday, 1972.

This examination of some groups within the Blackamerican religious experience beyond the phenomena of belief and practice is an attempt to explain why these sects and cults exist and seem to flourish in America. Washington's thesis is that the lack of outlet for expression within normative social relations accounts for the enormous amount of creativity within the world of black religion. (BRD)

1119   Washington, Joseph R. **Marriage in black and white.** Beacon, 1970.

Washington advances the thesis that widespread interracial intimacy will be a product of white, rather than black, initiative. The measure of this black-white intimacy will be the symbolic significance of such unions rather than the number of interracial marriages. (ED)

1120   Washington, Joseph R. **The politics of God.** Beacon, 1967.

Washington attempts to construct theories of the origins of color prejudice and develops the idea that such prejudice is at the heart of the preconscious white folk religion of this country. (CHR)

1121   Washington, Mary Helen. **Midnight birds: stories by contemporary black woman writers.** Anchor Books, 1980.

Black women are authors and subjects of stories which portray their struggle for freedom from the shackles of racism and sexism. Contributors include Toni Morrison, Alice Walker, Alexis De Veaux, Alice Childress, Gayle Jones, and Toni Bambara. (BRD)

1122   Waters, Ethel. **His eye is on the sparrow: an autobiography.** By Ethel Waters with Charles Samuels. Doubleday, 1951.

This is the unvarnished story of Waters' life from her childhood in Philadelphia through periods of depression and success. (BRD)

1123   Weaver, Robert C. **Dilemmas of urban America.** Harvard Univ. Pr., 1965.

A former administrator of the U.S. Housing and Home Finance Agency considers the housing problems arising from the metropolitan population explosion.   (BRD)

1124   Weaver, Robert C. **The Negro ghetto.** HBJ, 1948.

This book is about residential segregation in the North, the economic factors that have constantly operated, and the resulting costs. Proposals for resolving housing problems for Black Americans are explained.   (BRD)

1125   Weaver, Robert C. **Negro labor: a national problem.** HBJ, 1946.

This study of the problem of fitting blacks into the picture of reconversion describes the overall development of black employment during the war and the breakdown because of insufficient vocational training among them.   (BRD)

1126   Weaver, Robert C. **The urban complex: human values in urban life.** Doubleday, 1964.

The major concern of these seven essays is urban renewal in the federal sense and its relationship to the improvement of urban areas and to the betterment and development of the roles of minorities.   (LJ)

1127   Wesley, Charles Harris. **The collapse of the Confederacy.** Assoc. Pubs., 1938.

In this study of a downfall, Charles Wesley proposed to determine the sufficiency and availability of war resources, to describe moral and internal dissensions, to investigate cotton and slavery as factors in the struggle, and to review the use of blacks in military service.   (BRD)

1128   Wesley, Charles Harris. **Negro labor in the United States, 1850–1925: a study in American economic history.** Vanguard, 1927.

An important phase of the economic history of the United States is discussed here—the period of black labor from slavery in the South to the great exodus to the industrial life of the North. Also dealt with is the effect of that exodus on labor, economics, and social life.   (BRD)

1129   Wheatley, Phillis. **The poems of Phillis Wheatley.** Edited by Julian D. Mason, Jr. Univ. of North Carolina Pr., 1966.

The purpose of this book is to make readily available poems by the first significant black writer in America—a young Boston slave whose works were first published in London in 1773. (BRD)

1130   White, Walter Francis. **Fire in the flint.** Knopf, 1924.

In this novel of race relations in the South, a black doctor returns to establish a practice in his hometown. As a result, family members are violated and killed and his house visit to a sick white woman is misunderstood by a howling mob of whites. His efforts to live by his philosophy of tolerance and friendliness fail utterly. (BRD)

1131   White, Walter Francis. **Flight.** Knopf, 1926.

A black Creole girl acquires her race consciousness through a brief episode in Philadelphia where her child is born, and later in Harlem and in white Manhattan. The meanness and color snobbery of other blacks is also described.   (NYHT)

1132   White, Walter Francis. **How far the promised land?** Viking, 1955.

This study, completed just before White's death, is a report of the progress made by blacks during the last fifteen years. (BRD)

1133   White, Walter Francis. **A man called White.** Viking, 1948.

This is an autobiography of the former general secretary of the NAACP. Although a black, the author could easily pass for white—a fact which has advantages and disadvantages. His life story also reflects black history since 1906.   (BRD)

1134   White, Walter Francis. **Rising wind.** Doubleday, 1945.

This report on the status of black soldiers in Europe during World War I reveals that race relations were better abroad than at home, and best in the front lines.   (BRD)

1135   White, Walter Francis. **Rope and faggot: a biography of Judge Lynch.** Knopf, 1929.

This documented story of lynching in the South brings into

the open two aspects of lynching which are recognized but seldom admitted or discussed—sex and religion. (BRD)

1136   Wideman, John Edgar. **A glance away.** HBJ, 1967.

This novel covers a single day in the life of a young black who returns home after a year in an institution where he learned to kick his drug habit. (BRD)

1137   Wideman, John Edgar. **The lynchers.** HBJ, 1973.

In this novel which is prefaced by quotations from historical records of the brutality of black slavery and lynchings, the frustration and anger of blacks today are represented by four men who, in retaliation, plot the lynching of a white police-man in Philadelphia. (LJ)

1138   Wilkins, Roger. **A man's life: an autobiography.** Simon & Schuster, 1982.

Wilkens's memoirs portray him as a middle-class black man who graduated from law school, who worked in the Kennedy and Johnson administrations, who served as an Assistant U.S. Attorney General, who ran domestic programs for the Ford Foundation, and who wrote editorials for the *Washington Post* and the *New York* Times. (BRD)

1139   Wilkins, Roy. **Standing fast: the autobiography of Roy Wilkins.** Written with Tom Mathews. Viking, 1982.

These memoirs show that Wilkins worked nearly fifty years for the NAACP and served twenty years as its executive director. His earlier experiences were as a journalist for a black newspaper in Kansas City. (ATL)

1140   Wilkinson, Doris Y. and Taylor, Roland L., ed. **The black male in America: perspectives on his status in contemporary society.** Nelson-Hall, 1977.

These essays examine the relationship between cultural, economic, political, and legal structures in the United States, and the socialization experiences of black males. (BRD)

1141   Williams, John A., comp. **Beyond the angry black,** rev. ed. Cooper Square Pr., 1966.

Nineteen contributors discuss in essays, poems, and stories, the black in theater and fiction; prejudice within the black race; the terror of living in a segregated society; pressures behind discrimination; and the hatred engendered by such consideration. (BRD)

1142   Williams, John A. **Captain Blackman: a novel.** Doubleday, 1972.

This novel focuses on the injuries and efforts to save the life of a man who had been conducting seminars in black military history and who was badly wounded in Vietnam. (SR)

1143   Williams, John A. **!Click song.** Houghton, 1982.

In this novel of postwar New York City, a black novelist shows his experiences with publishing as the racial character of his material and the estimates of publishers and critics who constantly work against his endeavors to establish himself. (NYTBR)

1144   Williams, John A. **Flashback: a twenty-year diary of article writing.** Doubleday, 1973.

This collection has a dual focus—an analysis of various aspects of the American black experience, and a personal account of the problems of being a black writer in a white-oriented nation. (BRD)

1145   Williams, John A. **The Junior Bachelor Society.** Doubleday, 1976.

A group of middle-aged black men return with their wives to their hometown to honor the birthday of their old football coach and father figure. They play one last time as team members against a threatening enemy. (LJ)

1146   Williams, John A. **The King God didn't save: reflections on the life and death of Martin Luther King, Jr.** Coward, 1970.

This is an account of the life, achievements, and death of Dr. King. (BRD)

1147   Williams, John A. **The man who cries I am: a novel.** Little, 1967.

A Black American writer living in Amsterdam and dying of cancer uses time away from the hospital to recall the bitter circumstances of his marriage and life, and to make an important decision. (BRD)

1148   Williams, John A. **Night song.** Farrar, 1961.

This story chronicles the world of "cool" in Greenwich Village and the jazz night world which revolves around the dying life of an accomplished saxophonist. (BRD)

1149   Williams, John A. **Sons of darkness, sons of light; a novel of some probability.** Little, 1969.

Tensions in New York City run high after a white cop kills a black boy. (BRD)

1150   Williams, Sherley Anne. **Dessa Rose: a riveting story of the South during slavery.** Morrow, 1986.

Dessa Rose is an escaped slave who is sheltered by a white woman. This novel is about their friendship. (EPL)

1151   Williams, Sherley Anne. **Give birth to brightness: a thematic study in neo-black literature.** Dial, 1972.

Williams examines a number of significant twentieth-century black writers and concentrates on three: James Baldwin, Le Roi Jones, and Ernest J. Gaines. (C)

1152   Williams, Shirley. **The peacock poems.** Wesleyan Univ. Pr., 1975.

This collection of thirty-two poems begins with the birth of the poet's son and concludes with a description of his youth. (BRD)

1153   Willie, Charles V., editor. **Black/brown/white relations: race relations in the 1970s.** Transaction Bks., 1977.

Thirteen essays explore the phenomenon of institutional racism in America through description and analysis and strategies for institutional change. (BRD)

1154   Willie, Charles V. **The ivory and ebony towers: race relations and higher education.** Lexington Books, 1981.

Among the topics presented are the role and practice of desegregation, recruitment and financial aid for black students, enrollment issues, white students in black colleges, and the function and role of predominantly black colleges. (C)

1155   Willie, Charles V. **Oreo: a perspective on race and marginal men and women.** Parameter Pr., 1975.

Willie offers a new definition of the marginal man (one who rises above two social or cultural groups, freeing the different groups to work together) and cites the activities of Martin Luther King, Jr. to illustrate marginality's potential.   (LJ)

1156   Willie, Charles V. and Edmonds, Ronald R., ed. **Black colleges in America: challenge, development, survival.** Teachers College Press, 1978.

Essays supportive of public and private black colleges are concerned with three aspects—history and purpose; administration, financing, and governance; teaching and learning.   (C)

1157   Willie, Charles V.; Kramer, Bernard; and Brown, Bertram, ed. **Racism and mental health.** Univ. of Pittsburgh Pr., 1973.

This compilation of essays from two conferences of psychiatrists, sociologists, educators, demographers, etc., concerned with racism is from events at Syracuse University in 1970 and 1971.   (LJ)

1158   Wilmore, Gayrand S. **Black religion and black radicalism.** Doubleday, 1972.

In its analysis of the development of black religion in America from slavery to modern times, this study traces the logical currents which have impelled black churchmen into the center of the civil rights movement and explains why black religious institutions have always been the most reactionary and radical.   (BRD)

1159   Wilson, William Julius. **The declining significance of race: blacks and changing American institutions.** Univ. of Chicago Pr., 1978.

A sociologist traces the history of racial discrimination from slavery to the present and seeks to show that until the 1950s, the overwhelming majority of blacks were systematically excluded from the mainstream of American society. Affirmative action programs have scarcely touched the lives of the most desperately deprived, and class, not race, now determines opportunity and advancement.   (LJ)

1160   Woodson, Carter Godwin. **African background outlined, or, handbook for the study of the Negro.** Assoc. Pubs., 1936.

This book attempts to outline the African background of Black Americans. It is a compilation of information about African life, culture, and history with selected references for the study of Black American life and history.   (BRD)

1161   Woodson, Carter Godwin. **African heroes and heroines.** Assoc. Pubs., 1939.

Here is an account of the various black persons who have risen to prominence in the complicated history of tribal movement in Africa.   (BRD)

1162   Woodson, Carter Godwin. **A century of Negro migration.** Woodson, 1918.

Carter Woodson reviews the movements of blacks from the South to the North. He describes the dissolution of northern black communities by the return to the South of many of their members who followed the Union armies and tried to take some part in the reconstruction of the Confederate states after the Civil War. Westward migration is also discussed. (BRD)

1163   Woodson, Carter Godwin. **Education of the Negro prior to 1861: a history of the education of the colored people of the United States from the beginning of slavery to the Civil War.** Putnam, 1915.

In the period prior to 1835, many slaves were given schooling on the plantations, but, in the period after 1835, slavery became an industrial, rather than a patriarchal institution, and it was generally concluded that education would lead to too much self-assertion.   (BRD)

1164   Woodson, Carter Godwin., ed. **The mind of the Negro as reflected in letters during the crisis, 1800–1860.** Association for the Study of Negro Life, 1926.

Personal, private, and miscellaneous correspondence on subjects of slavery and the project of emigration to Liberia are presented in three sections.   (BRD)

1165   Woodson, Carter Godwin. **Mis-education of the Negro.** Assoc. Pubs., 1933.

After researching school methods and systems in different countries, this author-educator discusses the mistakes made in educating blacks. He holds that miseducation results from the black not having been taught to value himself at his proper worth. (BRD)

1166   Woodson, Carter Godwin. **The Negro in our history.** Assoc. Pubs., 1922.

This survey of black achievement from the earliest times in Africa to the first quarter of the twentieth century in America was intended for use as a textbook. (BRD)

1167   Woodson, Carter Godwin, ed. **Negro orators and their orations.** Assoc. Pubs., 1925.

The important speeches which were delivered by blacks in the United States from the first slavery protest to an address of thanksgiving at the close of World War I are presented in general chronological order with biographical notes of the authors and the circumstance under which each oration was delivered. (BRD)

1168   Woodson, Carter Godwin. **The Negro professional man and the community: with special emphasis on the physician and the lawyer.** Association for the Study of Negro Life and History, 1934.

Woodson's survey covered all large cities with a considerable black population and practically all of the South. Investigators studied communities where professional men lived, and their status and distribution in these communities. (BRD)

1169   Woodson, Carter Godwin. **The rural Negro.** Association for the Study of Negro Life and History, 1930.

This study deals with conditions among blacks in rural sections of the South, as to health, farming, tenancy and peonage, industry and trade, religion, education and recreation. (BRD)

1170   Woodson, Carter Godwin. **The story of the Negro retold.** Assoc.
        Pubs., 1936.

        This volume is adapted to high school students to provide
        them with background for greater self-respect and self-
        knowledge. (BRD)

1171   Work, John Wesley. **American Negro songs: a comprehensive col-
        lection of 230 folk songs, religious and secular.** Howell
        Book, 1941.

        The words and music of more than two hundred spirituals
        and work songs are provided with brief information on their
        origins and nature. (BRD)

1172   Wright, Charles. **Absolutely nothing to get alarmed about.** Farrar,
        1973.

        This journal, of sorts, sketches life in the ghetto and in gutter
        New York. It leans so heavily on Wright's perception of set-
        ting, character, and plot that it reads like a novel. (ATL)

1173   Wright, Charles. **Bloodlines.** Wesleyan Univ. Pr., 1975.

        In two long sequences of irregular sonnets and several long
        poems, the poet re-creates images of his past experience—
        prayer meetings, sexual encounters, and dreams. (YALE)

1174   Wright, Charles. **China trace.** Wesleyan Univ. Pr., 1977.

        This volume is the final part of a trilogy which includes *Hard
        Freight* and *Bloodlines*. (BRD)

        Winner: Edgar Allen Poe Award, 1976.

1175   Wright, Charles. **Hard freight.** Wesleyan Univ. Pr., 1973.

        Wright's second book of poems explores various exterior
        landscapes and one interior world—death. (LJ)

1176   Wright, Charles. **The messenger.** Farrar, 1963.

        This story is of a twenty-nine-year-old black from Missouri
        who works by day for a messenger service near Rockefeller
        Center where his travels expose him to diverse worlds. Inter-
        spersed flashbacks juxtapose vignettes about his life. (BRD)

1177   Wright, Charles. **The wig: a mirror image.** Farrar, 1966.

This story concerns the drive of a Harlem black to join the Great Society, that is, the white world. He changes his hair texture to be his badge of entry.   (BRD)

1178   Wright, Jay. **The double invention of Komo.** Univ. of Texas at Austin Pr., 1980.

This poem contains anthropology indebted to, but not restricted to, Komo initiation rites.   (C)

1179   Wright, Nathan. **Black Power and urban unrest: creative possibilities.** Hawthorn, 1967.

In this explanation of Black Power as vital to the growth, development, and peace of the nation, Wright tells why the movement becomes meaningless unless led by blacks. He presents proposals for developing skills among ghetto dwellers to become self-sufficient, and tells what roles churches, corporations, and individuals can play.   (BRD)

1180   Wright, Nathan. **Let's work together.** Hawthorn, 1968.

Based on the thesis that before black and white can work together each must work out their own problems, this book is concerned with the problems that each group must solve for themselves and those which involve cooperation and unity.   (BRD)

1181   Wright, Nathan. **Ready to riot.** Holt, 1968.

Describing Newark, New Jersey, as an example of urban blight, Wright presents an appeal aimed principally at white business leaders and the white power structure to change its ways.   (NR)

1182   Wright, Nathan, ed. **What black politicians are saying.** Hawthorn, 1972.

Wright attempts to show that a people's political revolution is underway and the black man is helping to spearhead it. Articles included are by Julian Bond, Fannie Lou Hamer, Jesse Jackson, Dick Gregory, John Conyers, and Shirley Chisholm.   (BRD)

1183   Wright, Richard. **Black boy: a record of childhood and youth.** Harper, 1945.

This autobiography includes years up to the time when Wright leaves the South and heads North.   (BRD)

1184   Wright, Richard. **Black Power: a record of reactions in a land of pathos.** Harper, 1954.

Wright reports on his trip to Africa's Gold Coast.   (BRD)

1185   Wright, Richard. **Color curtain: a report on the Bandung conference.** World, 1956.

This book records an event which was held together and separated by two factors—race and religion. Western commentators' confusion in handling a meeting of previously subject peoples—the conferees—rang the twin theme without pause.   (LJ)

1186   Wright, Richard. **Eight men.** World, 1961.

A posthumous volume of eight stories, each story centers on a black who is involved cruelly with his surroundings, but displays a desperate if qualified heroism.   (BRD)

1187   Wright, Richard. **Lawd today.** Walker & Co., 1963.

A posthumous novel written before *Native Son* which displays one day in the life of a black postal clerk in the Chicago of the Depression, burdened with debt and sharp frustration at being black.   (BRD)

1188   Wright, Richard. **Long dream.** Doubleday, 1958.

A Mississippi man, whose family wealth was gained through corrupt associations and dealings, emulates his father's behaviors with whites and blacks until he is forced to flee to France.   (BRD)

1189   Wright, Richard. **The outsider.** Harper, 1953.

The protagonist is a black man who works in the Chicago Post Office and succumbs to debt, drink, and women before a terrible subway accident involves him. He survives, but is pronounced dead as a result of mistaken identity.   (BRD)

1190   Wright, Richard. **Pagan Spain.** Harper, 1956.

Wright's report of an extended visit to Spain in 1954 when he entered into the life of the land and talked with people of all classes. (BRD)

1191   Wright, Richard. **12 million black voices: a folk history of the Negro in the United States.** Viking, 1941.

This text and picture folk history of the Black American is a burning commentary on three centuries of slavery, persecution, and want with reinforcement of some photographs from the Farm Security Administration. (BRD)

1192   Wright, Richard. **Uncle Tom's children: four novellas.** Harper, 1936.

Four stories reflect conflicts between whites and blacks in the South. It received *Story Magazine*'s prize for the best book length manuscript submitted by anyone connected with the Federal Writers' Project. (BRD)

Winner: Story Magazine's Prize, 1936.

1193   Wright, Richard. **White man, listen!** Doubleday, 1957.

In a series of lectures delivered in Europe from 1950 to 1956, Wright takes the psychological reactions of black people to the white oppressors using the literature of blacks as evidence of his thesis. (BRD)

1194   Wright, Sarah E. **This child's gonna live.** Delacorte, 1969.

In a Maryland black ghetto in the 1930s, residents are destitute and powerless to alter their fate. From this environment, the heroine is determined to escape with her children. (LJ)

1195   Yerby, Frank. **Benton's row.** Dial, 1954.

A Texas renegade entered a Louisiana bayou town in 1842 and took up with a circuit riding preacher's wife whom he later married. This is Sarah's story as she transcended family history with love. (BRD)

1196   Yerby, Frank. **Bride of liberty.** Doubleday, 1954.

This is a love story and a narrative of the American Revolution. (BRD)

1197 Yerby, Frank. **Captain rebel.** Dial, 1956.

This is. the story of a New Orleans gambler and opportunist who was the rebel captain of a small fleet of ships running arms and supplies from England through the Union blockade to the South.   (BRD)

1198 Yerby, Frank. **Devil's laughter.** Dial, 1953.

This novel spans a decade in the 1780s in the hazardous career of a young lawyer of means who is determined to help free the French masses from oppression.   (BRD)

1199 Yerby, Frank. **Fairoaks.** Dial, 1957.

This is the story of a southern aristocrat who lived a lie so thoroughly that eventually it came true.   (BRD)

1200 Yerby, Frank. **Floodtide.** Dial, 1950.

The protagonist who lived in Natchez in the 1850s is determined to overcome his poverty and live among the local aristocrats.   (BRD)

1201 Yerby, Frank. **Foxes of Harrow.** Dial, 1946.

Romance, historical detail, and a handsome hero are combined in this novel of Louisiana from 1825 to Civil War days.   (BRD)

1202 Yerby, Frank. **Golden Hawk.** Dial, 1948.

This story happens during the seventeenth century in the waters of the Caribbean where the master of the Seaflower is attracted to a woman pirate who is driven by her hatred of men.   (BRD)

1203 Yerby, Frank. **Pride's castle.** Dial, 1949.

Pride Dawson arrived penniless in New York, became a robber baron, and died a ruined man after discovering that nobody needed him.   (BRD)

1204 Yerby, Frank. **Saracen blade.** Dial, 1952.

This is a romantic story of an Italian armorer's son who was born in the same town at the same time as Emperor Frederick II.   (BRD)

1205   Yerby, Frank. **Serpent and the staff.** Dial, 1958.

This is the story of a young man who fought the poverty and degradation of his New Orleans birthplace for the wealth and position which the life of a physician offered. (BRD)

1206   Yerby, Frank. **Vixens.** Dial, 1947.

A Southern aristocrat who fought for the Union returns to New Orleans in 1866 to reestablish his ancestral home and marries a beautiful woman who proves to be mad. (BRD)

1207   Yerby, Frank. **Woman called Fancy.** Dial, 1951.

In 1880 at nineteen, Fancy fled from an arranged marriage to Augusta, Georgia, with no money and wearing her only dress, and began to establish her future through the men she met. (BRD)

1208   Yette, Samuel F. **The choice: the issue of black survival in America.** Putnam, 1971.

Yette explains that technocratic and scientific advancements have made traditionally inferior occupations superfluous, while the blacks' increasing unwillingness to accept the role assigned to them by white society poses a threat to that status quo. He describes government measure, proposals, and actions that are encouraging black genocide. (BRD)

1209   Young, Al. **Geography of the near past.** Holt, 1976.

This third volume of poems by the urban, black, poet-novelist evokes city life in New York, New Orleans, Denver, and Detroit. (C)

1210   Young, Al. **Snakes: a novel.** Holt, 1970.

This is the story of a young man and his grandmother who struggle to survive in Detroit—she by playing the numbers and he by playing the electric guitar. (BRD)

1211   Young, Al. **Who is Angelina? a novel.** Holt, 1975.

Angelina, black and in her late twenties, is recovering from an ended love affair and is unemployed. After several attempts to blot out the pain, she travels back to her roots and begins to piece together an appreciation of her true self. (BRD)

1212   Young, Whitney M. **Beyond racism: building an open society.** McGraw-Hill, 1969.

After discussing the background and present state of racism in the United States, Young presents a program that could enable America to move beyond racism to an open society of justice and equality.   (BRD)

1213   Young, Whitney M. **To be equal.** McGraw-Hill, 1964.

Whitney's theme is that the mere elimination of injustices and inequities is not enough—a special effort on the part of the entire white and black population must be made to help the black overcome the discrimination gap.   (BRD)

Chapter 4

Black Illustrators and Their Works

Black illustrators are featured alphabetically. A description of their illustrative style, technique, use of color language, and composition precedes a title-ordered bibliography of their works. Content descriptions are not provided for these books because the nature of their graphic features is the focus of attention. The illustrative style description is a general one which may not apply to the artwork portrayed within each book.

An entry number in parentheses follows those books by black authors that appear in the bibliography sections. Books with non-black authors do not appear in the bibliography sections and only the entry number of the illustrator follows those titles in the index.

A glossary of art terms that may facilitate understanding of important concepts in this chapter appears in the appendixes.

1214   Andrews, Benny
Style: Expressionism using thin lines; collage
Medium: Pen and ink
Color language: Black and white predominate to express mood and ethnic strengths.
Composition: Open edged and stark

Appalachee Red: a novel. By Raymond Andrews. Dial, 1978. (517)
Benny Andrews' painting and watercolors including "Trash." ACA Galleries, 1972.
I am the darker brother. By Arnold Adoff. Macmillan, 1968.

1215   Barnett, Moneta
Style: Representational with expressionistic backgrounds. Strong lines are used to symbolize strength. Large blocks of pastel colors and some gouache are used to accent moods.
Medium: Pencil, pen and ink; charcoal
Color language: Bicolored drawings of muted pastels and earthtones
Composition: Large illustrations with color-opened, airy backgrounds are frameless and mood evoking.

The city spreads its wings: Poems. Edited by Lee Bennett Hopkins. Watts, 1970.
Eliza's daddy. By Ianthe Thomas. HBJ, 1976.
Europe for young travelers. By Elinor P. Swiger. Bobbs-Merrill, 1972.
First pink light. By Eloise Greenfield. Crowell, 1976. (96)
Fly, Jimmy, fly! By Walter Dean Myers. Putnam, 1974. (161)
A glorious age in Africa. By Daniel Chu and Elliott Skinner. Doubleday, 1965.
I am here. Yo estoy aqui. By Rose Blue. Watts, 1971.
James Weldon Johnson. By Opelia S. Egypt. Crowell, 1974. (72)
Let's go to an art museum. By Mary J. Borreson. Putnam, 1960.
Let's go to Colonial Williamsburg. By Mary J. Borreson. Putnam, 1962.
Let's go to Mt. Vernon. By Mary J. Borreson. Putnam, 1962.
Me and Neesie. By Eloise Greenfield. Crowell, 1975. (102)
A Mongo homecoming. By Mary Elting and Robin McKown. M. Evans, 1969.
My brother fine with me. By Lucille Clifton. Holt, 1975. (48)
Ready-made family. By Frances S. Murphy. Scholastic, 1953.
Sister. By Eloise Greenfield. Crowell, 1974. (309)

Time of trial, time of hope. By Milton Meltzer and August Meier. Doubleday, 1966.
Timothy's flower. By Jean Van Leeuwen. Random, 1967.

1216   Bible, Charles
Style: Representational
Medium: Pen and ink; pencil; water-based paint
Color language: Black and white are usually used with little or no other color. Where colors predominate, they are brushed into shapes without ink line borders.
Composition: Frameless illustrations bleed off pages of books for younger readers. All portray emotions of pain, worry, and discomfort.

Black means. . . . By Barney Grossman and Gladys Groom. Hill & Wang, 1970.
Brooklyn story. By Sharon Bell Mathis. Hill & Wang, 1970.   (154)
Eating at the Y. By Charles Bible. Privately published, 1974.
Hamdaani. By Nikki Giovanni. Holt, 1977.
Jennifer's new chair. By Charles Bible. Holt, 1978.
Spin a soft black song. By Nikki Giovanni. Hill & Wang, 1971. (83)

1217   Biggers, John Thomas
Style: Expressionism; realism
Medium: Pencil or charcoal
Color language: Black and white evoke seriousness.
Composition: Primarily depictions of black life in the rural South with some textured African scenes. Lines provide added detail and precision.

Ananse: the web of life in Africa. By John Biggers. Univ. of Texas Pr., 1962.
Aunt Dicey tales. By John M. Brewer. Steck, 1956.
Black artists of the new generation. By Elton C. Fax. Dodd, 1977.   (684)
Black Texans. By Alwyn Barr. Hertel, Jenkins & Co., 1974.
The cross timbers. By Edward E. Dale. Univ. of Texas Pr., 1966.
Dog ghost and other Negro folk tales. By John M. Brewer. Univ. of Texas Pr., 1957.
Harlem U.S.A. By John H. Clark. Macmillan, 1971.
Hawk. By Vivian Ayers. Hawk Books Ltd., 1957.
I, Momolu. By Lorenz Graham. Crowell, 1966.   (295)

1218   Brandon, Brumsic, Jr.
Style: Cartoon
Medium: Pen and ink; watercolor; chalk
Color language: Black and white in cartoon panels; pastels in storybooks
Composition: Cartoons occupy a double spread with symbolic drawing prefacing the four-panel cartoon. Watercolors are full-page drawings which bleed and have textual inserts.

Luther from inner city. By Brumsic Brandon. Eriksson, 1969.
Luther raps. By Brumsic Brandon. Eriksson, 1971.
Luther tells it as it is. By Brumsic Brandon. Eriksson, 1970.
Luther's got class. By Brumsic Brandon. Eriksson, 1975.
Outta sight, Luther. By Brumsic Brandon. Eriksson, 1972.
Right on, Luther. By Brumsic Brandon. Eriksson, 1971.
The six-button dragon. By Matt Robinson. Random, 1971.   (186)

1219   Brown, David Scott
Style: Primarily representational line drawings with cartoon aspects
Medium: Pen and ink; watercolor
Color language: Colors are used minimally.
Composition: Strong, bold lines are used to exemplify struggle and hope. Texture is accomplished with cross-hatching.

Benjamin Banneker: genius of early America. By Lillie Patterson. Abingdon, 1978.   (460)
Don't ride the bus on Monday: the Rosa Parks story. By Louise Meriwether. Prentice-Hall, 1973.   (427)
God's warrior. By Pat Holt. Abingdon, 1986.
A hero ain't nothin' but a sandwich. By Alice Childress. Coward, 1973.   (273)
Sure hands, strong heart: the life of Daniel Hale Williams. By Lillie Patterson. Abingdon, 1981.   (465)

1220   Brown, Margery W.
Style: Realism, expressionism
Medium: Pencil; charcoal
Color language: Black and white
Composition: Textured drawings

Animals made by me. By Margery W. Brown. Putnam, 1970.   (17)
I'm glad to be me. By Elberta Stone. Putnam, 1971.
Old Crackfoot. By G. Alfred. Obolensky, 1965.
The second stone. By Margery W. Brown. Putnam, 1974.   (269)

Yesterday I climbed a mountain. By Margery W. Brown. Putnam, 1977. (18)

1221 Bryan, Ashley F.
Style: Expressionism
Medium: Woodcuts; block prints; pencil; tempera; watercolor; ink sketches
Color language: Brilliant colors
Composition: Drawings emit emotional responses and suggest geographical expanse and characteristics, especially in African stories.

The adventures of Aku. By Ashley F. Bryan. Atheneum, 1976. (19)
Beat the story-drum, pum-pum. By Ashley F. Bryan. Macmillan, 1986. (20)
The cat's purr. By Ashley F. Bryan. Atheneum, 1985. (21)
The dancing Granny. By Ashley F. Bryan. Macmillan, 1977. (22)
I greet the dawn, poems. By Paul Laurence Dunbar. Atheneum, 1978. (285)
I'm going to sing: Black American spirituals. By Ashley F. Bryan. Atheneum, 1982. (23)
Jathro and Jumbie. By Susan Cooper. Atheneum, 1979.
Jim flying high. By Mari Evans. Doubleday, 1979. (75)
Lion and the ostrich chicks and other African folk tales. Retold by Ashley F. Bryan. Macmillan, 1986.
Moon, for what do wait? By Rabindranath Tagore. Atheneum, 1967.
The ox of the wonderful horns and other African folk tales. By Ashley F. Bryan. Atheneum, 1971. (24)
Turtle knows your name. By Ashley F. Bryan. Atheneum, 1989.
Walk together children: Black American spirituals. By Ashley F. Bryan. Atheneum, 1974. (25)
What a morning! By John Langstaff. Macmillan, 1987.

1222 Burroughs, Margaret G.
Style: Representational; expressionism
Medium: Lithographed line drawings
Color language: Black-and-white line drawings
Composition: Borderless line drawings in early works; later illustrations texturized with bold black accenting of black people probably reflects the artist's more developed social awareness.

Africa, my Africa. By Margaret G. Burroughs. Privately published, 1970. (601)

Did you feed my cow? By Margaret G. Burroughs. Crowell, 1955. (26)

For Malcolm. By Dudley Randall and Margaret G. Burroughs. Broadside, 1966.

Jasper the drummin' boy. By Margaret G. Burroughs. Viking, 1947. (270)

What shall I tell my children who are black? By Margaret G. Burroughs. MA/AH Publishing, 1968.

Whip me, whop me, pudding. By Margaret G. Burroughs. Praga Pr., 1966.

1223   Byard, Carole M.
Style: Expressionism and cartoon styles with shading
Medium: Watercolor; pen and ink; pencil or charcoal
Color language: Conservative use of colors to emphasize and dramatize
Composition: Drama, spirit, and wisdom of African culture are captured in shading techniques.

Africa dream. By Eloise Greenfield. Crowell, 1977.   (93)

Arthur Mitchell. By Tobi Tobias. Crowell, 1975.

Cornrows. By Camille Yarbrough. Coward, 1981.   (237)

Grandmama's joy. By Eloise Greenfield. Putnam, 1980.   (98)

Have a happy. . .: a novel. By Mildred Pitts Walter. Lothrop, 1989.   (493)

I can do it by myself. By Lessie J. Little and Eloise Greenfield. Crowell, 1978.   (141)

Nomi and the magic fish. By Phumla Mbane. Doubleday, 1972.

The Sycamore tree and other African folktales. By Lee Po. Doubleday, 1974.

Under Christopher's hat. By Dorothy Callahan. Scribner, 1972.

Willy. By Helen H. King. Doubleday, 1971.   (134)

Willy. By Lore Shoberg. McGraw-Hill, 1974.

1224   Campbell, Elmer Simms
Style: Representational; expressionism; cartoon
Medium: Pen and ink
Color language: Black and white without shading
Composition: Borderless illustrations effect drama through their size and page position. Heavy lines are used to evoke power.

Cuties in arms. By Elmer S. Campbell. McKay, 1942.

More cuties in arms. By Elmer S. Campbell. McKay, 1943.
Popo and Fifina. By Langston Hughes and Anna Bontemps. Macmillan, 1932. (9)
Southern road: Poems. By Sterling A. Brown. HBJ, 1932. (596)

1225   Carty, Leo
Style: Impressionism and expressionism through line-and-wash technique
Medium: Watercolor; ink with pen and brush
Color language: Black and white express serious themes and gentle color combinations convey warmth and security.
Composition: Borderless, full-page bleeds

50,000 names for Jeff. By Anne Snyder. Holt, 1969.
The house on the mountain. By Eleanor Clymer. Dutton, 1971.
I love Gram. By Ruth Sonneborn. Viking, 1971.
Nat Turner. By Judith B. Griffin. Coward, 1970. (111)
Sidewalk story. By Sharon Bell Mathis. Viking, 1971. (157)
A tree for Tompkins Park. By Dawn C. Thomas. McGraw-Hill, 1971. (224)
Where does the day go? By Walter Dean Myers. Parents Magazine Pr., 1969. (164)

1226   Cooper, Floyd
Style: Expressionism
Medium: Watercolor
Color language: Lively colors with shading create a muted effect.
Composition: Illustrations consume the pages with vivid emotional portrayals and inserted text.

Grandpa's face. By Eloise Greenfield. Philomel Bks., 1988. (99)

1227   Crews, Donald
Style: Expressionism; photography
Medium: Gouache
Color language: Predominantly bright
Composition: Geometric shapes are used frequently.

ABC of ecology. By Harry Milgrom. Macmillan, 1972.
ABC science experiments. By Harry Milgrom. Crowell, 1970.
Bicycle race. By Donald Crews. Greenwillow, 1985. (54)
Blue sea. By Robert Kalan. Greenwillow, 1979.
Carousel. By Donald Crews. Greenwillow, 1982. (55)
Eclipse, darkness in daytime. By F. M. Branley. Crowell, 1973.
Flying. By Donald Crews. Greenwillow, 1986. (56)

Fractions are parts of things. By J. Richard Dennis. Crowell, 1971.
Freight train. By Donald Crews. Greenwillow, 1978.   (57)
Harbor. By Donald Crews. Greenwillow, 1982.   (58)
Light. By Donald Crews. Greenwillow, 1981.   (59)
Parade. By Donald Crews. Greenwillow, 1983.   (60)
Rain. By Robert Kalan. Greenwillow, 1978.
School bus. By Donald Crews. Greenwillow, 1984.   (61)
The talking stone. By Dorothy de Wit. Greenwillow, 1979.
Ten black dots. By Donald Crews. Scribner, 1968.   (62)
Truck. By Donald Crews. Greenwillow, 1980.   (63)
We read: A to Z. By Donald Crews. Harper, 1967.   (64)

1228   Crichlow, Ernest T.
Style: Realism; naturalism; and expressionism through line drawings and lithography
Medium: Pencil and wash; watercolor; pen and ink with brush applied color wash
Color language: Subdued
Composition: Illustrations reflect the dignity of man and the artist's respect for childhood and the attending emotions. Black skin is drawn with texture and subdued colors support the serious nature of the accompanying stories.

African folktales. By Jessie A. Nunn. Funk & Wagnalls, 1971.
Benjamin Banneker. By Claude Lewis. McGraw-Hill, 1970.
Captain of the Planter. By Dorothy Sterling. Doubleday, 1958.
Corrie and the Yankee. By Mimi C. Levy. Viking, 1959.
Enter in. By Laura Lewis. Pilot Books, 1959.
Forever free. By Dorothy Sterling. Doubleday, 1963.
Freedom train. By Dorothy Sterling. Doubleday, 1954.
Galumph. By Brenda Lansdown. Houghton, 1963.
Lift every voice. By Dorothy Sterling and Benjamin Quarles. Doubleday, 1965.
Lincoln's birthday. By Clyde Robert Bulla. Crowell, 1966.
The magic mirrors. By Judith B. Griffin. Coward, 1971.   (110)
Maria. By Joan M. Lexau. Dial, 1964.
Mary Jane. By Dorothy Sterling. Doubleday, 1959.
Twelve o'clock whistle. By Jerrold Beim. Morrow, 1946.
Two is a team. By Lorraine and Jerrold Beim. HBJ, 1945.
Unsung Black Americans. By Edith Stull. Grosset, 1971.
We shall live in peace: the teachings of Martin Luther King, Jr. Edited by Deloris Harrison. Hawthorn, 1968.   (412)
William. By Anne W. Guy. Hale, 1961.

1229   Cummings, Pat
Style: Representational; cartoon; expressionism; impressionism; gouache technique used
Medium: Ink; charcoal pencil; finger paints; crayons
Color language: Varied
Composition: Detailed patterns are used with contrasting colors. Texture is created with cross-hatching and stipple.

Beyond dreamtime. By Trudie MacDougall. Coward, 1978.
C.L.O.U.D.S. By Pat Cummings. Lothrop, 1986.   (66)
Chilly stomach. By Jeannette Franklin Caines. Harper, 1986.   (28)
Fred's first day. By Cathy Warren. Lothrop, 1984.
Good news. By Eloise Greenfield. Coward, 1977.   (97)
Jimmy Lee did it. By Pat Cummings. Lothrop, 1985.   (67)
Just us women. By Jeannette Franklin Caines. Harper, 1982.   (30)
My mama needs me. By Mildred Pitts Walter. Lothrop, 1983. (231)
Playing with mama. By Cathy Warren. Lothrop, 1986.
The secret of the Royal Mounds. By Cynthia Jameson. Coward, 1980.
Springtime bears. By Cathy Warren. Lothrop, 1987.
Storm in the night. By Mary Stolz. Harper, 1988.

1230   De Carava, Roy
Style: Photography
Medium: Camera
Color language: Black and white

The movement: documentary of a struggle for equality. By Lorraine Hansberry. Simon & Schuster, 1964.
The sweet flypaper of life. By Langston Hughes. Hill & Wang, 1967.   (794)

1231   De Veaux, Alexis
Style: Expressionism; photography
Medium: Pen and ink; camera
Color language: Black and white, primarily
Composition: Stark line drawings with little texture

Don't explain: a song of Billie Holiday. By Alexis De Veaux. Harper, 1980.   (655)
An enchanted hair tale. By Alexis De Veaux. Harper, 1987.   (68)
LiChen/second daughter first son. By Alexis De Veaux. Ba Tone Press, 1975.

Na-ni; a story and pictures. By Alexis De Veaux. Harper, 1973. (69)

Spirits in the street. By Alexis De Veaux. Anchor Books, 1973. (656)

1232 Dillon, Leo and Diane
Style: Expressionism using gouache and halftones
Medium: Watercolor; pen and ink
Color language: Thick and bold, especially in stories about Africa; black-and-white illustrations in history books
Composition: Strong, bold lines in African stories; thin detailed, regular lines in East Indian stories. Texture achieved through color or small irregular lines. Geographical and climatic settings and moods emerge.

Ashanti to Zulu. By Margaret Musgrove. Dial, 1976.
Behind the back of the mountain. By Verna Aardema. Dial, 1973.
Brother to the wind. By Mildred Pitts Walter. Lothrop, 1985. (230)
Burning star. By Eth Clifford. Houghton, 1974.
Children of the sun. By Jan Carew. Little, 1980. (32)
Claymore and Kilt. By Sorche Nic Leodhas. Holt, 1967.
Dark venture. By Audrey W. Beyer. Knopf, 1968.
Gassire's lute. Translated by Alta Jahlow. Dutton, 1971.
Hakon of Rogen's saga. By Erik C. Haugaard. Holt, 1973.
Honey, I love, and other love poems. By Eloise Greenfield. Crowell, 1978. (100)
The hundred penny box. By Sharon Bell Mathis. Viking, 1975. (155)
Listen children. Edited By Dorothy Strickland. Bantam, 1982.
The people could fly: American black folk tales. By Virginia Hamilton. Knopf, 1985. (331)
The porcelain cat. By Mildred P. Hearn. Little, 1987.
The ring in the prairie. By John Bierhorst and Henry R. Schoolcraft. Little, 1970.
Shamrock and spear. By Frances M. Pilkington. Bodley Head, 1966.
A slave's tale. By Erik C. Haugaard. Houghton, 1965.
Song of the boat. By Lorenz Graham. Crowell, 1975. (92)
Songs and stories from Uganda. By William M. Serwadda. Crowell, 1974.
Tales from Scandinavia. By Frederick Laing. Silver Burdett, 1979.
The third gift. By Jan Carew. Little, 1974. (33)
Two pairs of shoes. By P. L. Travers. Viking, 1980.

The untold tale. By Erik C. Haugaard. Houghton, 1971.

Whirlwind is a ghost dancing. By Natalie M. Belting. Dutton, 1974.

Who's in the rabbit's house? By Verna Aardema. Dial, 1977.

Why Heimdall blew his horn, tales of the Norse gods. By Frederick Laing. Silver Burdett, 1969.

Why mosquitoes buzz in people's ears. By Verna Aardema. Dial, 1975.

1233 Douglas, Aaron

Style: Cubistic aspect and silhouette technique

Medium: Ink and brush

Color language: Black and white with gray shadings

Composition: An African floral motif is used in pictures which allows room for imagination. Character forms are fluid and lyrical.

Black magic. By Paul Morand. Heinemann, 1929.

Caroling dusk. By Countee Cullen. Harper, 1927. (639)

God's trombones. By James Weldon Johnson. Viking, 1927. (820)

Plays of Negro life: a source-book of Native American drama. By Alain Le Roy Locke and Montgomery Gregory. Negro Univ. Pr., 1970. (872)

1234 Douglas, Stephanie

Style: Cartoon; naive; collage

Medium: Crayon; pen

Color language: Bold with various intensity levels

Composition: Rich texture; some one-dimensional facial expressions

Good, says Jerome. By Lucille Clifton. Dutton, 1973. (46)

Three wishes. By Lucille Clifton. Viking, 1976. (51)

1235 Fax, Elton Clay

Style: Representational; expressionism; cartoon; scratchboard technique with dominant use of lines

Medium: Pen and ink; pencil

Color language: Black and white

Composition: Shading and texture are created by parallel lines, cross-hatching, and stippling. Interpretation of the human body with faces shows intensity and emotions. Strong storytelling qualities.

Almena's dogs. By Regina Woody. Farrar, 1954.

Avalanche patrol. By Montgomery Atwater. Random, 1951.

Buffalo Bill. By Delores Garst. Messner, 1948.

Cotton from Jim. By Clara Baldwin. Abingdon, 1954.

Famous harbors of the world. By Eugene F. Moran. Random, 1953.

Garvey: the story of a pioneer black nationalist. By Elton Clay Fax. Dodd, 1972. (685)

Genghis Khan and the Mongol horde. By Harold Lamb. Random, 1954.

George Washington Carver, scientist. By Shirley Graham and George D. Lipscomb. Messner, 1944. (308)

Love of this land. By James Robinson. Christian Education Pubs., 1956.

Mateo of Mexico. By Ella H. Kepple. Friendship Pr., 1958.

Melinda's happy summer. By Georgene Faulkner. Hale, 1965.

Melinda's medal. By Georgene Faulkner. Messner, 1945.

More tales from the story hat. By Verna Aardema. Coward, 1966.

The Na of Wa. By Verna Aardema. Coward, 1960.

Olwe. By Verna Aardema. Coward, 1960.

Paul Cuffee: America's first black captain. By J. Johnson. Dodd, 1970.

A present from Rosita. By Celeste Edell. Messner, 1953.

Rustlers on the high range. By Montgomery Atwater. Random, 1952.

The seven wishes of Joanna Peabody. By Genevieve Gray. Lothrop, 1972.

Sitting Bull. By Doris S. Garst. Messner, 1946.

Skid. By Florence Hayes. Houghton, 1948.

The sky god stories. By Verna Aardema. Coward, 1960.

Taiwo and her twin. By Letta Schatz. McGraw-Hill, 1964.

Take a walk in their shoes. By Glennette Turner. Dutton, 1990. (228)

Tales from the story hat. By Verna Aardema. Coward, 1960.

Terrapin's pot of sense. By Harold Courlander. Holt, 1957.

Through black eyes. By Elton Clay Fax. Dodd, 1974.

Tommy two wheels. By Robert N. McClean. Friendship Pr., 1943.

Trumpeter's tale. By Jeanette Eaton. Morrow, 1955.

West African vignettes. Translated by Jacques Leger. American Society of African Culture, 1963.

1236   Feelings, Tom

Style: Realism; expressionism; cartoon; sketches

Medium: Pen; pencil; watercolor; line and wash

Color language: Vibrant colors establish the mood of African settings. Black and white convey serious messages and provide contrasts.

Composition: Texture is created with shading and cross-hatching, and sometimes with tissue paper. Illustrations reflect the range of human emotions in the stories.

African crafts. By Jane Kerina. Lion Publishing Corp., 1970.

Black folktales. By Julius Lester. R. W. Baron, 1969. (136)

Black is the color. By Ruth Duckett Gibbs. Center for Media Development, 1973. (81)

Black pilgrimage. By Tom Feelings. Lothrop, 1972. (289)

Bola and the Oba's drummer. By Letta Schatz. McGraw-Hill, 1967.

The Congo. By Robin McKown. McGraw-Hill, 1968.

Daydreamers. By Eloise Greenfield. Dial, 1981. (95)

From slave to abolitionist. By Lucille S. Warner. Dial, 1976.

Jambo means hello; Swahili alphabet book. By Muriel Feelings. Dial, 1974. (76)

Moja means one; Swahili counting book. By Muriel Feelings. Dial, 1971. (77)

Negro heritage reader for young people. Edited by Alfred E. Cain. Educational Heritage, 1965.

Now Sheba sings the song. By Maya Angelou. Dial, 1987. (523)

Panther's moon. By Ruskin Bond. Random, 1969.

A quiet place. By Rose Blue. Watts, 1969.

Something on my mind. By Nikki Grimes. Dial, 1978. (113)

Song of the empty bottles. Compiled by Osmond Molarsky. Walck, 1968.

Tales of Temba. By Kathleen Arnott. Walck, 1969.

To be a slave. By Julius Lester. Dial, 1968. (418)

The Tuesday elephant. By Nancy Garfield. Crowell, 1968.

When the stones were soft. Compiled by Eleanor Heady. Funk and Wagnalls, 1968.

Zamani goes to market. By Muriel Feelings. Seabury, 1970. (78)

1237   Ford, George Cephas

Style: Expressionism

Medium: Pen and ink; ink wash

Color language: Predominant use of dark brown

Composition: Frameless, bleeding illustrations exude strength from the intensity of dark shading.

African beginnings. By Olivia Vlahas. Viking, 1967.

Alesia. By Eloise Greenfield and Alesia Revis. Philomel Bks., 1981. (311)

Battle-ax people. By Olivia Vlahas. Viking, 1968.

The best time of day. By Valerie Flournoy. Random, 1978.

Daba's travels. By Bambato. Pantheon, 1971.

Darlene. By Eloise Greenfield. Methuen, 1980.   (94)

Ego tripping and other poems for young people. By Nikki Giovanni. Lawrence Hill Bks., 1973.   (82)

Freddie found a frog. By Alice J. Napjus. Van Nostrand Reinhold, 1969.

Little boy black. By Alfred W. Wilkes. Scribner, 1971.   (499)

Muhammad Ali. By Kenneth Rudeen. Crowell, 1976.

Paul Robeson. By Eloise Greenfield. Crowell, 1975.   (104)

Ray Charles. By Sharon Bell Mathis. Crowell, 1973.   (156)

The singing turtle and other tales of Haiti. By Philippe Thoby-Marcelin and Pierre Marcelin. Farrar, 1971.

Stories from Nyasiza. By Pierre Marcelin and Philippe Thoby-Marcelin. Viking, 1967.

Tales told near a crocodile: stories from Nyanza. By Humphrey Harman. Viking, 1967.

Tales told near a crocodile: the singing turtle. . . . By Humphrey Harman. Farrar, 1971.

Walk on! By Mel Williamson. Third World Press, 1972.   (235)

1238   Fufuka, Mahiri (Morgan, Sharon A.)
Style: Realism; expressionism
Medium: Pencil
Color language: Black and white
Composition: Dominance is created with detail and shading.

My daddy is a cool dude and other poems. By Karama and Mahiri Fufuka. Dial, 1975.   (80)

Nguzo Saba: the seven principles of nation building. By Karama and Mahiri Fufuka. Privately printed, 1972.

Poochie. By Ted Pontiflet. Dial, 1978.

1239   Gilchrist, Jan Spivey
Style: Impressionism
Medium: Watercolor
Color language: Pastels
Composition: Illustrations reflect moods and feelings, and show respect for children.

Children of long ago: poems. By Lessie Jones Little. Philomel Bks., 1988.   (140)

Nathaniel talking. By Eloise Greenfield. Black Butterfly Children's Bks., 1988.   (103)

1240   Harrington, Oliver Wendell
Style: Expressionism; cartoon
Medium: Crayon and ink
Color language: Single color inside ink outline
Composition: Lines are used effectively to convey moods, emotions, and texture.

Bootsie and others. By Oliver W. Harrington. Dial, 1958.
Hezekiah Horton. By Ellen Tarry. Viking, 1942. (210)
Laughing on the outside. By Philip Sterling. Grossett, 1965.
Runaway elephant. By Ellen Tarry. Viking, 1950. (212)

1241   Haskett, Edythe Rance
Style: Expressionism
Medium: Watercolor; pen and ink
Color language: Reflects nature without transferring specific moods.
Composition: Frameless illustrations bleed and use vibrant color blocks and patterns to symbolize African environment.

Some gold, a little ivory: country tales from Ghana and the Ivory Coast. By Edythe Rance Haskett. Day, 1971. (122)

1242   Hodges, David
Style: Representational realism
Medium: Pen and ink; pencil; watercolor
Color language: Only black and white are used in books on race relations to support seriousness of theme.
Composition: Shapes are used to convey mood while texture is created from lines and shading.

The Bannekers of Bannaky Springs. By Deloris Harrison. Hawthorn, 1970. (340)
Harriet Tubman. By Frances T. Humphreville. Houghton, 1967.
Joseph Henry, father of American electronics. By Patricia Jahns. Prentice-Hall, 1970.
Martin Luther King. By Edward Clayton. Prentice Hall, 1968.
Nat Love. By Harold W. Felton. Dodd, 1969.
Thurgood Marshall: fighter for justice. By Lewis H. Fenderson. McGraw-Hill, 1969. (291)
William C. Handy. By Elizabeth R. Montgomery. Garrard, 1968.

1243   Holder, Geoffrey
Style: Impressionism
Medium: Pen and ink

Color language: Appropriate to geographical reality of the Caribbean region
Composition: Frameless ink sketches

Black gods, green islands. By Geoffrey Holder. Doubleday, 1959. (765)
Caribbean cookbook. By Geoffrey Holder. Viking, 1973. (764)

1244 Hollingsworth, Alvin C.
Style: Expressionism
Medium: Line and wash
Color language: Pastel shades
Composition: Balanced; dominant aspects complement story themes.

Black out loud. By Arnold Adoff. Macmillan, 1970.
I'd like the Goo-gen-heim. By A. C. Hollingsworth. Reilly & Lee, 1970. (125)

1245 James, Harold L.
Style: Realism; cartoon
Medium: Pen and ink; pencil
Color language: Black and white with gray shadings
Composition: Detailed and textured drawings

Bed-Stuy beat. By Rose Blue. Watts, 1970.
Black soldier. By John Clarke. Doubleday, 1968.
The buffalo soldiers in the Indian wars. By Fairfax Downey. McGraw-Hill, 1969.
A guy can be wrong. By Barbara Rinkoff. Crown, 1970.
How many blocks is the world? By Rose Blue. Watts, 1970.
I think I saw a snail. By Lee Bennett Hopkins. Crown, 1969.
Member of the gang. By Barbara Rinkoff. Crown, 1968.
Mira! Mira! By Dawn C. Thomas. Lippincott, 1970. (222)
Mystery at Lane's End. By Evelyn L. Fiore. Doubleday, 1968.
Ollie's go-kart. By Anne Huston. Seabury, 1971.
Safari the singer. By Eleanor B. Heady. Follett, 1972.
Susie King Taylor, Civil War nurse. By Simeon Booker. McGraw-Hill, 1969. (263)
Tessie. By Jesse Jackson. Harper, 1968. (403)
Time of fearful night. By Alice Wellman. Putnam, 1970.

1246 Johnson, Eugene Harper
Style: Realism
Medium: Watercolor and ink; pencil; line and wash; charcoal

Color language: Sparing and dramatic use of color
Composition: Texture is created by using lines.

Albad the oaf. By Burl Ives. Abelard-Schuman, 1965.
Bamba: an African adventure. By Andree Clair. HBJ, 1962.
Daniel Boone: taming the wilds. By Katherine E. Wilkie. Garrard, 1960.
Elephant outlaw. By Louis A. Stinetorf. Lippincott, 1956.
A fox named Rufus. By Elizabeth Ladd. Morrow, 1960.
Frederick Douglas; slave-fighter-freeman. By Arna Bontemps. Knopf, 1959. (254)
The French Foreign Legion. By Wyatt Blassingame. Random, 1955.
Julie's heritage. By Catherine Marshall. Longmans, Green, 1957.
Kalena. By Esma R. Booth. Longmans, Green, 1958.
Kenny. By E. Harper Johnson. Holt, 1957.
Ladder to the sky. By Ruth F. Chandler. Abelard-Schuman, 1959.
The little brown hen. By Patricia Martin. Crowell, 1960.
Lone Hunter's first buffalo hunt. By Donald E. Worcester. Walck, 1958.
Matthew Henson: Arctic hero. By Sheldon N. Ripley. Houghton, 1966.
Meeting with a stranger. By Duane Bradley. Lippincott, 1964.
Musa, the shoemaker. By Louis A. Stinetorf. Lippincott, 1959.
Piankky the great. By E. Harper Johnson. Nelson, 1962.
The red drum's warning. By Willis Lindquist. McGraw-Hill, 1958.
The story of George Washington Carver. By Arna Bontemps. Grossett, 1954. (261)
War pony. By Donald Worcester. Walck, 1961.

1247 Lawrence, Jacob Armstead
Style: Expressionism; cartoon
Medium: Gouache
Color language: Poster color in brilliant and flat shades
Composition: Lines reflect story mood and enhance visual literacy qualities. Stylized drawings have exaggerated character features.

Aesop's fables. By Jacob Lawrence. Windmill, 1970.
Harriet and the promised land. By Jacob Lawrence. Windmill, 1966. (415)
Hiroshima. By John Hersey. Limited Editions Club, 1983.
One-way ticket. By Langston Hughes. Knopf, 1949. (784)

1248   Lee, George L.
Style: Representational; cartoon
Medium: Pen and ink wash
Color language: Dark colors and shades predominate
Composition: Styles are used simultaneously. Texture is smooth.

Interesting people: Black American history makers. By George L. Lee. McFarland & Co., Ltd., 1989.   (135)

1249   Lewis, Samella
Style: Expressionism; realism
Medium: Serigraph
Color language: Appropriate to story mood
Composition: Smooth and textured qualities are varied. Strong visual literacy qualities are present.

Art: African American. By Samella Lewis and Ruth Waddy. HBJ, 1975.
Benny, Bernie, Betye, Noah and John: five black artists. By Samella Lewis and Ruth Waddy. Contemporary Bks., 1971.
Black artists on art, vol. I. By Samella Lewis and Ruth Waddy. Contemporary Bks., 1969.
Black artists on art, vol. II. By Samella Lewis and Ruth Waddy. Contemporary Bks., 1971.   (863)
Portfolio on contemporary American artists. By Samella Lewis and Ruth Waddy. Contemporary Bks., 1972.

1250   Lilly, Charles
Style: Expressionism
Medium: Charcoal; pencil
Color language: Dark colors and shades predominate
Composition: Framed and borderless illustrations are decoratively supportive of text.

Growin'. By Nikki Grimes. Dial, 1977.
Mukasa. By John Nagenda. Macmillan,1973.
The peppermint pig. By Nina Bawden. Lippincott, 1975.
Philip Hall likes me, I reckon maybe. By Bette Greene. Dial, 1974.
Runaway to freedom. By Barbara Smucker. Harper, 1977.
Soup and me. By Robert N. Peck. Knopf, 1975.
Underground to Canada: Runaway to freedom. By Barbara Smucker. Harper, 1977.
When the rattlesnake sounds. By Alice Childress. Coward, 1975.   (275)

1251   Lloyd, Errol
Style: Impressionism with pointillist technique
Medium: Line and wash
Color language: Colors and shapes highlight the illustrations.
Composition: Full-page illustrations use strong dominance features against abstract backgrounds.

Doctor Shawn. By Petronella Breinberg. Crowell, 1975.   (13)
My brother Sean. By Petronella Breinberg. Bodley Head, 1973.
Nini at carnival. By Errol Lloyd. Crowell, 1978.
Shawn goes to school. By Petronella Breinberg. Crowell, 1974.
    (15)
Shawn's red bike. By Petronella Breinberg. Crowell, 1976.

1252   Lynch, Lorenzo
Style: Representational with paint and sketching
Medium: Pen and ink; watercolor; crayon
Color language: Bright and dull hues are used.
Composition: Lines are used as borders within borderless and bleeding illustrations.

Baba and Mr. Big. By C. Everard Palmer. Bobbs-Merrill, 1972.
    (165)
Big sister tells me that I'm black. By Arnold Adoff. Holt, 1976.
The black is beautiful beauty book. By Melba Miller. Prentice-Hall, 1974.
A bottle of pop. By James Holding. Putnam, 1972.
The fastest quitter in town. By Phyllis Green. Young Scott Bks., 1972.
The hot dog man. By Lorenzo Lynch. Bobbs-Merrill, 1970.   (142)

1253   McCannon, Dindga
Style: Expressionism
Medium: Pen and ink
Color language: Appropriate to moods of stories
Composition: Reflect moods strongly

Children of night. By Edgar White. Lothrop, 1974.
Omar at Christmas. By Edgar White. Lothrop, 1974.   (233)
Peaches. By Dindga McCannon. Lothrop, 1974.
Sati, the Rastafarian. By Edgar White. Lothrop, 1973.   (234)
Speak to the winds. By Kofi Asare Opoku. Lothrop, 1975.

1254   Marlow, Eric
Style: Realism

Medium: Acrylics
Color language: Bright color accents
Composition: Lines convey emotions without providing texture.

Rosa Parks. By Eloise Greenfield. Crowell, 1973.   (105)

1255   Miller, Donald George
Style: Expressionism; realism
Medium: Pen and ink; watercolor
Color language: Black and white, earthtones, or a combination used in frameless illustrations.
Composition: Shading and texture are created with lines in frameless illustrations which exude strength of message. Pictures are placed alternately color and black and white.

Between the devil and the sea. By Brenda A. Johnson. HBJ, 1974.   (404)
A bicycle from Bridgetown. By Dawn C. Thomas. McGraw-Hill, 1975.   (220)
The black BC's. By Lucille Clifton. Dutton, 1970.   (37)
Creoles of color of New Orleans. By James Haskins. Crowell, 1975.   (349)
Daniel Hale Williams: open-heart doctor. By Lewis H. Fenderson. McGraw-Hill, 1971.   (290)
Langston Hughes, American poet. By Alice Walker. Crowell, 1973.   (229)
Negro heritage reader for young people. By Alfred E. Cain. Educational Heritage, 1965.
Proudly we hail. By Vashti Brown. Houghton, 1968.
Searchers of the sea. By Charles M. Daugherty. Viking, 1968.

1256   Morton, Lee Jack
Style: Realism
Medium: Charcoal
Color language: Appropriate to story moods
Composition: Created with media overlay of charcoal over ink

Animal stories from Africa. By Marguerite P. Dolch. Garrard, 1975.
A birthday present for Katheryn Kenyatta. By C. A. Russell. McGraw-Hill, 1970.
The freedom ship of Robert Smalls. By Louise Meriwether. Prentice-Hall, 1971.   (428)
Leroy oops. By Barbara Glasser. Cowles, 1971.
Pragmatic humanist: the Whitney M. Young, Jr. story. By R. W. Bruner. McKay, 1971.

1257   Owens, Carl
Style: Expressionism
Medium: Ink with pen and brush
Color language: Black and gray predominate
Composition: Frameless illustrations bleed.

African herdboy: a story of the Masai. By Jean Bothwell. HBJ, 1970.
Your hand in mine. By Sam Cornish. HBJ, 1971.   (53)

1258   Parks, Gordon
Style: Photographic realism
Medium: Camera
Color language: Subject and theme appropriate
Composition: Poetic images are combined with bleeds and bordered photographs.

Born black. By Gordon Parks. Lippincott, 1971.   (964)
Gordon Parks: whispers of intimate things. By Gordon Parks. Viking, 1971.   (968)
In love. By Gordon Parks. Lippincott, 1971.
J. T. By Jane Wagner. Van Nostrand Reinhold, 1969.
Moments without proper names. By Gordon Parks. Viking, 1975.
A poet and his camera. By Gordon Parks. Viking, 1968.

1259   Pinkney, Jerry
Style: Realism; folk art; cartoon
Medium: Watercolor; pencil; pen and ink
Color language: Appropriate to text and usually vibrant
Composition: Lines are used compulsively for definition, emotions, mood, and texture. Drama is effected with bleeding edges, borders alternating color and black and white, size, and page position.

The adventures of spider. By Joyce Arkhurst. Little, 1964.   (1)
Apples on a stick: the folklore of black children. By Barbara Michels and Bettye White. Coward, 1983.   (158)
Babushka and the pig. By Ann Trofimuk. Houghton, 1969.
The beautiful blue jay. By John W. Spellman. Little, 1967.
Childtimes: a three-generation memoir. By Eloise Greenfield and Lessie Jones Little. Crowell, 1979.   (310)
The clock museum. By Ken Sobol. McGraw-Hill, 1967.
Cora Annett's Homerhenry. By Cora Annett. Addison-Wesley, 1970.

Count on your fingers African style. By Claudia Zaslavsky. Crowell, 1980.

Craftsmanship, a tradition in Black America. RCA, 1976.

Even tiny ants must sleep. By Harold J. Saleh. McGraw-Hill, 1967.

Femi and old grandaddie. By Adjai Robinson. Coward, 1972.

Folktales and fairytales of Africa. By Lila Green. Silver Burdett, 1967.

The Great Minu. By Beth P. Wilson. Follett, 1974.   (505)

The green lion of Zion Street. By Julia Fields. McElderry Bks., 1988.

Half a moon and one whole star. By Crescent Dragonwagon. Macmillan, 1986.

J. D. By Mari Evans. Doubleday, 1973.   (74)

Jahdu. By Virginia Hamilton. Greenwillow, 1980.   (117)

Ji-nongo-nongo means riddles. By Verna Aardema. Four Winds Pr., 1978.

Juano and the wonderful fresh fish. By Thelma Shaw. Addison-Wesley, 1969.

Kasho and the twin flutes. By Adjai Robinson. Coward, 1973.

The king's ditch. By Francine Jacobs. Coward, 1971.

Kostas the rooster. By Traudl Flaxman. Lothrop, 1968.

Mary McLeod Bethune. By Eloise Greenfield. Crowell, 1977.   (101)

Mildred Murphy, how does your garden grow? By Phyllis Green. Addison-Wesley, 1977.

Mirandy and Brother Wind. By Patricia C. McKissack. Knopf, 1988.   (152)

Monster myths of ancient Greece. By William Wise. Putnam, 1981.

More tales of Uncle Remus; further adventures of Brer Rabbit, his friends, enemies, and others. By Julius Lester. Dial, 1988.   (139)

The patchwork quilt. By Valerie Flournoy. Dial, 1985.   (79)

The porcupine and the tiger. By Fern Powell. Lothrop, 1969.

Prince Littlefoot. By Berniece Freschet. Ginn, 1973.

Rabbit makes a monkey of Lion. By Verna Aardema. Dial, 1988.

Rabbit redux. By John Updike. Franklin Library, 1981.

Roll of thunder, hear my cry. By Mildred D. Taylor. Dial, 1976.   (483)

Rosie and Mr. William Star. By Eve Bunting. Houghton, 1981.

Song of the trees. By Mildred D. Taylor. Dial, 1975.   (216)

Strange animals of the sea. National Geographic Soc., 1987.

Tales from Africa. By Lila Green. Silver Burdett, 1979.

The tales of Uncle Remus: the adventures of Brer Rabbit. By Julius Lester. Dial, 1987. (416)

The talking eggs: a folktale from the American South. By Robert D. San Souci. Dial, 1989.

This is music for kindergarten and nursery school. By Adeline McCall. Allyn & Bacon, 1965.

Tonweya and the eagles. By Rosebud Yellow Robe. Dial, 1979.

The traveling frog. By Vsevolod M. Garshin and translated from the Russian. . . by Marguerita Rudolph. McGraw-Hill, 1966.

Turtle in July. By Marilyn Singer. Macmillan, 1989.

The twin witches of fingle fu. By Irv Phillips. L. W. Singer, 1969.

Two friends and a lost bill. By Jeanette Catherwood. American Printing House for the Blind, 1977.

Wild, wild sunflower child Anna. By Nancy W. Carlstrom. Macmillan, 1987.

Yagua days. By Cruz Martel. Dial, 1976.

1260   Shearer, John
Style: Photographic realism
Medium: Camera
Color language: Black and white, often quite dark to evoke special mood
Composition: Vary in size; edges bleed

I wish I had an Afro. By John Shearer. Cowles, 1970. (193)

Little man in the family. By John Shearer. Delacorte, 1972. (194)

1261   Shearer, Ted
Style: Expressionism; cartoon
Medium: Charcoal
Color language: Predominantly black with single other color accent
Composition: Frameless; bleeding illustrations

Billy Jo Jive and the case of the midnight voices. By John Shearer. Delacorte, 1982.

Billy Jo Jive and the case of the missing pigeons. By John Shearer. Delacorte, 1978. (189)

Billy Jo Jive and the walkie-talkie caper. By John Shearer. Delacorte, 1981. (190)

The case of the missing ten speed bike. By John Shearer. Delacorte, 1976. (191)

The case of the sneaker snatcher. By John Shearer. Dell, 1977. (192)

Quincy. By Ted Shearer. Bantam, 1972.
Quincy's world. By Ted Shearer. Grossett, 1978.

1262   Steptoe, John
         Style: Representational; cartoon; expressionism; collage
         Medium: Watercolor; collage; paint; pencil and wash
         Color language: Strong, warm, with vitality
         Composition: Urban environment is like a character. Textured
              illustrations have strong visual literacy qualities.

All the colors of the race. By Arnold Adoff. Lothrop, 1982.
All us come cross the water. By Lucille Clifton. Holt, 1973.   (35)
Baby says. By John Steptoe. Lothrop, 1988.   (199)
Birthday. By John Steptoe. Holt, 1972.   (200)
Daddy is a monster . . . sometimes. By John Steptoe. Harper,
     1980.   (201)
Jeffrey Bear cleans up his act. By John Steptoe. Lothrop, 1983.
     (202)
The little tree growing' in the shade. By Camille Yarbrough. Put-
     nam, 1987.
Marcia. By John Steptoe. Viking, 1976.   (478)
Mother Crocodile: an Uncle Amadou tale from Senegal. By Rosa
     Guy. Delacorte, 1981.   (114)
Mufaro's beautiful daughters: an African tale. By John Steptoe.
     Lothrop, 1987.   (203)
My special best words. By John Steptoe. Viking, 1974.   (204)
OUTside INside poems. By Arnold Adoff. Lothrop, 1981.
Roses. By Barbara Cohen. Lothrop, 1984.
She come bringing me that little baby girl. By Eloise Greenfield.
     Lippincott, 1974.   (106)
Stevie. By John Steptoe. Harper, 1969.   (205)
The story of jumping mouse. By John Steptoe. Lothrop, 1984.
     (206)
Train ride. By John Steptoe. Harper, 1971.   (207)
Uptown. By John Steptoe. Harper, 1970.   (479)

1263   Temple, Herbert
         Style: Realism; cartoon
         Medium: Pen and ink; crayon
         Color language: Color is used to connote life; its absence con-
              notes death.
         Composition: Large illustrations have smooth textures on flat, ex-
              aggerated features.

The Ebony cook book. By Freda DeKnight. Johnson, 1962.
The legend of Africania. By Dorothy W. Robinson. Johnson, 1974.
Negro firsts in sports. By Andrew S. N. Young. Johnson, 1963.

1264   Thompson, Mozelle
Style: Expressionism
Medium: Watercolor; charcoal
Color language: Limited to grey, yellow, and white
Composition: Lines are used economically.

Lift every voice and sing. By James Weldon Johnson and John
    Rosamond Johnson. Hawthorn, 1970.   (405)
Pumpkinseeds. By Steven A. Yezback. Bobbs-Merrill, 1969.

1265   White, Charles Wilbert
Style: Realism
Medium: Pen and ink
Color language: Most of work is in black and white.
Composition: Detailed and textured drawings; portraits with dra-
    matic background of strong hatched lines

Four took freedom. By Philip Sterling and Rayford Logan. Double-
    day, 1967.
Give me a child. By Sarah E. Wright and Lucy Smith. Kraft, 1955.
Images of dignity. By Charles White. Ward Ritchie Pr., 1968.

1266   Williamson, Mel
Style: Realism
Medium: Pen and ink; crayons
Color language: Black and white
Composition: Greatly detailed; reflect scenic energy and rhythm

Walk on! By Mel Williamson and George Ford. Third World Press,
    1972.   (235)

Appendixes

Awards and Prizes

The American Book Award

1983   Thomas, Joyce Carol. *Marked by fire.* Avon, 1982.

American Institute of Graphic Arts Certificate of Excellence

1974   Carew, Jan. *The third gift.* Little, 1974.

Art Books for Children Citation

1973   Steptoe, John. *Stevie.* Harper, 1969.

1974   Feelings, Muriel. *Moja means one; Swahili counting book.* Dial, 1971.

1975   Feelings, Muriel. *Moja means one; Swahili counting book.* Dial, 1971.

1976   Feelings, Muriel. *Jambo means hello; Swahili alphabet book.* Dial, 1974.

1979   Crews, Donald. *Freight train.* Greenwillow, 1978.

1983   Feelings, Muriel. *Moja means one; Swahili counting book.* Dial, 1971.

Boston Globe-Horn Book Award

1974   Feelings, Muriel. *Jambo means hello; Swahili alphabet book.* Dial, 1974.

1975   Greenfield, Eloise. *She come bringing me that little baby girl.* Lippincott, 1974.

       Mathis, Sharon Bell. *The hundred penny box.* Viking, 1975.

1976   Graham, Lorenz. *Song of the boat.* Crowell, 1975.

1983   Hamilton, Virginia. *Sweet whispers, Brother Rush.* Putnam, 1982.

1987   Steptoe, John. *Mufaro's beautiful daughters: an African tale.* Lothrop, 1987.

1988   Hamilton, Virginia. *Anthony Burns: the defeat and triumph of a fugitive slave.* Knopf, 1988.

       Taylor, Mildred D. *The friendship.* Dial, 1987.

Carter G. Woodson Book Award

1974   Greenfield, Eloise. *Rosa Parks.* Crowell, 1973.

1988   Haskins, James. *Black music in America: a history through its people.* Crowell, 1987.

Children's Book of the Year Award

1979   Breinberg, Petronella. *Sally-Ann's skateboard.* Bodley Head, 1979.

Children's Book Showcase Award

1976   Graham, Lorenz. *Song of the boat.* Crowell, 1975.

       Taylor, Mildred D. *Song of the trees.* Dial, 1975.

Christopher Award

1987   Flournoy, Valerie. *The patchwork quilt.* Dial, 1985.

1988   Taylor, Mildred. *The gold Cadillac.* Dial, 1987.

Coretta Scott King Award

1970 Patterson, Lillie. *Martin Luther King, Jr.: man of peace*. Garrard, 1969.

1971 Rollins, Charlemae Hill. *Black troubadour: Langston Hughes*. Rand McNally, 1970.

1972 Fax, Elton, C. *Seventeen black artists*. Dodd, 1971.

1973 Robinson, Jackie. *I never had it made*. Putnam, 1972.

1974 Mathis, Sharon Bell. *Ray Charles*. Crowell, 1973.

1977 Haskins, James. *The story of Stevie Wonder*. Lothrop, 1976.

1978 Greenfield, Eloise. *Africa dream*. Day, 1977.

1979 Davis, Ossie. *Escape to freedom; a play about young Frederick Douglass*. Viking, 1978.

Grimes, Nikki. *Something on my mind*. Dial, 1978.

1980 Myers, Walter Dean. *The young landlords*. Viking, 1979.

Yarbrough, Camille. *Cornrows*. Coward, 1979.

1981 Bryan, Ashley. *Beat the story drum, pum-pum*. Atheneum, 1980.

Portier, Sidney. *This life*. Knopf, 1979.

1982 Guy, Rosa. *Mother Crocodile: an Uncle Amadou tale from Senegal*. Delacorte, 1981.

Taylor, Mildred D. *Let the circle be unbroken*. Dial, 1981.

1983 Hamilton, Virginia. *Sweet whispers, Brother Rush*. Putnam, 1982.

1984 Clifton, Lucille. *Everett Anderson's good-bye*. Holt, 1983.

Walter, Mildred Pitts. *My mama needs me*. Lothrop, 1983.

1985 Myers, Walter Dean. *Motown and Didi: a love story*. Viking, 1984.

1986 Flournoy, Valerie. *The patchwork quilt*. Dial, 1985.

Hamilton, Virginia. *The people could fly: American black folk tales*. Knopf, 1985.

1987 Walter, Mildred Pitts. *Justin and the best biscuits in the world*. Lothrop, 1987.

1988 Steptoe, John. *Mufaro's beautiful daughters: an African tale*. Lothrop, 1987.

Taylor, Mildred D. *The friendship*. Dial, 1987.

1989   McKissack, Patricia C. *Mirandy and Brother Wind*. Knopf, 1988.

Myers, Walter Dean. *Fallen angels*. Scholastic, 1988.

Coretta Scott King Honorable Mention Book

1971   Angelou, Maya. *I know why the caged bird sings*. Random, 1970.

Chisholm, Shirley. *Unbought and unbossed*. Houghton, 1970.

Graham, Lorenz. *Every man heart lay down*. Crowell, 1970.

Jordan, June and Bush, Terri. *The voice of the children*. Holt, 1970.

1974   Childress, Alice. *A hero ain't nothin' but a sandwich*. Coward, 1973.

Clifton, Lucille. *Don't you remember?* Dutton, 1973.

Hunter, Kristin. *Guests in the promised land*. Scribner, 1973.

1976   Graham, Shirley. *Julius K. Nyerere: teacher of Africa*. Messner, 1975.

Greenfield, Eloise. *Paul Robeson*. Crowell, 1975.

Myers, Walter Dean. *Fast Sam, Cool Clyde and Stuff*. Viking, 1975.

Taylor, Mildred D. *Song of the trees*. Dial, 1975.

1977   Clifton, Lucille. *Everett Anderson's friend*. Holt, 1976.

Taylor, Mildred D. *Roll of thunder, hear my cry*. Dial, 1977.

1978   Greenfield, Eloise. *Mary McLeod Bethune*. Crowell, 1977.

Haskins, James. *Barbara Jordan*. Dial, 1977.

Patterson, Lillie. *Coretta Scott King*. Garrard, 1977.

1979   Grimes, Nikki. *Something on my mind*. Dial, 1978.

Hamilton, Virginia. *Justice and her brothers*. Greenwillow, 1978.

Patterson, Lillie. *Benjamin Banneker: genius of early America*. Abingdon, 1978.

1980   Gordy, Berry. *Movin' up; Pop Gordy tells his story*. Harper, 1979.

Greenfield, Eloise and Little, Lessie Jones. *Childtimes: a three-generation memoir*. Crowell, 1979.

Haskins, James. *Andrew Young, man with a mission*. Lothrop, 1979.

Haskins, James. *James Van Der Zee, the picture takin' man.* Dodd, 1979.

Southerland, Ellease. *Let the lion eat straw.* Scribner, 1979.

1981 De Veaux, Alexis. *Don't explain: a song of Billie Holiday.* Harper, 1980.

Greenfield, Eloise. *Grandmama's joy.* Collins, 1980.

1982 Childress, Alice. *Rainbow Jordan.* Coward, 1981.

Greenfield, Eloise. *Daydreamers.* Dial, 1981.

Hunter, Kristin. *Lou in the limelight.* Scribner, 1981.

1983 Bryan, Ashley. *I'm going to sing: Black American spirituals.* Atheneum, 1982.

Caines, Jeannette Franklin. *Just us women.* Harper, 1982.

Lester, Julius. *This strange new feeling.* Dial, 1982.

1984 Hamilton, Virginia. *Magical adventures of Pretty Pearl.* Harper, 1983.

Haskins, James. *Lena Horne.* Coward, 1983.

Thomas, Joyce Carol. *Bright shadow.* Avon, 1983.

Walter, Mildred D. *Because we are.* Lothrop, 1983.

1985 Hamilton, Virginia. *A little love.* Philomel Bks., 1984.

1986 Hamilton, Virginia. *Junius over far.* Harper, 1985.

Walter, Mildred Pitts. *Trouble's child.* Lothrop, 1985.

1987 Bryan, Ashley. *Lion and the ostrich chicks and other African folk tales.* Atheneum, 1986.

Hansen, Joyce. *Which way freedom?* Walker, 1986.

1988 Mebane, Mary. *Mary.* Viking, 1981.

Council on Interracial Books for Children Award

1969 Mathis, Sharon Bell. *Sidewalk story.* Viking, 1971.

1973 Taylor, Mildred D. *Song of the trees.* Dial, 1975.

Edgar Allen Poe Award

1976 Wright, Charles. *China trace.* Wesleyan Univ. Pr., 1977.

Houghton-Mifflin Literary Fellowship Award

1966   Walker, Margaret. *Jubilee*. Houghton, 1966.

International Board on Books for Young People (Honor): United States

1984   Hamilton, Virginia. *Sweet whispers, Brother Rush*. Putnam, 1982.

1988   Hamilton, Virginia. *The people could fly: American black folk tales*. Knopf, 1985.

Irma Simonton Black Award

1975   Greenfield, Eloise. *She come bringing me that little baby girl*. Lippincott, 1974.

Jane Addams Book Award

1956   Bontemps, Arna Wendell. *Story of the Negro*. Knopf, 1948.

1976   Greenfield, Eloise. *Paul Robeson*. Crowell, 1975.

Jefferson Cup Award

1989   Hamilton, Virginia. *Anthony Burns: the defeat and triumph of a fugitive slave*. Knopf, 1988.

John Newbery Honor Book

1949   Bontemps, Arna Wendell. *Story of the Negro*. Knopf, 1948.

1976   Mathis, Sharon Bell. *The hundred penny box*. Viking, 1975.

John Newbery Medal Award

1973   Hamilton, Virginia. *M. C. Higgins, the great*. Macmillan, 1974.

1977   Taylor, Mildred D. *Roll of thunder, hear my cry*. Dial, 1976.

Juniper Prize for Poetry

1980   Clifton, Lucille. *Two-headed woman*. Univ. of Massachusetts Pr., 1980.

Lewis Carroll Shelf Award

1973   Lester, Julius. *The knee-high man, and other tales*. Dial, 1972.

1978   Steptoe, John. *Stevie*. Harper, 1969.

Nancy Block Memorial Award

1971   Jordan, June and Bush, Terri. *The voice of the children*. Holt, 1970.

New Jersey Institute of Technology New Jersey Author Award

1967   Crews, Donald. *We read: A to Z.* Greenwillow, 1967.

New York Times Choice of Best Illustrated Children's Books of the Year

1985   Hamilton, Virginia. *The people could fly: American black folk tales.* Knopf, 1985.

1986   Crews, Donald. *Flying.* Greenwillow, 1986.

Notable Children's Books (American Library Association)

1979   Myers, Walter Dean. *The young landlords.* Viking, 1979.

1980   Bryan, Ashley. *Beat the story-drum, pum-pum.* Atheneum, 1980

Crews, Donald. *Truck.* Greenwillow, 1980.

1981   Greenfield, Eloise. *Daydreamers.* Dial, 1981.

Guy, Rosa. *Mother Crocodile: an Uncle Amadou tale from Senegal.* Delacorte, 1981.

Hamilton, Virginia. *The gathering.* Greenwillow, 1981.

Taylor, Mildred D. *Let the circle be unbroken.* Dial, 1981.

1982   Bryan, Ashley. *I'm going to sing: Black American spirituals.* Atheneum, 1982.

Crews, Donald. *Carousel.* Greenwillow, 1982.

Hamilton, Virginia. *Sweet whispers, Brother Rush.* Putnam, 1982.

1983   Hamilton, Virginia. *Magical adventures of Pretty Pearl.* Harper, 1983.

Hamilton, Virginia. *Willie Bea and the time the Martians landed.* Greenwillow, 1983.

1985   Bryan, Ashley. *The cat's purr.* Atheneum, 1985.

Flournoy, Valerie. *The patchwork quilt.* Dial, 1985.

Hamilton, Virginia. *The people could fly: American black folk tales.* Knopf, 1985.

1986   Hansen, Joyce. *Which way freedom?* Walker & Co., 1986.

1987   De Veaux, Alexis. *An enchanted hair tale.* Harper, 1987.

Lester, Julius. *The tales of Uncle Remus: the adventures of Brer Rabbit.* Dial, 1987.

Steptoe, John. *Mufaro's beautiful daughters: an African tale.* Lothrop, 1987.

Taylor, Mildred D. *The friendship.* Dial, 1987.

1988   Greenfield, Eloise. *Grandpa's face.* Philomel, 1988.

Greenfield, Eloise. *Under the Sunday tree; poems.* Harper, 1988.
Hamilton, Virginia. *Anthony Burns: the defeat and triumph of a fugitive slave.* Knopf, 1988.

Hamilton, Virginia. *In the beginning; creation stories from around the world.* HBJ, 1988.

Hansen, Joyce. *Out from this place.* Walker, 1988.

Lester, Julius. *More tales of Uncle Remus; further adventures of Brer Rabbit, his friends, enemies, and others.* Dial, 1988.

McKissack, Patricia C. *Mirandy and Brother Wind.* Knopf, 1988.

Myers, Walter Dean. *Scorpions.* Harper, 1988.

Other Award

1986   Hamilton, Virginia. *The people could fly: American black folk tales.* Knopf, 1985.

1987   Guy, Rosa. *My love, my love, or the peasant girl.* Holt, 1985.

Parents' Choice Award for Illustration in Children's Books

1980   Bryan, Ashley. *Beat the story drum, pum-pum.* Atheneum, 1980.

Pulitzer Prize

1950   Brooks, Gwendolyn. *Annie Allen.* Harper, 1949.

Randolph Caldecott Honor Book

1972   Feelings, Muriel. *Moja means one; Swahili counting book.* Dial, 1971.

1975   Feelings, Muriel. *Jambo means hello; Swahili alphabet book.* Dial, 1974.

1979   Crews, Donald. *Freight train.* Greenwillow, 1978.

1981   Crews, Donald. *Truck.* Greenwillow, 1980.

1987   Steptoe, John. *Mufaro's beautiful daughters: an African tale.* Lothrop, 1987.

Randolph Caldecott Medal

1984   Steptoe, John. *The story of Jumping Mouse.* Lothrop, 1984.

Regina Medal

1981   Baker, Augusta. *The golden lynx and other tales.* Lippincott, 1960.

School Library Journal "Best Books of the Year" Award

1980   Crews, Donald. *Truck.* Greenwillow, 1980.

1981   Childress, Alice. *Rainbow Jordan.* Coward, 1981.

1982   Hamilton, Virginia. *Sweet whispers, Brother Rush.* Putnam, 1982.

1984   Crews, Donald. *School bus.* Greenwillow, 1984.

1985   Hamilton, Virginia. *The people could fly: American black folk tales.* Knopf, 1985.

1986   McKissack, Patricia C. *Flossie and the fox.* Dial, 1986.

1987   Steptoe, John. *Mufaro's beautiful daughters: an African tale.* Lothrop, 1987.

1988   Greenfield, Eloise. *Grandpa's face.* Philomel Bks., 1988.

Hamilton, Virginia. *Anthony Burns: the defeat and triumph of a fugitive slave.* Knopf, 1988.

Lester, Julius. *More tales of Uncle Remus; further adventures of Brer Rabbit, his friends, enemies, and others.* Dial, 1988.

Myers, Walter Dean. *Fallen angels.* Scholastic, 1988.

Story Magazine's Prize

1936   Wright, Richard. *Uncle Tom's children.* Harper, 1936.

Vernon Rice Drama Desk Award

1986   Bullins, Ed. *Five plays.* Bobbs, 1969.

Yale Series of Younger Poets

1942   Walker, Margaret. *For my people.* Yale Univ. Pr., 1942.

Glossary of Art Terms

1267 **bleed** When an illustration extends to the very edge of a printed page, it is said to bleed. To accomplish this, the page is first printed and then trimmed along the edge of the picture. (Quick)

1268 **block print** Such a design is printed by means of one or more carved or engraved blocks of wood or metal.

1269 **cartoon** Usually humorous, a cartoon is a sketch or drawing which satirizes, symbolizes, or caricatures some action or person.

1270 **collage** The technique of creating art by pasting onto a surface various materials of contrasting textures and patterns, such as paper, cloth, wood, photographs, feathers, shells, etc.

1271 **color language** The artist's use of color to convey emotions, moods, strength, time, etc.

1272 **composition** Also called design; composition is the way in which an artist organizes the elements of line, color, shape, and texture into a unified whole with unity, balance, and a sense of rhythm.

1273 **crosshatch** Two or more intersecting series of parallel lines. *See also* **hatch.**

1274 **cubism** Painting style in which natural forms are reduced to their geometrical equivalents and the organization of the planes of the object represented are not realistic.

1275 **etch** A photoengraving term which means to produce an image on a printing plate by chemical or electrolytic action. When used in offset lithography, it refers to solutions used on the nonprinting areas of the plate or in the water to keep nonprinting areas on the plate from accepting ink.

1276 **expressionism** A style of art characterized by heavy lines that define forms, sharply contrasting colors, and symbolic treatment causing it to lean toward abstraction.

1277 **folk art** This style of art usually shows agrarian settings, chubby and jovial characters who display provincial dress and mannerisms. It may also be characterized by the use of earthtones or muted autumn-like colors.

1278 **gouache** A type of watercolor painting that uses opaque rather than transparent colors. The finished painting often looks like an oil painting. *See also* **poster color.**

1279 **halftone** A halftone is produced by photographing artwork through a screen. This produces the effect of tones being represented by a series of tiny, evenly spaced dots of varying size and shape. Any gray tone can be produced out of tiny black dots with white spaces between them.

1280 **hatch** To mark with closely set parallel lines for shading in drawing. *See also* **crosshatch.**

1281 **impressionism** A style of painting characterized by short brush strokes of bright colors used to re-create the impression of light on objects.

1282 **lithography** The process of producing a figure or image on a flat, specially prepared stone or plate in such a way that it will absorb and print with special inks.

1283   medium   The mode of expression chosen by an artist, such as oil painting, sculpture, or etching. Also the tools or materials used, such as an etching needle, a camera, or a certain kind of paint. (Quick)

1284   motif   A distinctive and recurring form, shape, figure, etc., in an artistic work.

1285   naive   A layman's art which combines the influences present in the folk art and in the original. The painter tends to present only the clearly outlined aspects of his visual world and demonstrates an almost exclusive adherence to frontal posture and profile.

1286   naturalism   The artistic style in which the subject is drawn as it actually appears in nature and is almost photographic in detail.

1287   overlay   A transparent or translucent film attached to artwork carrying additional detail to be reproduced. In multicolor printing, these overlays may represent the simple separation of the colors to be printed. (Quick)

1288   photography   The mechanical reproduction of the visual facts of an object, person, or scene with a camera. It is not a subjective creative expression.

1289   pointillism   An art technique in which the juxtaposition of points or spots of pure colors are optically mixed by the viewer.

1290   poster color   A coarser version of gouache. *See also* **gouache.**

1291   realism   The artistic treatment of forms, colors, space, etc., as they appear in actuality or in ordinary visual experience. *See also* **representational.**

1292   representational   The practice of realistic representation in art when the artist adheres rather close to the appearance of the object.

1293   scratchboard   This is essentially an ink technique. In practice, a specially surfaced white board is covered with india ink, producing a uniformly black surface. When the board is dry it is possible to scratch very fine lines into the ink, revealing the white board underneath. Numerous stipple, dot, and crosshatch patterns can be made with ease and great control. Drawings done in this technique can be reproduced as line engravings, rather than as more expensive halftones.

1294 **serigraph** An original color process of pressing pigments through a silk screen with a stencil design.

1295 **silhouette** A representation of the outlines of an object filled in with black or some other uniform color.

1296 **sketch** A rough drawing representing the chief features of an object or scene.

1297 **stipple** To paint by small short touches that together produce an even or softly graded shadow.

1298 **style** A manner of expressing thoughts and feelings in art.

1299 **technique** A method through which an art style is produced. Painting techniques include watercolor, gouache, poster color, and tempera. Graphic techniques include woodcut, linocut, cardboard cutout, wood engraving, scratchboard, and stone lithography.

1300 **tempera** Strictly speaking, tempera is an opaque watercolor paint consisting of pigment ground in water and mixed with egg yolk. Tempera is also used to describe a poster paint that uses glue or gum as a binder. It also allows for loose, uninhibited brush strokes.

1301 **texture** The quality of pictures which reflects how the object would feel if it could be touched. Artists create textural imagery by using line, color, and shape.

1302 **visual literacy** The ability to interpret or read graphic symbols, pictures, or illustrations. Illustrations which are easy to "read" are said to have strong visual literacy qualities.

1303 **wash** A sweep or a splash of color made by or as if by a long stroke of a brush; a thin coat of paint.

1304 **watercolor** In this technique, whites are opaque. In watercolor painting, the paper creates the white and a color can be built up with several applications of a diluted color, but no color can be covered by overpainting. The painter may use tissues, sponges, and other materials to create patterns. Razor blades are often used to create various textures and effects. (Quick)

1305 **woodcut** A printing made from a wooden block with a pictorial design cut with the grain.

Bibliography

Campbell, Dorothy W. *Index to Black American Writers in Collective Biographies.* Englewood, Colo.: Libraries Unlimited, 1983.

Jones, Dolores B. *Children's Literature Awards and Winners.* Detroit, Mich.: Gale Research, 1983.

Page, James A. and Roh, Jae Min. *Selected Black American, African, and Caribbean Authors.* Englewood, Colo.: Libraries Unlimited, 1985.

Quick, John. *Artists' and Illustrators' Encyclopedia.* New York: McGraw-Hill, 1969.

Shockley, Ann Allen. *Living Black American Authors.* New York: R. R. Bowker Co., 1973.

Sims, Rudine. *Shadow and Substance: Afro-American Experience in Contemporary Children's Fiction.* Urbana, Ill.: National Council of Teachers of English, 1982.

Spradling, Mary Mace. *In Black and White,* 2d ed. Kalamazoo, Mich.: Kalamazoo Public Library, 1976.

Stanford, Barbara D. and Amin, Karima. *Black Literature for High School Students.* Urbana, Ill.: National Council of Teachers of English, 1978.

Ward, Martha E. and Marquardt, Dorothy A. *Authors of Books for Young People.* Metuchen, N.J.: Scarecrow, 1979.

234

Index

Throughout this index, distinctions are made to enhance clarity. Only black authors and illustrators are indexed. Book titles are followed by the principal author's last name in parentheses. Illustrators' names are followed by (illus.). The numbers which follow index terms are references to the entry numbers rather than pagination.